SERVICES TRADE
AND
DEVELOPMENT

SERVICES TRADE AND DEVELOPMENT

The Experience of Zambia

*Edited by Aaditya Mattoo
and Lucy Payton*

A copublication of Palgrave Macmillan
and the World Bank

1 2 3 4 10 09 08 07

A copublication of The World Bank and Palgrave Macmillan.

Palgrave Macmillan
Houndmills, Basingstoke, Hampshire RG21 6XS and
175 Fifth Avenue, New York, N. Y. 10010
Companies and representatives throughout the world

Palgrave Macmillan is the global academic imprint of the Palgrave Macmillan division of St. Martin's
Press, LLC and of Palgrave Macmillan Ltd.

Macmillan® is a registered trademark in the United States, United Kingdom and other countries. Palgrave® is a registered
trademark in the European Union and other countries.

ISBN-10: 0-8213-6849-4
ISBN-13: 978-0-8213-6849-7
eISBN-10: 0-8213-6850-8
DOI: 10.1596/978-0-8213-6849-7

Library of Congress Cataloging-in-Publications Data

Services trade and development : the experience of Zambia / edited by Aaditya Mattoo and Lucy Payton.
         p. cm.
      Includes bibliographical references and index.
      ISBN 978-0-8213-6849-7 (pbk.) — ISBN 978-0-8213-6983-8 (hardback) — ISBN 978-0-8213-6850-3
      (electronic (pbk.)) — ISBN 978-0-8213-6984-5 (electronic (hardback))
         1. Service industries—Zambia—Evaluation.   2. Service industries—Government policy—Zambia.
      3. Free trade—Zambia. 4. International trade. I. Mattoo, Aaditya. II. Payton, Lucy.

HD9988.Z33S47 2007
338.4096894—dc22

2007000445

Cover photos: Corbis.

CONTENTS

Figures

Tables

ACKNOWLEDGMENTS

Many people have contributed to this project: experts on particular services sectors, individuals working on the problems of least developed countries, and a wide range of stakeholders in Zambia. Gaia Narciso (on estimating the impact of services availability), Gael Raballand and Charles Kunaka (on road transport), Ndung'u Gathinji, then at ECSAFA (on accountancy), and Allaeddin Twebti each made substantial contributions to the book.

Within the Zambian Government, Dipak Patel, then Minister of Commerce, Trade, and Industry in Zambia, initiated this project and provided critical support and encouragement. His staff—David Chilipamushi (Permanent Secretary) Mwila Mukosa-Daka, and most of all, Dorothy Tembo (Director, Foreign Trade, Ministry of Commerce, Trade, and Industry)—played a critical role in helping identify key issues.

The rich interaction with stakeholders in Zambia could be the subject of a separate book. Here we can only express our gratitude to the individuals listed at the end of chapter 1 for sharing with us their time and insights. We are particularly grateful to Chawe Mpande-Chuulu from the COMESA Secretariat and Manenga Ndulu from the University of Zambia.

Within the World Bank, the individual experts who helped us are too numerous to even list and we mention only a few. Bernard Hoekman provided support and guidance from beginning to end. Without the help of the World Bank Zambia Country Team—Ohene Owusu Nyanin, Marie Sheppard, and in particular, Jos Verbeek—and the trade coordinator for Southern Africa, Fahrettin Yagci, this project would not have been possible. Ahmet Soylemezoglu, Sam Maimbo, and Tony Thompson provided valuable advice on the financial services chapter. Alan Gelb, Kathie Krumm, and Richard Newfarmer as peer reviewers, and Uri Dadush,

Sudhir Shetty, Julia Nielson, and David Satola all commented thoughtfully and critically on the manuscript. We thank John Panzer, Mark Juhel, Philippe Dongier, and Latifah Merican for their support of the project. Maureen Mwikisa and Michelle Chester provided outstanding administrative support.

CONTRIBUTORS

Mohammad Amin is Private Sector Development Specialist in the Enterprise Analysis Unit, The World Bank.

Jens Arnold is with the Economics Department of the Organisation for Economic Co-operation and Development in Paris, and is also a lecturer of Economics at the Fondation Nationale des Sciences Politiques.

Olivier Cattaneo is with the International Trade Department of the World Bank, Washington, DC, and is Research Associate with the Groupe d'Economie Mondiale de Sciences-Po, Paris.

Boutheina Guermazi is Senior Regulatory Specialist with the Policy Division of the Global Information and Communications Technologies Department, The World Bank.

José de Luna Martinez is Senior Financial Economist in the Financial and Private Vice Presidency, The World Bank.

Aaditya Mattoo is Lead Economist with the Trade Team of the Development Research Group, The World Bank.

Lucy Payton is with the Trade Team of the Development Research Group, The World Bank.

Charles E. Schlumberger is Principal Air Transport Specialist with the Transport Division, The World Bank.

CONTRIBUTORS

Mohammad Amin is Private Sector Development Specialist in the Enterprise Analysis Unit, The World Bank.

Jens Arnold is with the Economics Department of the Organisation for Economic Co-operation and Development in Paris, and is also a lecturer of Economics at the Fondation Nationale des Sciences Politiques.

Olivier Cattaneo is with the International Trade Department of the World Bank, Washington, DC, and is Research Associate with the Groupe d'Economie Mondiale de Sciences-Po, Paris.

Boutheina Guermazi is Senior Regulatory Specialist with the Policy Division of the Global Information and Communications Technologies Department, The World Bank.

José de Luna Martinez is Senior Financial Economist in the Financial and Private Vice Presidency, The World Bank.

Aaditya Mattoo is Lead Economist with the Trade Team of the Development Research Group, The World Bank.

Lucy Payton is with the Trade Team of the Development Research Group, The World Bank.

Charles E. Schlumberger is Principal Air Transport Specialist with the Transport Division, The World Bank.

ABBREVIATIONS

ADSL	asymmetric digital subscriber line
ADS-B	Automatic Dependent Surveillance-Broadcast
AML	anti–money laundering
ATC	Airport Traffic Control
ATM	automated teller machine
BASA	bilateral air service agreement
BCPs	Basel Core Principles
BPO	business process outsourced
CAZ	Communications Authority of Zambia
CGS	credit guarantee scheme
COMESA	Common Market for Eastern and Southern Africa
DDACC	direct debit and credit clearing
DSL	digital subscriber line
DTIS	Diagnostic Trade Integration Study
ECA	Electronic Communications Act
ECSAFA	Eastern Central and Southern African Federation of Accountants
ECOWAS	Economic Community of West African States
EPA	Economic Partnership Agreement
FDI	foreign direct investment
FSAP	Financial Sector Assessment Program
FSDP	Financial Sector Development Plan
GATS	General Agreement on Trade in Services
GDP	gross domestic product

GEF	Global Environment Facility
GNSS	Global Navigation Satellite Systems
GoZ	Government of Zambia
GPS	Global Positioning System.
HIPC	Heavily Indebted Poor Countries
IACM	Mozambique Civil Aviation Institute
IASB	International Accounting Standards Board
IATA	International Air Transport Association
ICAO	International Civil Aviation Organization
ICT	Information and Communications Technology
IDA	International Development Association
IFRS	International Financial Reporting Standards
IGW	international gateway market
IMF	International Monetary Fund
IOM	International Organization for Migration
ISA	International Standards on Auditing
ISP	Internet service provider
ITU	International Telecommunications Union
KYC	Know Your Customer
LDCs	least developed countries
LLU	local loop unbundling
MCDSS	Ministry of Community Development and Social Services
MFI	microfinance institution
MFN	most favored nation
MIDA	Migration for Development in Africa
MMP	Mexican Migration Project
NACL	National Airports Corporation Limited
NBFI	non-bank financial institution
NELMP	National Employment and Labor Market Policy
NGO	nongovernmental organization
NPL	nonperforming loan
OBA	output-based assitance
OECD	Organisation for Economic Co-operation and Development
OWWA	Overseas Workers Welfare Administration
PIA	Pensions and Insurance Authority
POEA	Philippines Overseas Employment Administration
POP	point of presence
POS	point of sale
PTC	Post and Telecommunications Corporation
RCDF	Rural Communications Development Fund

RQAN	Return of Qualified Africans
RTRN	Regional Trunk Road Network
SAA	South African Airways
SACU	South African Customs Union
SADC	Southern African Development Community
SARPs	Standards and Recommended Practices
SAWP	Seasonal Agricultural Worker Programme
SI	statutory instrument
SMEs	small and medium enterprises
T&T	tourism and travel
UNDP	United Nations Development Fund
UNESCO	United Nations Educational, Scientific and Cultural Organization
USOAP	Universal Safety Oversight Audit
VAT	value added tax
VoIP	Voice over Internet Protocol
WTO	World Trade Organization
YD	Yamoussoukro Decision
ZASTI	Zambian Air Services Training Institute
ZAWA	Zambia Wildlife Authority
ZCC	Zambian Competition Commission
ZEGA	Zambian Export Growers Association
ZICA	Zambian Institute of Certified Accountants
ZNCB	Zambia National Commercial Bank
ZSIC	Zambia State Insurance Corporation

1

SERVICES TRADE FOR ZAMBIA'S DEVELOPMENT: AN OVERVIEW

Aaditya Mattoo and Lucy Payton

Introduction

To say that the least developed countries (LDCs) have a major stake in services trade is to invite incredulity or derision. The first comes from those who see services trade as largely irrelevant to the LDCs' development agenda. The second comes from those who see few benefits from past market opening by LDCs. These views have had a powerful influence on international services trade negotiations. Pascal Lamy in his previous role as European Union (EU) commissioner for trade said that the EU would make no market-opening demands of LDCs at the World Trade Organization (WTO). Then the WTO's Hong Kong Ministerial Declaration stated that LDCs would not be expected to undertake new services commitments (box 1.1). The LDCs generally have endorsed this stance, offering little on services in multilateral, bilateral, or regional negotiations. Are these developments a sensible evolution of policy or a recipe for further marginalization of LDCs?

To address this question, we undertake an assessment of services trade in a particular LDC, Zambia. The choice of a single country is motivated by the evidence of rapidly diminishing returns to cross-country analyses. The choice of Zambia is motivated by a request from the Zambian Ministry of Commerce, Trade, and Industry. But there are other reasons: Zambia is an LDC whose economic performance has not been affected by conflict, which derives nearly two-thirds of its output from services (much higher than the LDC average), and which has seen significant services liberalization since the 1990s.

That, in principle, services and services trade matter for Zambia's development is immediately obvious. Services include finance, communications, transport, distribution, health, education, and tourism. Services "trade" encompasses cross-border trade in road and air transport; consumption by foreigners of tourism services; foreign direct investment (FDI) in banking, communication, and distribution; and temporary migration of doctors and teachers. It should, therefore, hardly need arguing that services are critical to Zambia's overall economic performance and the well-being of its people, and that the constraints on service sector development because of small markets and limited endowments could be alleviated by greater regional and global integration.

But, in practice, Zambia has so far derived only limited benefits from services trade. It has underperformed in terms of its services exports and in terms of widening access to services for its firms, farms, and households. Its exports of tourism services have grown but at one-tenth of the rate in Botswana and Tanzania—appreciation of the Zambian kwacha (K) is, at best, a partial explanation. From finance and accounting to telecommunications and international transport, despite a significant degree of liberalization and even after allowing for the low income levels in Zambia, access to services remains low and highly unequal—being available at affordable prices primarily to the affluent in urban areas and to the larger firms.

We believe that the current crisis of access in Zambia, and hence the diminishing faith in reform, are attributable to the fact that the government and donor organizations behaved *as if* they had complete faith in the power of markets. They moved aggressively, but unevenly, on the elimination of barriers to entry, sluggishly on the development of regulations to deal with market failure, and only notionally on the implementation of access-widening policies. The result is that access has been undermined by the persistence of barriers to competition in telecommunications and transport, the weakness and inappropriateness of regulation in banking and accounting, and the absence of meaningful access policies in virtually all sectors. One irony is that only limited liberalization has been accomplished in precisely those sectors (for example, telecommunications) where successful outcomes could have been achieved even without progress in the other dimensions of reform, whereas barriers have been completely eliminated in sectors (for example, financial services) where successful outcomes depended critically on complementary reforms.

For Zambia, neither the domestic reform agenda nor international negotiations will quietly disappear. Zambia is continuing to implement services reform. It is also engaged in services trade negotiations, in the WTO under the General Agreement on Trade in Services (GATS), with the EU in the context of the Economic Partnership Agreements (EPAs), and potentially within both the Common Market for Eastern and Southern Africa (COMESA) and the Southern African Development Community (SADC). International negotiations can be harnessed to deliver much-needed reform, but there is also a danger that unbridled mercantilism could produce outcomes that are antithetical to development. Zambian policy makers and trade negotiators need to be fully informed about the opportunities to expand trade in services—unilaterally, regionally, and multilaterally—and about the domestic preconditions for successful services liberalization. That is a key rationale for the present study.

The issues we raise in this study of Zambia will resonate with policy makers in other LDCs. Despite greater openness to competition, especially in the mobile segment, monopolies in international telephony still exist in countries like Bangladesh and Ethiopia. Although West Africa has begun to develop a regional market for air transport, evidence suggests that other countries in Africa, such as Nigeria and Mozambique, are continuing to restrict the entry of foreign airlines. Like Zambia, other LDCs, such as Mali and Uganda, have eliminated all barriers to foreign investment in banking, and have seen the increasing presence of foreign banks; however, the state of access to credit and other banking services has not significantly improved.

The challenge is to ensure that international commitments reflect good economic policy rather than the dictates of domestic political economy or international negotiating pressure. In particular, it is essential to distinguish between the areas in which liberalization is prevented solely by the political power of vested interests—to which reciprocal market opening is an antidote—and the areas in which regulatory or other problems need to be remedied before the full benefits of liberalization can be realized.

Today, market access in services is negotiated internationally, for example, at the WTO, or regionally. Policy advice and assistance for regulatory reform is provided by multilateral institutions and other agencies. There is virtually no link between two processes, just as at the country level, little coordination exists between sectoral ministries or regulators and trade negotiators. This disconnect persists even though it is clear that, in some areas, improved regulation—ranging from prudential regulation in financial services to procompetitive regulation in a variety of network-based services—is critical to realizing the benefits of services liberalization in many sectors. Policy intervention also will be necessary to widen access to services because liberalization per se will not always deliver adequate access to the poor. Regulatory institutions and access-widening mechanisms can be costly and require sophisticated skills. The Doha Declaration contains innumerable references to assistance, but not one of these regulations is binding. It is

Box 1.1. The Least Developed Countries and the WTO Services Negotiations

In the services negotiations at the WTO, the least developed countries (including Zambia) have pursued three goals: retaining flexibility in making liberalizing commitments, securing commitments from other countries in sectors and modes of export interest to them, and obtaining assistance to enhance the capacity of their services sectors. They have so far succeeded in achieving only the first goal.

Over the last decade, the international trading community has made fewer and fewer demands for liberalization of the LDCs. The General Agreement on Trade in Services (GATS), which went into effect in January 1995, states in Article IV on the Increasing Participation of Developing Countries notes that "[p]articular account shall be taken of the serious difficulty of the least-developed countries in accepting negotiated specific commitments in view of their special economic situation and their development, trade and financial needs." In September 2003, the WTO adopted the "Modalities for the Special Treatment for Least-Developed Country Members in the Negotiations on Trade in Services" (henceforth, LDC Modalities), which accepted that "[t]here shall be flexibility for LDCs for opening fewer sectors, liberalizing fewer types of transactions, and progressively extending market access in line with their development situation. LDCs shall not be expected to offer full national treatment, nor are they expected to undertake additional commitments under Article XVIII of the GATS on regulatory issues which may go beyond their institutional, regulatory, and administrative capacities." The December 2005 Hong Kong Ministerial Declaration went even further, stating, "We recognize the particular economic situation of LDCs, including the difficulties they face, and acknowledge that they are not expected to undertake new commitments." The right to hold back in most cases has been exercised. For example, in the Uruguay Round, Zambia promised openness only in a few business services, construction, health, and tourism, and not in communications, finance, or transport. In the current round of negotiations, it has so far offered no improvements.

With respect to the other two goals, the LDCs have had less success. Beginning with GATS Articles IV and XIX, and continuing the with the LDC Modalities and the Hong Kong Ministerial Declarations, there have been exhortations to members to "give special priority to providing effective market access in sectors and modes of supply of export interest to LDCs, through negotiated specific commitments...." The LDC Modalities notes that "It is recognized that the temporary movement of natural persons supplying services (Mode 4) provides potential benefits to the sending and recipient Members. LDCs have indicated that this is one of the most important means of supplying services internationally. Members shall to the extent possible... consider undertaking commitments to provide access in mode 4, taking into

Box 1.1. (continued)

account all categories of natural persons identified by LDCs in their requests." Countries have largely ignored these exhortations and promised little in the area of greatest export interest for the LDCs, the provision of services through the movement of unskilled workers.

Assistance to develop their services sectors has also not been forthcoming in the WTO context despite the acknowledgment, for example, in the LDC Modalities that "[t]he importance of trade in services for LDCs goes beyond pure economic significance due to the major role services play for achieving social and development objectives and as a means of addressing poverty, upgrading welfare, improving universal availability and access to basic services, and in ensuring sustainable development, including its social dimension. LDCs are facing serious difficulty in addressing a number of complex issues simultaneously, and lack institutional and human capacities to analyse and respond to offers and requests. This should be factored into the negotiating process in general and regarding the individual requests made to LDCs."

There are, however, signs that the political climate may now be more conducive to mobilizing assistance for the LDCs. The Hong Kong Ministerial Declaration requires members to provide "targeted and effective technical assistance and capacity building for LDCs" in accordance with LDC Modalities "to strengthen their domestic services capacity, build institutional and human capacity, and enable them to undertake appropriate regulatory reforms." Members are asked to take measures, in accordance with their individual capacities, aimed at increasing LDC participation in services trade, including "strengthening programmes to promote investment in LDCs, with a view to building their domestic services capacity and enhancing their efficiency and export competitiveness; reinforcing export/import promotion programmes; promoting the development of LDCs' infrastructure and services exports through training, technology transfer, enterprise level actions and schemes, intergovernmental cooperation programmes, and where feasible, financial resources; and improving the access of LDCs' services and service suppliers to distribution channels and information networks, especially in sectors and modes of supply of interest to LDCs."

Technical assistance is to be provided to LDCs to carry out national assessments of trade in services in overall terms and on a sectoral basis, and to assess interests in and gains from services trade. The present study is intended to be a contribution to such an assessment.

Sources: WTO General Agreement on Trade in Services 1995; WTO's Hong Kong Ministerial Declaration 2005; WTO's The Modalities for the Special Treatment for Least Developed Country Members in the Negotiations on Trade in Services (WTO Document TN/S/13), available from www.wto.org.

vital to establish a credible link between policy advice and technical and financial assistance, on the one hand, and liberalization commitments, on the other. In establishing such a link, the Ministries of Commerce can play an important dual role: domestically becoming more powerful advocates for reform on the strength of the external assistance they can mobilize, and internationally articulating demands for aid more effectively because of the domestic reform momentum they can generate. In this process of developing an "aid-for-services trade" agenda, the present study is a first contribution.

Method and scope of analysis

The method and scope of the Zambian analysis were rooted in addressing the following sets of issues.

Objectives

The broad objective of the exercise was to examine how Zambia could implement *services trade reform*—unilaterally, regionally, or multilaterally—to achieve its development goals (see figure 1.1). One dimension is managing its own liberalization to improve the performance of its services sectors, leading to increased productivity of resources employed in these sectors and increased availability of services for firms, farms, and households. Another linked dimension is enhancing Zambia's ability to export services through reforms at home and by eliminating impediments abroad.

Taking stock of services policy and performance

Before developing new policies, it is necessary to assess the state of current services policies, as well as the structure and performance of services sectors. How policy affects services trade is often obscure, even in more advanced countries. Developing countries' ability to design policy, as well as to use negotiations to facilitate domestic reform and obtain improved access to foreign markets, can be aided by better knowledge of the *barriers* to foreign participation in their own markets, and the barriers their exporters face in foreign markets. Information about the *structure* and *performance* of domestic services markets, especially in a comparison with those of other similar countries, can create the basis for a meaningful diagnostic exercise.

Regulatory diagnostics, distributional concerns, and external assistance

Research on services trade indicates that sound domestic regulation is often critical to realizing the benefits of services liberalization. Yet many developing coun-

Figure 1.1. Structure of the Exercise

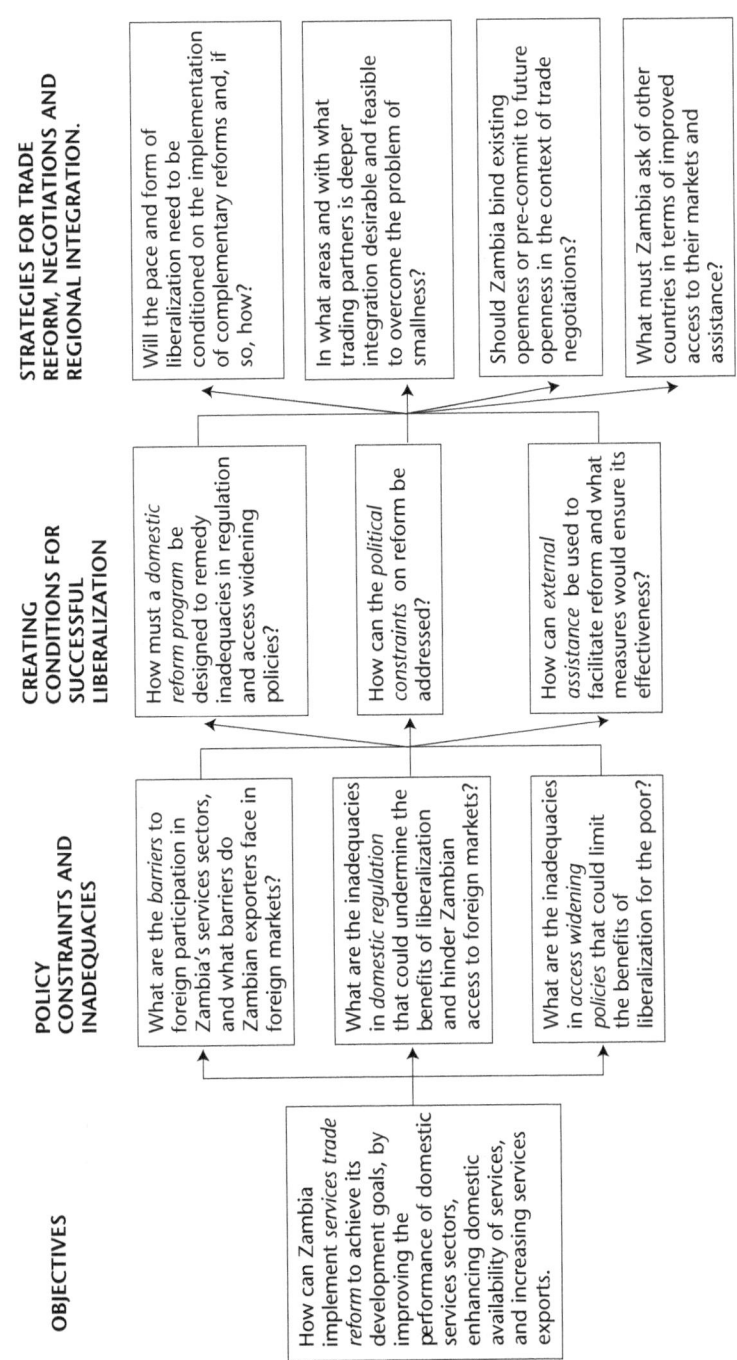

OBJECTIVES

How can Zambia implement *services trade reform* to achieve its development goals, by improving the performance of domestic services sectors, enhancing domestic availability of services, and increasing services exports.

POLICY CONSTRAINTS AND INADEQUACIES

What are the *barriers* to foreign participation in Zambia's services sectors, and what barriers do Zambian exporters face in foreign markets?

What are the inadequacies in *domestic regulation* that could undermine the benefits of liberalization and hinder Zambian access to foreign markets?

What are the inadequacies in *access widening policies* that could limit the benefits of liberalization for the poor?

CREATING CONDITIONS FOR SUCCESSFUL LIBERALIZATION

How must a *domestic reform program* be designed to remedy inadequacies in regulation and access widening policies?

How can the *political constraints* on reform be addressed?

How can *external assistance* be used to facilitate reform and what measures would ensure its effectiveness?

STRATEGIES FOR TRADE REFORM, NEGOTIATIONS AND REGIONAL INTEGRATION.

Will the pace and form of liberalization need to be conditioned on the implementation of complementary reforms and, if so, how?

In what areas and with what trading partners is deeper integration desirable and feasible to overcome the problem of smallness?

Should Zambia bind existing openness or pre-commit to future openness in the context of trade negotiations?

What must Zambia ask of other countries in terms of improved access to their markets and assistance?

Source: Authors.

tries have weak regulatory institutions, and remedying these weaknesses is costly and difficult because regulation requires sophisticated skills, particularly in a world of rapidly changing technologies. Thus, a key issue is the design of regulatory frameworks in limited capacity environments.

The diagnostic exercise needs to distinguish between (1) services sectors in which a clear benefit is evident from the immediate introduction of international competition; and (2) services sectors in which liberalization must be conditioned on remedying weaknesses, for example, in existing mechanisms for prudential or procompetitive regulation, alleviating adjustment costs, and ensuring universal access in liberalized markets. On the export side, the exercise needs to assess services sectors for export potential (by one or more modes), if foreign barriers are eliminated, and those for which the development of incipient export capacity needs further domestic reform or international assistance.

Apart from identifying policy constraints and inadequacies, the diagnostic exercise ideally would examine the political constraints to reform. An economic analysis of such constraints is inevitably inadequate, but nevertheless it may be possible to identify the winners and losers from particular reforms and assess their relative political power (for example, on the basis of stakeholder concentration). Such an analysis, even if it is crude, could reduce the political naivety of economic policy advice.

Finally, this diagnostic exercise must produce prescriptions regarding the types of interventions that would remedy the weaknesses in policy and overcome the existing political constraints. It is useful to distinguish between remedial actions that a country can undertake unilaterally and those that need external assistance. External support could range from technical assistance for regulatory improvements to funding for voluntary retirement and universal access mechanisms.

Strategies for trade liberalization, international negotiations, and regional integration

This component needs to assess, from the country's broader development perspective, the desirability of unilateral liberalization, as well as the extent and form of engagement in alternative international negotiating forums.

Strategies for unilateral action and international negotiations must consider the particular constraints on services liberalization in Zambia. If regulatory weaknesses prevent the country from reaping the full benefits of liberalization, then policy makers need to know whether and how liberalization needs to be conditioned on the implementation of complementary reforms. Negotiators may need to push for the gradual implementation of trade agreements as well as for technical assistance. Demands for technical assistance can be explicitly incorporated in the trade negotiations. Or these demands can be addressed to international development organizations and donors as part of the "aid-for-trade" agenda. This component of the exercise should help negotiators articulate demands for assistance.

Negotiators must decide whether to bind their immediate or gradual market opening in the context of international trade agreements. Binding lends credibility to the reform program and can obtain a negotiating benefit. But a balance must be struck between the gain in credibility and the loss in flexibility. It may be best for a country to bind aspects of the agreement along some dimensions but not others.

A negotiating strategy must specify offensive interests as well. The program should provide Zambia with an analysis to develop requests to be made of its trading partners, in terms of improved access to their markets and assistance.

The program should assess the desirability and feasibility of greater regional integration of services markets from Zambia's perspective. Should Zambia liberalize services faster in the regional context than multilaterally? Is regulatory cooperation—harmonization or mutual recognition of qualifications, technical standards, prudential regulation, and so on—more feasible and desirable regionally? Here, we must address the key questions of "what, where, and how much?"

Sectoral coverage

To gain a broad perspective on trade reform challenges, we cover a wide range of services sectors in this study, including the following: finance, telecommunications, accounting, air transport, road transport, distribution, and tourism. We examine the possible temporary migration of the unskilled and skilled, which is currently the key "trade" dimension of the health care and education sectors. We do not cover the electricity and water sectors, in part because the services dimension pertains only to their distribution, and because these sectors raise reform issues that go beyond the scope of the present study. Moreover, we do not provide a fuller treatment of export interests in business process outsourcing and accounting because our investigations established that, at this stage, Zambia has only limited capacity in these areas.

Mission in Lusaka

At the invitation of the Ministry of Commerce, Trade, and Industry, the team spent three weeks in Lusaka in March 2006. We met sector experts, regulatory authorities, line ministries, donors, and private sector stakeholders to discuss the state of policy, regulation, and performance in each sector, to hear about current reform initiatives and constraints to reform, and to identify strategies for reform and trade negotiations. A list of meeting participants can be found in annex I.

Box 1.2. Trade in Services: Four Modes of Supply

Services include activities as disparate as transport of goods and people, financial intermediation, communications, distribution, hotels and restaurants, education, health care, construction, and accounting. In contrast to merchandise trade, services are often intangible, invisible, and perishable, and usually require simultaneous production and consumption. The need in many cases for proximity between the consumer and the producer implies that one of them must move to make an international transaction possible. Because the conventional definition of trade—where a product crosses the frontier—would miss out on a whole range of international transactions, it is now customary to define "trade in services" widely to include four modes of supply:

- Mode one: cross-border supply, which is analogous to trade in goods, and arises when a service crosses a national frontier, for example, the purchase of software or transport by a consumer from a supplier located abroad
- Mode two: consumption abroad, arises when the consumer travels to the territory of service supplier, for example, to purchase tourism, education, or health services
- Mode three: commercial presence involves foreign direct investment, for example, when a foreign bank, telecommunications, or retailing firm establishes a branch or subsidiary in the territory of a country
- Mode four: movement of individuals, for example, when independent service providers or employees of a multinational firm temporarily move to another country.

The role of services and the services trade

As discussed in chapter 2, services matter in Zambia because they make a significant contribution to national income and because they affect the performance of other sectors of the economy. The services trade matters, at least in principle, because it offers Zambia the opportunity to overcome the constraints of limited endowments of capital and skills as well as the smallness of its markets.

Services in the Zambian Economy

The performance of the services sector is vital for growth and poverty reduction in Zambia, first of all, because it is already the largest part of Zambia's economy. Nearly 64 percent of Zambia's gross domestic product (GDP) is now generated in services, compared with 56 percent a decade earlier and 47 percent in other Sub-Saharan African countries (excluding South Africa). Close to 90 percent of Zambia's economic growth in the period from 1965 to 2002 and half of the country's GDP growth over the period from 2000 to 2004 has come from the services sector. Although services have done well relative to other sectors of the economy, their performance has hardly been impressive. The average annual growth of the services sector has been just 3 percent in the period from 1965 to 2002, compared with the overall GDP growth of 1.4 percent. Within services sectors, the largest contributors to growth have been community and social services, real estate and business services, and wholesale and retail trade, rather than sectors like tourism, transport and communications, and finance and insurance, which tend to reflect broader economic dynamism. Creating a more dynamic services sector must be a priority in Zambia.

Measured exports of services have grown at about 16 percent over the last three years—at the same rate as nontraditional exports—and currently constitute about 13 percent of Zambian exports. Tourism exports are perceived to have grown substantially over recent years. Despite this increase, on the export front, too, Zambia has not as yet realized the development potential of its services sectors.

Services and Overall Economic Performance

Apart from their direct contribution to GDP, services affect other sectors of the economy and the productive potential of Zambians. Widening access to services like finance, communication, and transport, as well as education and health care, must be a critical element of any growth enhancement and poverty reduction program. Inadequate access to services not only hurts Zambians in their role as consumers, but also perpetuates poverty by undermining the productivity of firms and farms as well as their ability to engage in trade. Moreover, the positive impact of access to efficient services sectors can be amplified because of the synergies between services sectors: access to insurance services can enhance farmers' ability to access credit; availability of telecommunications services helps financial service providers reach firms and farms in outlying areas; and the development of tourism depends critically on the availability and affordability of transport services.

In the Investment Climate Surveys (World Bank 2002), a large proportion of Zambian firms identify inadequacies in finance, telecommunications, and transport as a major or severe obstacle to their operations, and these proportions are higher than in many other countries. The analysis of data for a cross-section of Sub-Saharan countries suggests that if Zambian firms had access to banking services at the same average level as their South African counterparts, their productivity would be 6 percent higher, and if they were also to enjoy the access to telecommunications services that South African firms currently have, they could be 13 percent more productive (Arnold, Mattoo, and Narciso 2006).

Supply-side problems attributable to the weakness of services are preventing Zambia from meeting its full potential as a producer and exporter of agricultural goods. Juxtaposing district-level averages of farm yields of cotton and maize with district-level services performance indicators, reveals a significant correlation between farm productivity and the local performance of transport and the cost of obtaining finance (Ajwad, Balat, and Porto 2005). This is consistent with the fact that in those districts in which access to these services is better, farmers of cotton and maize tend to enjoy higher yields per hectare.

Zambian firms and farms can benefit from access to export markets and compete with imports only if they have access to efficient and competitively priced services. Sub-Saharan African exporters like Zambia today pay transport costs that are at least five times greater than the tariffs they face in industrial country markets. Zambia's ability to export tourism services and horticulture depends critically on the state of road and air transport, and its ability to participate in the growing market for business process outsourcing depends on the state of its telecommunications services.

A recent study of 42 countries found that Zambian firms have the second-highest share of "indirect" costs, most of which are attributable to services-related inputs into production—energy, transport, telecom, water, insurance, marketing, travel, independent professionals, and accounting (Eifert, Gelb, and Ramachandran 2005). In fact, the share of indirect costs in Zambian firms is on average 22 percent of gross value added, which is more than twice the share of labor costs. The study found that the high level of indirect costs attributable to the high prices of services inputs is likely to have undermined the competitiveness of Zambian firms in export markets.

The Potential Role of the Services Trade

Services "trade" can play a central role in determining the state of services, because it encompasses cross-border trade in road and air transport; consumption by foreigners of tourism services; FDI in banking, communication, and distribution; and temporary migration of doctors and teachers. Greater regional and global integration could, in principle, alleviate the constraints on the development of Zambia's services sector because of its limited endowments of capital and skills and its small market. Foreign providers can bring the capital, skills, and technology that are used intensively in sectors like telecommunications and finance. This does not mean that only foreign or entirely foreign suppliers would provide these services. As in mobile telephony, insurance, and aviation, Zambian firms are likely to continue to operate, and even foreign firms are likely to have Zambian owner-ship and employees. But the mere fact of being open to foreign entry makes these markets more contestable and can help ensure that the desired quality of services will be provided most efficiently.

Small economies like Zambia's derive another type of benefit from integration. Given the large economies of scale in services industries, incentives to invest would be greater if the Zambian market were not segmented from neighboring markets. Telecom companies can spread the fixed cost of establishing transmission facilities, and insurance companies can spread the risk they bear over a larger market. For any given level of scale economies, more entry, and hence greater competition, in a larger, regionally integrated market would result.

The sectors covered in this study reveal a high degree of openness with virtu-ally no restrictions on FDI (table 1.1). Furthermore, unlike some LDCs whose open markets have been largely ignored by foreign investors, in Zambian sectors ranging from banking to mobile telephony, foreign firms dominate, and in sectors like distribution and tourism, they have a significant share. (For a full description of the initial state of policy in the early 1990s and the subsequent policy changes, please see chapter 2.)

Some areas have already benefited from openness

Mobile telephony was opened to international competition in 1995 and has since seen an increase in the number of subscribers of 300,000, whereas fixed-line telephony, which has remained a de facto monopoly, saw an increase over the same period of less than 20,000 subscribers. In tourism, although there is some concern about the generous tax incentives the foreign investor, Sun International, was granted, its investments (a total of $120 million in two hotels with 385 rooms) have created 350 permanent jobs, supported by 500 or more casual and contract workers, and have significantly boosted economic activity in Livingstone and the neighboring area (Mosi-oa-Tunya national park and the rapids). In insurance, since the liberalization of the sector in 1992, nonlife premium rates have dropped—for example, motor vehicle insurance premium rates fell from 10 to 16 percent of the value of the car in 1992 to 6 percent today.

But in other areas, openness has not so far led to improved access to services

Significant foreign investment in the banking sector has meant that foreign banks today account for more than two-thirds of total assets, loans, and deposits. How-ever, credit to the private sector is only 8 percent of gross domestic product (GDP), which is lower than the level registered in 1990 and the level in most other Sub-Saharan African countries. Although international air transport grew by 7 percent per year between 1995 and 2004, domestic traffic declined at an average of

Table 1.1. Restrictions on Trade and Foreign Presence

Sector	Openness to Services Trade	Share of Sector Held by Foreign Firms
Banking	<u>Mode 1</u>: Capital market liberalized. Cross-border lending and borrowing are permitted by both banks and households. <u>Mode 3</u>: Private and foreign ownership is permitted (up to 100 percent). Foreign banks must be licensed to operate in their home country.	Six foreign banks own 67 percent of the total assets of the sector, with 76 percent of loans and 64 percent of deposits.
Insurance	<u>Mode 1</u>: Cross-border purchasing of insurance services is not permitted unless it can be proven that the type of insurance required is not available in Zambia. <u>Mode 3</u>: Private and foreign ownership permitted (up to 100 percent). Foreign firms must be incorporated locally to open a branch.	Five foreign-owned and part-foreign-owned companies control 17 percent of the market share, in terms of gross written premium.
Telecom (fixed)	<u>Mode 1</u>: Callback services and Voice over IP (VoIP) are illegal and there are high access charges for call termination through the incumbent. <u>Mode 3</u>: Private and foreign ownership permitted in principle (30 percent of equity must be domestically owned). The Zamtel de facto monopoly on international gateway limits competition for international services. VoIP and callback services are illegal.	No foreign investment in the sector. In terms of cross-border supply of services, there are reports of widespread use of callback services and VoIP services on the international segment.
Telecom (mobile)	<u>Mode 1</u>: Callback services and VoIP are illegal and there are high access charges for call termination through the incumbent. <u>Mode 3</u>: Private and foreign-owned firms entry allowed to bid for competitively tendered licenses (at least 30 percent of equity must be domestically owned). Currently, four licenses have been allocated. All firms (foreign and domestic) must use Zamtel's international gateway.	Two foreign-owned cellular companies have 91 percent share of the market, with Celtel alone having 77 percent. As with fixed-line international calls, there are reports of widespread use of callback services and VoIP.

Air Transport	Mode 1: Committed to Fifth Freedom liberalization according to the Yamoussoukro Decision, which became fully binding in 2002, and in COMESA through the COMESA Legal Notice No. 2. In practice, denial of Fifth Freedom rights under bilateral air service agreement continues by both Zambia and other countries, thus leaving a sector that is only notionally open. Mode 3: No formal ownership restrictions.	The domestic and regional air traffic markets are currently served by two fully Zambian-owned carriers and by a few carriers on bilateral agreements with neighboring countries, Ethiopia and South Africa. On the intercontinental route, the only carrier is British Airways.
Accounting	Mode 3: No restrictions on foreign presence. Mode 4: Restrictions through economic means test on visa work permit requirements.	Of the nine accounting firms that have three or more partners, seven were linked to international networks.
Tourism	Mode 3: No restrictions on foreign investment. Mode 4: Limitations of the number of authorized intracorporate transferees.	The formal tourism sector is largely foreign owned in terms of the value of assets.

Source: Authors' compilation from World Bank documents.

5 percent per year. From finance and accounting to telecommunications and international transport, despite a significant degree of liberalization and even after allowing for the low income levels in Zambia, access to services remains low and highly unequal—being available at affordable prices primarily to the affluent in urban areas and to the larger firms.

Zambia has failed so far to exploit its advantage in, and reap the developmental benefits of, tourism

Currently, Zambia's main services export interest is in tourist.[1] But, in 2005, real growth of the travel and tourism sector was 10 times faster in Botswana and Tanzania than in Zambia, differences that cannot be explained by the appreciation of real exchange rate alone. Compared with its neighbors, Zambia has the second lowest (after Zimbabwe) rate of contribution of tourism to GDP (4 percent compared with about 10 percent for Botswana, Tanzania, Namibia, and South Africa) and employment (3.7 percent compared to more than 11 to 12 percent for Namibia and Botswana). Furthermore, the benefits have been unequally spread. Despite the high tourism potential of other poorer provinces, 82 percent of the tourists visit only the Victoria Falls and Mosi-oa-Tunya area, and 93 percent of employment in nature-based tourism activities is concentrated in Livingstone and the rapids. Preliminary cross-country estimates suggest that Zambia is receiving one-third less tourists than would be warranted by its fundamental endowments.

Why has liberalization produced such disappointing results in terms of access?

Because it is difficult even today to conceive of a set of feasible policies that would generate greater growth with equity in the Zambian context, one cannot be too hard on past failures of policy for the lack of success so far in attaining these goals. Moreover, although our focus here is on sector policies, the development of services sectors in Zambia was also strongly affected by economy-wide problems. For example, in the case of the financial sector, the main problems are macroeconomic and institutional rather than sectoral policies. (More comprehensive analysis of individual sectors and recommendations for reform are set out in the sector chapters.)

Nevertheless, there were important errors of policy. We believe that the current crisis of access in Zambia, and hence the diminishing faith in reform, are attributable to the fact that the government and donor organizations behaved *as if* they had complete faith in the power of the markets. They moved aggressively, but unevenly, on the elimination of barriers to entry, sluggishly on the development of regulations to deal with market failure, and only notionally on the implementation of access policies. The result is that access has been undermined by the following:

- Persistence of barriers to competition
- Weakness and inappropriateness of regulation
- Absence of meaningful access policy

This does not mean that the government and donors were naïve and did not appreciate the importance of the latter two dimensions. Rather they did what they could do quickly and relatively easily, which was to privatize and allow entry in some sectors.

One irony is that only limited liberalization has been accomplished in precisely those sectors in which successful outcomes could have been achieved even without progress in the other two dimensions of reform, whereas barriers have been completely eliminated in sectors for which successful outcomes depended critically on complementary reforms. For example, in basic telecommunications and transport, where the benefits of liberalization have been most convincingly and unconditionally demonstrated in international experience, liberalization either did not happen or happened half-heartedly. In telecommunications, a de facto monopoly still exists in fixed-line telephony although there is competition in mobile telephony, and in transport, important restrictions still affect international and domestic competition although some public incumbents have been liquidated. In contrast, in banking, not only was new domestic and foreign bank entry facilitated, but also capital account transactions were fully liberalized. Ten new bank licenses were issued between 1991 and 1994, increasing the number of commercial banks to 18. Nine bank failures between 1995 and 2001 were estimated to have caused losses to taxpayers and depositors equivalent to 7 percent of GDP.[2]

The need to improve regulatory mechanisms was appreciated, and the nature of action required was reasonably well understood. Thus, for example, the Banking and Financial Services Act of 1994 gave the central bank authority to issue prudential directives for banks and non-bank financial intermediaries; the Pensions and Insurance Authority (PIA) was established in 1997 to provide regulation and supervision of pensions and insurance schemes; and the Communications Authority of Zambia (CAZ) was set up in 1995. But implementing comprehensive improvements is necessarily a difficult and slow process. Thus, the 2002 Financial Sector Assessment Program found significant weaknesses in the PIA, and the CAZ lacks effective jurisdiction even today over the incumbent telecommunications operator, Zamtel. The revealed judgment seems to have been that liberalization could proceed before regulatory improvements were fully implemented (box 1.3).

The need for access-widening policies was probably felt in Zambia, although this is far from clear from the policy documents of the period. The appropriate form of such policies, however, is still not well understood outside a few sectors, such as telecommunications, and there is still hardly any evidence of their imple-

---

Box 1.3. Lessons from Privatization

The World Bank's Investment Climate Assessment Report of 2004 recapitulates the main lessons from the Bank's privatization review of Zambia. The review found that one of the reasons some privatized companies did not perform to the expected standard is that previously state-owned enterprises were released into a regulatory vacuum or into an inadequate or inappropriate regulatory framework. Such regulatory frameworks include the legal framework, the institutional design of the regulators, and the capacity of the regulators to discharge their mandates effectively. Reforms are needed at all three levels, especially in the infrastructure sector. To facilitate the growth of the private sector, a sound and predictable regulatory and policy framework needs to be designed and implemented. The privatization program was driven by the need to stop the financial hemorrhage to loss-making companies from the national budget and to enable potentially profitable companies to survive. But by delaying the launch of the privatization program until the last possible moment and not communicating with the public, many options were eliminated and the net benefit to the country was significantly lower than it might otherwise have been. The review recommends greater transparency in the privatization process as well as better efforts to communicate the government's rationale to the public.

Source: World Bank 2004b.

---

mentation in Zambia beyond social services. The poor record of public monopolies in widening access led many to see liberalization itself as the main vehicle for achieving improved access. It should have been clear, however, that the market would deliver nowhere near the socially desirable levels of access.

Sequences matter

As a result of the sluggishness in implementation and imagination, which created lags in the development of regulatory capacity and access-widening policies, a particular sequence of reform resulted. Did the sequence matter? Or was it right to simply "do what you can do when you can do it"?

Sometimes there is no good reason to hold back on liberalization even when regulatory reforms and access-widening policies take time to implement. This is true for reforms that are "additive" in that the benefit from trade reform is independent of the benefit from domestic reforms and each can be undertaken separately. Thus, there is no *economic* reason to wait to liberalize until a universal access policy is established, for example, in telecommunications. In other cases reforms are "multiplicative" in that Zambia would benefit more from trade reform if domestic reforms were also implemented (and vice versa), but the order in which the two are implemented does not matter. Thus, regulatory improvements and competition in transport are mutually beneficial, but the sequence is probably not critical.

In a number of situations, however, "sequences matter" in that if Zambia implements trade reform before the necessary domestic reform, then the long-term payoffs will be lower than if the opposite sequence had been followed. We believe that sequences of reform mattered and continue to matter in Zambia for both economic and political reasons. In these situations, if the complementary reform cannot be implemented instantaneously, then there is a case for gradual liberalization.

...within services for economic reasons

The failure to introduce full competition in a sector such as telecommunications has made it much more difficult to implement effective regulation because of the excessive economic and political power of a monopolistic incumbent. In other sectors, the problem has rather been too much competition too early leading to a form of "regulatory overshooting." For example, allowing new entry in banking without creating a mechanism to sift the sound institutions from the dubious led to disruptions that have had a durable effect on the development of the financial sector: the once-bitten Zambian depositor is skeptical of the benefits of banking and the once-bitten central bank more prudent than most, with stability on its mind. The result has been the implementation of excessively stringent regulation that has itself become an impediment to access.

...and political reasons

In telecommunications in Zambia, efforts to impose immediate liberalization have been rendered *infeasible* by an influential incumbent that is not equipped to survive under competitive conditions. In these circumstances, liberalization may need to be preceded by assistance to the incumbent to adjust to competitive conditions. Probably more serious are the situations in which increased inequality and the failure to ensure that the benefits of liberalization are widely shared make reform *unsustainable*. The failure to deal with access issues has made further progress in eliminating barriers more difficult and has created a serious danger of reversion to the inefficient instruments of the past (box 1.4).

Why does the sequencing of efficiency-enhancing and access-widening policies matter? For one simple reason: any policy is easier to admit when it leads to a Pareto improvement, that is, it makes at least some people better off and no one worse off. This is true at every point of time.[3] So if the objective is growth with equity, then it

**Box 1.4. From Colonialism to Kaundian Socialism,
from Conditionality to Empowerment:
The Present in Historical Context**

It is illuminating to divide the recent economic history of Zambia and its services sectors into four periods:

Phase I: Colonialism
The first phase, the colonial period, saw the emergence of a dichotomous economy: a mining-based urban core, with ownership of the means of production and the rights to mining in the hands of the Europeans, and African participation primarily as labor; and an agricultural periphery, with traditional tribal organization, including communal ownership, and traditional production technologies. Modern services sectors, transport, finance, and communication were developed primarily to serve colonial needs and to an extent the needs of the urban working class.

Phase II: State Capitalism
The period after independence in 1964 eventually saw the emergence of state capitalism with the appropriation by the state of the means of production in sectors ranging from mining to transport. Some effort was exerted to achieve a more egalitarian distribution of at least the consumption of goods and services, ranging from food to education and finance, through a system of artificially low prices, but these policies still had a big urban bias and an even bigger macroeconomic cost. Combined with exogenous negative shocks, notably the declining price of copper, the result was stagnation and a fiscal crisis.

Phase III: Liberalization
The crisis in the late 1980s marked the beginning of a period of liberalization with support from the World Bank and the International Monetary Fund (IMF). Ownership of state assets, including in services sectors, began to be transferred to the private sector (national and foreign) and there was a much greater reliance on the market for resource allocation. These policies, combined with exogenous positive shocks, notably the increasing price of copper, have at the end of the 1990s begun to deliver growth. But they have not delivered equity. For the bulk of the population, access to productive employment and essential goods and services is no better than it was in the 1980s, and in some cases, such as finance, it is probably worse, although there is unquestionably greater efficiency today in the production of services.

As demonstrated in our sectoral reports, liberalization is associated not with widened participation but with accentuated inequalities. It would always have been difficult to demonstrate the benefits of liberalization in the

---

Box 1.4. (continued)

short run, but in Zambia, the problem has been compounded by the weakness of policy, ranging from inadequate competition where it would have helped most to widen access like in telecommunications and transport, to overly stringent regulation that has itself become an impediment to access in accounting and finance, and, most of all, the absence of effective universal access policies in any sector. The result is a dangerous policy vacuum even as Heavily Indebted Poor Countries (HIPC) completion enables Zambia to shake off the shackles of conditionality.

Phase IV: A Return to State Capitalism
The stage may be set for the next phase, moving forward to a possibly diluted version of past state capitalism. Some signs are visible. The privatization of inefficient state-owned incumbents in telecommunications, electricity, and insurance was once imminent but has now been indefinitely deferred. At the same time, proposals have been put forward to create a new national reinsurance company and a national airline to take the place of the one that was liquidated a decade ago. Finally, the empowerment bill has been introduced, which combines elements of affirmative action in ownership and employment with preferential procurement. Some of these measures may serve distributional goals most effectively. But for those who believe that efficiency and growth are best achieved through private enterprise and the market, the challenge is to demonstrate that these instruments can be harnessed to achieve social goals.

Note: For a chronology of service sector reforms in Zambia, including World Bank and IMF support for those reforms, please see Annex A of the Country Economic Memorandum (World Bank 2004c).

---

makes sense to implement a bundle of growth and distributional policies together rather than to focus first on growth and then on redistribution. If we add to this a further dimension, the unequal distribution of the benefits of liberalization becomes apparent only with a lag. When it does, however, those who have not benefited (much) protest or vote against liberalization. Then further liberalization is halted or policies are reversed, which deprives the economy of (further) gains from efficiency.

...as well as in implementing goods and services reform
Sequence matters not just within individual services sectors but also, as Zambia's experience shows, in implementing goods and services reform (see box 1.5 for an example). Consider three stylized facts: the state of producer services affects comparative advantage in goods trade; firms and farms cannot move in and out of

Box 1.5. The Retail Distribution Sector in Zambia: Lessons for the Interplay between Services and Goods Reform

Before the economic reforms initiated in 1989, the state was significantly involved in setting the rules of agricultural production. On the output side, public intervention created a disconnect between farming incentives and comparative advantage: by dictating prices through a marketing board it granted cross-subsidies across crops and regions and from mining to agriculture. After the scheme was abolished, the area under cultivation for maize fell by 23 percent between 1990/91 and 1996/97, while the cultivation of groundnuts and cotton increased substantially (IMF 1999). From an efficiency point of view, the marketing board scheme had obvious disadvantages, and its costly production and distribution scheme became a substantial fiscal burden, taking up 13.7 percent of the budget in 1990.

But at the same time, public intervention did more than just distort the allocation of resources in the output market. It provided farmers with subsidized inputs, credit, extension services, and implicit insurance and transport subsidies by means of uniform pricing across regions and time. The abolition of the marketing boards without any proactive access policies meant that these services become difficult to access for many farmers, and in some remote areas served by none of the emerging private purchasers, farmers had to return to subsistence farming. Many of those farmers found they had lost the necessary seed stocks and practical knowledge while producing only maize as a cash crop during the subsidized period (Winters, McCulloch, and McKay 2004).

At the same time, the liberalization of the Zambian distribution sector allowed the inflow of foreign retail companies, which replaced a part of the traditional retail structures with modern supermarkets. Shoprite of South Africa (Africa's largest retailer, which currently is present in 18 countries) is operating 18 modern supermarkets throughout Zambia, while Spar (another South-African-based retail firm) is following suit. Foreign direct investment in the distribution sector represents opportunities for efficiency improvements in retail, resulting in better quality, more choice, and lower prices for consumers, and in upstream agricultural production. The latter, however, depends on whether local producers are able to participate in these opportunities.

Many potential suppliers of supermarkets, in particular smallholder farmers, are finding it difficult to meet the stringent requirements of a modern business. As a result, Shoprite initially imported 90 percent of its fresh produce from South Africa. When the company arrived in 1995, it found the quality and quantities provided by individual local smallholder farmers too low and too unreliable. Surmounting these difficulties requires organizational assistance, extension services, and credit, which many farmers find difficult to access. Farmers' cooperatives provided with technical assistance from donor-funded organizations have since managed to supply the supermarkets and have demonstrated the potential effectiveness of such complementary policies for integrating local smallholders into modern value chains. In the case of one cooperative that has been organized with donor support and is now supplying Shoprite outlets, farmers' cash incomes have increased from $2–$3 a month to $50–$70 a month, and local access to health care and education services has increased. An alternative source of essential services has been the supermarkets themselves. Through a fully owned sourcing subsidiary for fresh produce, they are providing farmers with extension services and technical assistance, albeit not with credit. Agricultural experts of the retailer's subsidiary visit farms, give advice on crop sequence, and provide inputs.

Local capacities in the production of agricultural goods have proven responsive to this kind of services assistance. Shoprite is now sourcing 90 to 95 percent of the fresh produce from local Zambian farmers. Box figure 1 demonstrates how the bilateral trade patterns between Zambia and South Africa for two food products are related to the entry of South African retailers into Zambia. Around the initial entry in October 1995, one can observe increased imports of meat and vegetable oils from South Africa, but these trends have now reversed as local sourcing options have become viable for the foreign retailers.

Box Figure 1. Trends in Imports of Select Food Products from South Africa to Zambia

Production, processing, and preserving of meat and meat products

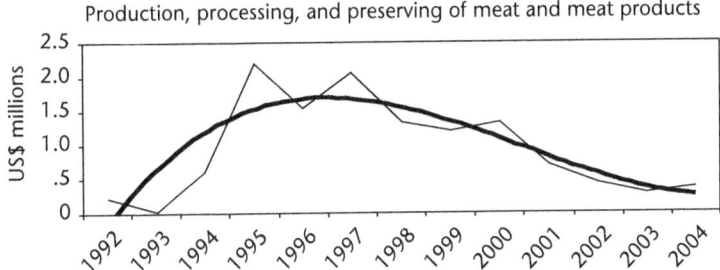

Manufacture of vegetable and animal oils and fats

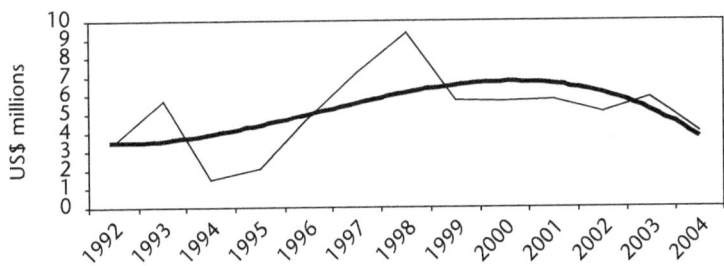

Source: UN Comtrade data; data obtained from the Central Statistical Office in Lusaka.

Note: The first Shoprite store in Zambia was opened in October 1995.

(*Box continues on the following page.*)

Box 1.5. (continued)

   Political pressure to source locally has certainly played its role in the provision of these services by the retailers themselves, and transport and customs difficulties add to the attractiveness of the local provision of fresh produce. Regardless of whether donor goodwill, political pressure, or border delays caused the provision of services where they took place, the modern supermarkets would have found it difficult to source locally had local quality not genuinely improved.

   The Zambian experience in distribution services is an example of two things: the importance of access to services for goods production and the importance of getting the sequence of policies right. The fact that when essential services are withdrawn, farmers can be forced to exit the market economy and lose valuable skills and investments, and the fact that farmers need precisely these skills and investments to upgrade and supply foreign retailers, suggest that the liberalization process should be accompanied by proactive measures that prevent a disruption of services. Freeing markets without enhancing access to services beyond the level provided by markets may reduce the opportunities and benefits of openness.

   Source: Authors' compilation based on interviews in Zambia.

---

production without cost; and it can be hard for firms to borrow in bad times. Thus, the sequence of reform can have durable affects on the structure of production. In particular, if goods liberalization happens in a context in which access to services is limited, then certain service-intensive firms and farms can be driven out of the market by rivals located in countries with wider access to services, and they may find it too costly to reenter even when services reform does eventually take place. In the same way, trade policy for goods may affect services sectors. For example, high tariffs and excise duties on certain inputs make the tourism industry less competitive.

Looking ahead: What needs to be done to improve access?

The chapters that follow set out the key issues and a program for reform for each sector. In chapter 2, Jens Arnold and Aaditya Mattoo draw on available evidence to describe the actual and potential importance of services and services trade in Zambia's economy. In chapter 3, Jens Arnold, Boutheina Guermazi, and Aaditya Mattoo look at the telecommunications sector and argue that its performance has been undermined by barriers to entry and by the weakness of the sector regulator. They find that the use of cross-subsidies by the public provider, Zamtel, has failed to widen access to services. In chapter 4, José de Luna Martinez looks at the banking sector and finds that access to banking services in Zambia has not improved since liberalization of the sector in the 1990s. Much of this is attributable to macroeconomic, institutional, and regulatory weaknesses that have been identified in recent assessments. Little effort has been made on the part of policy makers to pursue interventions to widen access to financial services among the poor.

In chapter 5, Charles Schlumberger looks at the air transport sector. Although the economy, particularly the export sector, would benefit from liberalization, Zambia has rejected requests from foreign airlines to pass through Lusaka en route to other countries. The government should support regional liberalization efforts, reform and strengthen the Civil Aviation Authority, and address the cripplingly high cost of fuel. In chapter 6, Olivier Cattaneo finds that the cost of doing business in the tourism sector is hampering growth. The tax system favors certain providers and certain regions in which tourism establishments already have a high concentration. Furthermore, strong evidence suggests that national parks are not being well managed with serious risk of depletion of tourism resources. In chapter 7, Mohammad Amin and Aaditya Mattoo address migration policy. They argue that Zambia would gain from pursuing bilateral agreements that promote temporary migration. On the one hand, industrial countries may be willing to accept a higher level of unskilled immigration if they could be certain that it was temporary. On the other hand, concerns about brain drain in a source country like Zambia would be greatly alleviated if emigration was temporary. In each chapter, the authors set out a strategy for domestic reform, identify requirements for technical and financial assistance, and propose an approach to international trade negotiations. The key recommendations for each sector are set out in table 1.2.

In this section, we take a horizontal view of the four types of actions that would enable Zambia to benefit from the services trade.

Eliminating Remaining Barriers to Entry

Good regulation and access policies can help, but competition itself is a powerful instrument to widen access in sectors like transport and telecommunications. In these sectors, the case for introducing meaningful competition immediately by eliminating barriers at home and abroad is overwhelming, based on international experience and evidence specific to Zambia. A different type of problem arises in a service sector like tourism for which Zambia has a comparative advantage but is unable to exploit it because regulatory barriers impede entry by Zambian and foreign services providers.

Table 1.2. Key Recommendations, by Sector

Sector	Recommendations for domestic reform (liberalization, regulation, and access for the poor)
Telecommunications	• Immediately make the Communications Authority of Zambia (CAZ) independent and bring Zamtel clearly under its jurisdiction by issuing a proper license; begin tariff rebalancing by Zamtel; allow competition in the international gateway to currently licensed operators. • Over the next year, enhance the regulatory capacity of CAZ; restructure Zamtel so that it can operate on a commercial basis; institute a meaningful universal access policy. • At the end of the year, allow free entry into the international segment to new providers not currently present in the market.
Banking	• Continue to implement the Financial Sector Development Plan (FSDP) to improve the macroeconomic and institutional environment for banking. • Strengthen the regulatory framework as set out in the FSDP but ensure that regulation, particularly if applied to microfinance institutions, is not unduly burdensome for the poor. • Identify appropriate proactive policies to widen access to financial services.
Air Transport	• Fully liberalize entry into the sector and grant Fifth Freedom rights when requested by third countries. • Address inefficiencies in the fuel market that lead to the highest price of fuel in the region. • Focus on (1) the creation of an autonomous Civil Aviation Authority, with administrative and financial independence, (2) development of regulation and technical guidance material, and (3) capacity building for continued surveillance obligations.

Recommendations for technical and financial assistance[a]	Recommendations for international services trade negotiations
• Strengthen CAZ, especially its capacity to ensure inter-connection and guarantee competitive conditions (estimated requirements: $2.7 million). • Institute policies that promote universal access and the develop-ment of national telecommunica-tions backbone, and supplement investment in these areas by the private sector and the government (estimated requirements: $15 million).	• To lend credibility to the reform program, precommit under the General Agreement on Trade in Services (GATS) to eliminate all impediments to competition in all segments of the telecommunication market at the end of the year. • Cooperate regionally to ensure efficient access to the East African Submarine Cable System (EASSy) fiber-optic submarine cable, in particular by developing regional interconnection guidelines and creating a regional dispute resolution mechanism.
• Continue implementation of the FSDP. • Support the creation of a Credit Information Bureau. • Evaluate and implement of banking regulation in light of access needs. • Develop and implement pro-active policies to widen access to financial services.	• Bind existing openness under the GATS to create policy certainty. • Evaluate the benefits of creating a more integrated regional market by harmonizing regulation. Support moves to create a more integrated regional market by harmonizing regulation.
• Regulatory reform and capacity building. The typical cost for such a project ranges from $1 to $3 million. • Upgrade the domestic airport infrastructure. Request funding for the establishment of Global Navigation Satellite System (GNSS)approaches, the cost of which is about $1 million for six to eight approaches.	• Support the full implementation of conti-nentwide liberalization up to and including Fifth Freedom rights as set out in the Yamoussoukro Decision (YD). • Given the slow progress at the continental level, focus negotiation efforts regionally, on liberalization initiatives in COMESA and SADC. • In parallel, negotiate bilateral air service agreements (BASAs) that set out conditions similar to YD. • Use various international forums to eliminate protectionist arrangements between third countries, upon whose routes Zambia relies, and support inclusion of air traffic rights in the GATS.

(Table continues on the following page.)

Table 1.2.   (continued)

Sector	Recommendations for domestic reform (liberalization, regulation, and access for the poor)
Tourism	• Eliminate impediments and distortions created by regulatory policy, in particular, the licensing process and other legal requirements for opening a business in the tourism sector. • Rationalize the tax system; apply incentives equally to all regions of the country and to all providers, national and foreign. • Reform and lend coherence to the mandate of the six public institutions that manage the sector. In particular, for the management of national parks, ensure selection processes and performance incentives that promote conservation, local employment, and infrastructure development.
Migration	• No recommendations for reform.

Source: Authors.

Note: a. These figures are rough estimates of the costs of the project components, based on World Bank experience in contexts similar to Zambia. For more accurate projections of the costs, deeper country-specific analysis would need to be undertaken.

In **telecommunications,** Zamtel's de facto monopoly in the international segment (because of a prohibitive license fee) must end, because it is inefficient in itself and because it is inhibiting the expansion of all other telecommunication market segments. Profits from the international segment have not found their way to financing the expansion of the rural network; rather, they cross-subsidize services for urban households that are already in possession of a phone line and for government departments that do not pay their bills (see box 1.6 for observations on the political economy of reform). At the same time, Zamtel's monopoly inflicts losses upon mobile service providers that must use its gateway, depriving them of

Recommendations for technical and financial assistance[a]	Recommendations for international services trade negotiations
• Streamline impediments to doing business in the sector. • Improve national park and game area management. A recent UNDP/GEP study recommended that $50 million be invested.	• Cooperate regionally to facilitate the movement of tourists, for example, by issuing regional visas, which will enable countries to package their individual attractions. • Cooperate regionally on conservation issues, for example, where there is cross-border movement of wildlife.
• Strengthen the capacity to manage unskilled and skilled migration, especially to screen and certify potential emigrants and facilitate the return and integration of returning migrants.	• Existing agreements like the GATS offer limited hope of increased labor mobility, because they seek primarily to induce host countries to make commitments to allow entry. Zambia may do better by negotiating temporary migration agreements bilaterally with countries like the United Kingdom (along the lines of Spain-Ecuador, Caribbean-Canada, and Poland-Netherlands) with reciprocal obligations: Zambia agrees to screen, select, and facilitate return, and the host country undertakes to repatriate skilled workers at the end of an agreed-on period.

resources that could have been invested in the expansion of their networks. Discriminatory practices in Internet access undermine the growth of other dynamic firms. Our estimates suggest that introducing full competition could provide another 30,000 Zambians with access to fixed-line telephones, and the gains in mobile access could be comparable.

In **aviation**, openness is vital for a small market like Zambia, which has a stake in tourism and horticulture. This openness has been accomplished in principle through ambitious regional agreements, but these agreements have unfortunately failed so far to sweep away protection in Zambia and abroad. Somewhat unusually, Zambia allowed its loss-making national airline to be liquidated in the mid-1990s and liberalized entry into its market. Furthermore, the implementation of up to Fifth Freedom liberalization in the African Union was agreed in the Yamoussoukro Decision (YD), which became fully binding in 2002.[4] Over the three years since it became fully binding, however, the agreement has had little impact on Zambia and its neighbors. Given the failure of YD, COMESA has agreed to liberalize air transport services among its member states with regulations and a mechanism similar to the YD. But here, too, implementation has been partial and subject to delays. As a consequence, Zambia's international air transport remains primarily based on relatively restrictive bilateral air service agreements (BASAs). According to reports, South Africa is keen to protect its national airline's interests on routes between Zambia and South Africa, and has denied Fifth Freedom rights to other countries like the Arab Republic of Egypt to fly the vital Lusaka-Johannesburg route. But Zambia, too, has denied Fifth Freedom rights to Ethiopia and Nigeria to fly the same route. Most recently, for reasons that are difficult to understand, Zambia denied Kenya the right to fly the Lusaka-Harare route. It would be in Zambia's interests to push for the full implementation of YD, and for liberalization within COMESA, and to negotiate, as far as possible, BASAs with other countries under similar conditions (no capacity constraints, up to Fifth Freedom).

In **tourism**, regulatory impediments to entry and operation have shut Zambian entrepreneurs out of a sector in which the country has a comparative advantage. Investment in tourism has been stifled by the high cost, in terms of time and money, and the lack of predictability of licensing and administrative requirements to open and operate a business. Up to 74 licenses are required (no exhaustive list exists), which can take between six months and one year to obtain, and can cost as much as K 10 million for a five-room guest house. As a result, two-thirds of hospitality establishments are unclassified and a large proportion of the tourism sector inhabits the informal economy. In our tourism sectoral report, we estimate that improvements in the business climate and infrastructure could lead to 51 percent or nearly 300,000 more tourists every year.[5] The government must review all administrative and licensing requirements with a view toward removing measures that do not serve any valid policy objective, while ensuring that any measure serving a valid policy objective does so efficiently, transparently, and predictably, seeking ultimately to reduce the cost of compliance with licensing requirements.

Improving the Quality of Regulation to Remedy Market Failure

Good regulation is a precondition for efficient competitive markets, and Zambia faces contrasting challenges. In a number of sectors, from telecommunications to transport, the regulatory framework is weak; in others, such as financial services, auditing, and accounting, it is inappropriately strong. Both problems need to be remedied to widen access.

In **telecommunications**, the enforcement capacity and regulatory independence of the Communication Authority of Zambia (CAZ) are vital, but the regulator is ill-equipped, legally and technically, to ensure efficient interconnection and competitive conditions. Zamtel must be issued a proper license to bring it unambiguously under the ambit of the regulatory regime. The division of power between the CAZ and the Zambian Competition Commission needs to be clarified. Donor support in terms of technical and financial assistance is needed to strengthen regulatory capacity. In our sectoral report, we estimated such assistance to cost $2.7 million.

In **aviation**, too, the regulatory framework and oversight mechanism need to be improved to support the implementation of Zambia's Air Transport Policy. According to the latest Universal Safety Oversight Audit of the International Civil Aviation Organization (ICAO), shortfalls in the regulatory framework and oversight mechanism include a lack of technical guidance material and the poor structure of the Department of Civil Aviation. ICAO particularly noted weak implementation of surveillance obligations and the failure to resolve safety issues. These shortcomings need to be remedied to ensure the development of a safe, secure, efficient, and reliable air transport sector, as well as to support international liberalization, because all liberalization frameworks have provisions to refuse granting traffic rights for safety reasons. The typical cost of a remedial action ranges from $1 to $3 million.

Regulation of **banking** in Zambia must be sensitive to the needs of the population, if banks are to be encouraged to serve the poor and small and medium-size enterprises (SMEs) and, in particular, if microfinance institutions (MFIs) are brought under the umbrella of Bank of Zambia supervision. International regulation, such as anti–money laundering regulation, if applied with no discretion, is not well designed for countries in which only 10 percent of land is registered and much of the population live in temporary dwellings and work informally (see box 1.4).[6] Most SMEs are not registered, do not pay taxes, and do not have audited accounts. Therefore, they cannot access financial services offered by banks. Banks in the past have relied on group monitoring and personalized relations to give loans for productive investments carried out by this part of the population and required only a national identity card. However, Know Your Customer (KYC) rules make such lending illegal if the customer cannot provide documentary proof of residence or proof of employment in the formal sector. Several bank managers stated that these rules were effectively hindering them from making loans to SMEs and individuals that usually they would have made. Finally, a proposal to regulate MFIs could have the benefit of protecting depositors, enhancing stability, and mobilizing resources for MFIs from donors and the formal sector. However, the regulation must be carefully designed so as not to inhibit the development of this nascent sector.

In **accounting and auditing,** appropriate standards should be developed for SMEs because International Financial Reporting Standards (IFRSs) and the International Standards on Auditing (ISA) are primarily directed at the accounting and reporting needs of listed companies and other large public interest entities, such as nonlisted financial institutions and major state-owned enterprises.[7] At the same time, Zambia uses U.K. qualifications and training requirements in auditing and accounting, implying high international mobility of professionals but also high costs and limited domestic relevance of their services. The Zambian Centre for Accountancy Studies trains accountants to sit for the U.K.-based examination at a cost of almost $7,000 whereas it costs a Kenyan student only $1,650 to train and sit for the local Certified Public Accountant examinations. The majority of businesses in Zambia are not listed, but rather are private limited companies or unincorporated small business entities for whom the cost of employing accountants, adopting and applying IFRSs, or undergoing audits outweighs the benefits and becomes one more barrier to their entry into the formal economy. The International Accounting Standards Board (IASB), in fact, has begun a slow process of developing more appropriate standards for SMEs. Even if an IFRS-based SME accounting standard were issued, it is far from certain that it would respond to the needs of Zambian or African SMEs. It is, therefore, necessary to develop locally appropriate accounting standards and corresponding qualification and training standards for professionals, and to assess the desirability of subjecting SMEs to mandatory audits. The Zambian Institute of Chartered Accountants (ZICA) is in the process of developing a local professional qualification with local examinations, but as we argue below, these tasks are best undertaken at the regional level. On the basis of past experience in Zambia, the required assistance is estimated to be around $1 million

Policies to Increase Access for the Poor

Even an efficient, competitive market will not necessarily deliver socially desirable levels of access to services, so a policy priority must be the institution of effective and efficient access-widening policies. This task is perhaps the most difficult and few definite prescriptions transcend the specificity of services sectors, country institutions, and the distribution of political power. Nevertheless, certain broad principles are emerging based on experience in Zambia as well as other countries.

Instruments that distort the functioning of markets often fail to improve access to services or do so at a high cost in terms of efficiency

Skepticism about the ability of private enterprise and the market to deliver socially desirable levels of access has often led to the complete displacement of both, as occurred in Zambia in the 1970s. Thus, public monopolies emerged with administratively set prices kept artificially low for certain categories of users or types of services products through a system of explicit or implicit cross-subsidies. Such interventions nearly always led to inefficient production as public monopolies were not subject to any discipline and inefficient allocation, because the price mechanism was not replaced by any meaningful allocative criteria. Despite the sacrifice of efficiency, the interventions in many cases did not result in any improvement in equity because subsidies were captured by the better-connected, better-located, and wealthier segments of the population. Thus, Zamtel used the revenue from its high-cost international calls to subsidize the cost of domestic calls made by its existing customers, who are overwhelmingly urban and wealthy, with hardly any investment in the expansion of services to the rural poor. Similarly, the water utility used subsidies from the government to keep prices below cost for the urban public elite, but it invested little in the expansion of services in rural areas.

If programs are designed to reach their target, and if there is the institutional capacity to implement them and avoid political capture, they can have an equalizing effect. Despite the widespread acknowledgment of the failure of Lines of Credit as a sustainable means of increasing access, the Enterprise Development Project in Zambia may be a relatively successful example of providing scarce medium-term lending for investment and export production to SMEs (OED 2004). One of the key characteristics of this project was that the funds were channeled through an institution, the Bank of Zambia, that had the capacity and diligence to monitor the on-lending. In addition, the facility allowed local banks to decide freely on on-lending rates, thereby allowing competition between banks receiving funds from the project (World Bank 2003a). In the same way, although the institution of a marketing board for the distribution and marketing of agricultural production was widely criticized for being inefficient and corrupt, it did ensure more equitable access to services in a country that suffers from major weaknesses in transport and distribution services (see box 1.5). Both these schemes, however, furthered equity goals at high cost and held out the risk of fostering unsustainable models of development.

New instruments do better at reconciling equity with efficiency

Hard and soft commands to providers can work, but they must be designed realistically and flexibly, to allow the private sector to choose the most efficient and sustainable means of extending access. To get providers to expand their opera-

Box 1.6. Some Observations on the Political Economy of Reform

Why do we see in Zambia the persistence of poor policy in some areas? Discussions with stakeholders in Zambia suggest a standard explanation: those who gain (or are not hurt) from current policies are economically and politically powerful interest groups, whereas those who lose have little economic and political power.

The persistence of monopoly in telecommunications is hardest to explain given the overwhelming evidence that reforms are likely to produce widespread benefits for all sections of society. Although security concerns are presented by those in the Ministry of Communications and Transport as an important reason for holding back, a more plausible explanation is that politically influential stakeholders may lose or at least fear losses from liberalization. First of all, significant resistance to reform comes from the influential incumbent, Zamtel. Given its current administered price structure (artificially high international prices and artificially low local prices) as well as a general lack of efficiency, Zamtel cannot deal with competition in the international segment. The experience of other countries suggests that many Zamtel employees would be able to find lucrative employment with new entrants, but some are likely to prefer the security of employment in a public monopoly to the uncertain world of competition. Secondly, a key element of equipping Zamtel to face competition would involve tariff rebalancing. The resultant increase in local call prices is likely to be resisted by the politically vocal urban consumers, although the prospect of more competitive mobile telephony may dilute such opposition. Finally, although Zamtel is hardly a cash cow, there are suggestions that some of its revenues benefit politically influential entities. The lack of transparency in the firm's accounts, and our inability to obtain access to them, lends some credence to this view. Some form of transparent compensation (for example, voluntary retirement schemes, cheaper mobile telephony) could be used to persuade the incumbent's employees and urban consumers to accept reform, but it is hard to devise a socially acceptable compensation package for dubious beneficiaries like political parties.

In banking, the issue is why the government has not done more to improve access to credit and other banking services. Note, first of all, that Zambia places no restrictions on international transactions on the capital account. The result is that those who can borrow from abroad, that is, the large firms and the urban rich, are partially insulated from the "crowding out" caused by large government deficits. The pressure from these politically powerful entities for broader fiscal reform is consequently weaker than in regimes for which external borrowing is not an option. Secondly, burdensome regulatory requirements relating to documentation or collateral do not hurt the concentrated interests of the large firms or the urban rich, but rather the diffuse interests of small enterprises and the rural poor. The managers of foreign banks stated that their primary if not exclusive focus was on corporate clients. The manager of a Zambian bank did profess an interest in broad-based lending, but in response to a question about Know-Your-Client rules, stated that "these are the documentation requirements—if you can't meet them, hard luck." Finally, powerful donor interests, in the current climate of concern about terrorism and drugs, are placing a greater emphasis on regulatory changes that protect the integrity of financial systems than on those that ensure wider access to financial services. Several banks suggested that a fear of being black-listed prevented them from even exploring less burdensome alternatives to regulatory requirements.

In accounting, the issue is that the local profession is geared almost entirely toward the lucrative large firm market. Of the big four accounting firms' focus, only one revealed an interest in developing products for the small and medium-size enterprise (SME) market. The revealed preference of the profession is to perpetuate and apply, with limited differentiation, international accounting and auditing standards. The Zambian Institute of Chartered Accountants (ZICA) has made an effort to develop a local technician and professional qualification, but it has done little to develop appropriate accounting and auditing standards for SMEs. The question of whether it might be desirable to exempt SMEs from burdensome statutory audits provoked a ZICA official to say, "but audits are where our revenue comes from." Even the development of a Zambia-specific qualification is a mixed blessing because it will have the effect of further segmenting the Zambian market from the regional market and confer greater market power on local accountants. As it is, all countries in the region are applying restrictive immigration and work permit rules to protect their own professionals from foreign competition that would potentially benefit diffuse consumer interests.

In the case of transport services, too, the current constellation of political forces could produce perverse results. On the face of it, Zambia is a land-locked country and seems to be a victim of high transportation costs. But a closer look demonstrates that Zambia itself maintains certain restrictions on both air and road transport. To understand why, the focus needs to shift from exporting interests, which do suffer from these restrictions, to import competing interests and domestic transport service providers who benefit. Thus, discussions with South African distributors of horticultural products revealed that an important reason for local sourcing was the high cost of transporting products from neighboring countries. Similarly, Zambian restrictions on foreign entry in cabotage, as well as the regional requirement that international transporters move products between two foreign countries only if they pass through their own country, serve to benefit Zambian transporters. If, as seems likely, Zambia's import competing interests and transporters are better organized than exporting and other consumer interests, then it would help explain why landlocked Zambia has adopted restrictive transport policies.

tions to unserved parts of the country, governments sometimes place explicit roll-out obligations in licenses. For example, Vodacom of South Africa was induced by such a scheme to set up more than 3,500 phone shops, mostly in South Africa's townships, to provide 22,000 community phones in disadvantaged areas (World Bank 2004a). Under this scheme, the provider bears the risk and cost of the expansion, and thus has every incentive to make sure that it is efficient and sustainable. Business and telecenters that follow commercial models from the start, in general, are more effective than those that receive subsidies. This has been demonstrated in Zambia, as the business center started by Zamnet and Zamtel in the Chipata Chamber of Commerce stopped functioning as soon as subsidies ended in 2001, whereas the Coppernet telecenter in Choma has functioned without subsidies since it opened in 2000.

In South Africa, in response to government "moral suasion," the representatives of the financial services industry signed the Financial Sector Charter in 2003 in which they undertook to increase the number of poor people with a bank account from 32 percent to 80 percent by 2008. To achieve this goal, the key players in the sector have collaborated to design the Mzansi account, which offers fewer services, but that has lower charges on transactions such as cash deposits and automated teller machine (ATM) withdrawals. The product has been highly successful, with 180,000 new customers in the first six weeks. Thus, government pressure has pushed banks to innovate and to engineer a product that is sustainable and even profitable. In fact, the South African Stanbic Bank is considering introducing a similar product in Zambia. This example emphasizes that allowing banks to decide on the extent, process, and technology of the expansion not only avoided conflict with the regulator, but also resulted in the kind of innovation and sectorwide coordination necessary to achieve the objective.

Fiscal incentives to providers are often the best inducement to get them to serve the poor and remote. Competitive allocation of performance-based subsidies has proved to be an efficient instrument of access. So that subsidies do not have the downsides described above, governments and donors prefer to subsidize the connection cost, and not the cost of the service itself. The subsidy is explicitly tied to increasing access, so that it cannot be captured by those who are already customers. Zambia is in the process of pursuing this approach in basic telecommunications with World Bank support, and this approach has shown positive results in a variety of contexts, from the rural electrification program in Guatemala to the rural telecommunication program in India. The key to the success of these projects is that the subsidies are allocated competitively and on the basis of revealed performance to the provider that demands the least subsidy. Furthermore, obligations stipulate only the end goal, leaving the choice of technology, in terms of product design or mode of delivery, to the imagination of the providers.

A direct transfer to poor households in the form of cash or a voucher to enable them to purchase services is, in principle, the most effective policy, but the administrative costs of selecting households are high and the policy is prone to capture. This approach has so far been applied internationally more for the purchase of social services, such as health care and education, as well as to provide cash for food. In principle however, it could be widened to other areas. Such direct transfers are being administered currently by the Ministry of Community Development and Social Services (MCDSS) in the Kalomo District in Zambia. The transfer is targeted at those in need of cash for food and other basic services and to increase their ability to make investments in seeds, for example. In contrast to receiving transfers in kind (as distributed by nearly all transfer programs in Zambia), the critically poor households receive transfers in cash, which they can use flexibly according to their own priorities. The German agency that is helping to implement the project has found that empowering consumers to decide how to allocate their resources has a stronger poverty impact than transfers in kind. However, a large investment in the selection process is necessary to ensure the subsidy is not captured.

The government should see universal access in a horizontal context and exploit the synergies between services sectors to increase the likelihood of achieving access goals.
Focus on a single sector may itself be a problem. It is in the nature of services, such as insurance, banking, energy, telecommunications, postal, and water, that they are interdependent, as the provision of one may be made easier by access to another. If policies are designed to enable the consumption of more than one service, providers are able to exploit economies of scale as well as benefit from the positive spillovers from the consumption of complementary services.

The irony is that postliberalization Zambia has seen several induced or spontaneous breakups of service providers: the postal, telecommunications, and banking services have separated into Zampost, Zamtel, and the National Savings and Credit Bank; the marketing board that provided transport, distribution, and a range of other services has been replaced by specialized private service providers. Furthermore, regulatory restrictions prevent banking and insurance services from being provided by the same financial institution. These separations have often arisen from efficiency considerations. The question is whether the equity gains from bundling can be reaped without sacrificing any efficiency gains that arise from separation.

One approach is to exploit economies of scale by allowing multiple services providers to offer their products through the same distribution network. Given that banks have found it a challenge to serve poor and rural areas because of the nature of demand, which is small but transaction intensive, many countries have moved toward "correspondent banking" as a way to broaden the range of delivery points and allow for small-scale banking. Banks outsource services typically undertaken at branches, like receiving loan applications, making deposit withdrawals, and paying invoices, to nonfinancial institutions with a significant network of outlets, such as convenience stores or lottery houses. This has been highly successful in Brazil, for example, where it was estimated that the cost of providing banking services through the already existing post office was but 0.5 percent of the cost of building a new branch (Schmukler and Gozzi 2006).[8]

Building effective and strong partnerships between state-owned postal operators and financial institutions has proven to be a complex and cumbersome process, as the divorce of Zampost and the National Savings and Credit Bank demonstrates. A recent report on lessons for expanding access to financial services through the postal networks highlights two particular weaknesses that have undermined the potential for public-private partnerships: first, private banks are loath to work with an institution that is not run on a commercial basis, that depends on a nontransparent provision of subsidies between the separate services being offered by the post office, and that has little tradition of accountability (World Bank 2006b). The lack of investment in information and communication technology (ICT) in many postal networks in Africa is another problem, which again makes the argument for bundling access to postal and banking services with access to telecommunications networks.

Bundling services can help providers exploit the positive spillovers arising from their joint consumption. The experiments of Grameen Bank in Bangladesh have brought to attention a point that had been overlooked by the designers of telecom rollout obligations: that the ability of consumers to pay for communications services will be enhanced if they have access to finance. Local entrepreneurs in Bangladesh use microloans from Grameen Bank to cover the cost of a handset and the connection fee for a mobile phone from Grameen Telecom. This has enabled local entrepreneurs to provide mobile payphone services in their local community, while repaying the up-front investment over two to three years, plus a minimum monthly usage charge for the line. Each village payphone covers about 2,500 people. Furthermore, by working with an established local institution, the telecom company has experienced high cost recovery despite its lack of familiarity or ability to enforce contracts in the local context (Lawson and Meyenn 2000).

This is the approach underlining the recent "Zyonse" product that has been developed by the National Resources Institute to be offered to smallholder farmers in Zambia. The packaged financial product being offered consists of insurance, primarily covering weather insurance, and production credit and the collateralization of produce to improve crop marketing and ease access to commodity finance. The product will be offered by financing banks, with the insurance cover provided by credible insurance companies. Farmers ultimately pay the insurance premium, but it may be initially financed by the banks. The loan covenants require farmers to deposit and market their produce using the warehouse receipt system (Onumah 2005).

In general, bundling of services will create a significant regulatory challenge to ensure competitive and cost-based access to shared networks—a problem that motivated some of the separations. The report on post office banking concluded that, if banks are to use the postal network, they must continue to remain institutionally separate from the post office and come under central bank supervision. Regulating access to networks has proved to be a challenge even within a single sector.[9] These problems are not insurmountable, however, and the potential benefits in terms of access provide good reason to look for solutions.

Priorities for International Engagement

Zambia's international engagement can help mobilize assistance for, and lend credibility to, domestic reform, can deliver improved access to foreign markets, and can further deeper regional integration.
Zambia is engaged in services trade negotiations, in the WTO under the GATS, with the EU in the context of the EPAs, and potentially within both COMESA and SADC. Zambian policy makers and negotiators must address what is feasible and desirable in the different negotiating contexts.

International services trade negotiations thus far have not been powerful instruments of reform. In the Uruguay Round, the GATS instituted certain fundamental rules for trade in services, such as the requirements of transparency with regard to policy measures and nondiscrimination between trading partners (most-favored-nation, MFN, treatment). But the GATS framework for negotiating liberalization commitments has had limited results, with most countries choosing to commit legally only to maintaining the policy status quo or even less. Zambia's own involvement in the Uruguay Round was cautious, and it made liberal commitments only on certain professional and other business services, construction and related engineering services, health care and social services, and tourism and travel-related services (see annex 2). Even in these sectors, Zambia's commitments on the presence of natural persons were conservative, like those of most other countries.

Looking ahead, however, it would be wrong to rule out the possibility of beneficial engagement in bilateral, regional, and multilateral forums. In principle, international negotiations can deliver four things:

- Improved access to foreign markets and liberalization at home through a process of reciprocal market opening that is central to mercantilist trade negotiations.

Zambia's main services exports today are of tourism on which its trading partners impose few restrictions. Conversely, Zambia has a small market that is quite open, with the exception of the high fees for the international telecommunications gateway, some restrictions on air transport, and economic needs tests with regard to the movement of natural persons. So, its own market access does not offer a great deal of negotiating power. Furthermore, if Zambia does liberalize or bind its liberalization, its own interests would best be served by doing so on an MFN or nonpreferential basis. Doing so would give its consumers access to the best service providers in the world. Liberalizing on a preferential basis may improve the status quo in the short run (for example, reducing the gateway license fee only for European or South African providers), but granting a first-mover advantage to a second-best provider can have undesirable long-term consequences in services markets. Because services are often provided through establishment, they involve significant sunk costs that give an incumbent a strategic advantage. Once the second-best provider has established, it may be difficult for the best provider to enter even if Zambia subsequently liberalizes on an MFN basis. On these grounds, Zambia should depart from nonpreferential market opening only if its trading partners in a regional or bilateral context provide substantial incentives to do so.

- Credibility of existing and future reform through legally binding international commitments that are costly to revoke.

In cases in which the Zambian market is already open (for example, in banking services), promising to keep it open creates greater policy certainty, which could make the market more contestable and attract new firms. The key issue is whether the gain in credibility outweighs any loss in flexibility. In cases in which market opening should be deferred—for example, to give the incumbent (Zamtel) or regulator (CAZ) time to prepare for competition—Zambia also could make reform credible through binding commitments to future liberalization. Such commitments avoid the danger of perpetual infancy, and hence perpetual protection, by confronting incumbents and regulators with a credible deadline by which time they must be equipped to deal with openness.

- External assistance from more affluent trading partners to facilitate adjustment, improve regulation, and institute effective policies for universal access.

Zambia is well placed to mobilize such assistance. The consensus-based approach to international negotiations gives small countries like Zambia an important say in the advancement of multilateral liberalization, in particular, because the interests of these countries are only imperfectly aligned with the broader liberalization agenda. Because they have preferential access to the markets of the industrial countries, further multilateral liberalization, in certain areas, would erode rather than enhance their access to these markets. Accommodating the interests of the small and poor countries by providing them with "aid for trade" is desirable in itself, but also is necessary to ensure smooth and expeditious progress in the Doha Round or the EPA negotiations, especially in an intellectual and political climate that is geared toward ensuring a fair outcome for these countries.[10]

- **Deeper integration that creates a single market in one or more sectors through regulatory harmonization and infrastructural coordination.**

To create stronger incentives for investment and to reap the benefits of scale without sacrificing competition, Zambia needs to be part of a more integrated market. Integration requires a certain degree of regulatory harmonization, which has benefits but also costs. The former will dominate in situations in which national regulation can be improved, as in the case of telecommunications services. But in situations in which national regulations are optimal, the benefits of international harmonization in terms of greater competition in integrated markets must be weighed against the costs of departing from nationally appropriate regulations. For example, harmonizing accounting standards with the EU may give Zambian accountants access to the larger EU market, but this harmonization leads to a higher degree of local inappropriateness than if standards were harmonized with neighboring countries. The choices are simpler when it is possible to have separate standards, for example, one for exporters and one for companies that serve the domestic market, as may be feasible in accountancy.

Table 1.3 summarizes the main recommendations.

Three bundles naturally emerge:

- Aid for trade and commitment to reform in the WTO and EPA contexts
- Cooperation on migration in the EPA or bilateral context
- Deeper integration in the regional COMESA and SADC context

Aid for Services Trade: A Priority in the Doha Agenda and EPA Contexts

The critical elements of the aid-for-trade agenda relate to services. The Ministry of Commerce must continue to play an influential role at the interface of interna-

Table 1.3. Priorities for International Engagement in Alternative Forums

	WTO	EPA	COMESA/SADC
Reciprocal market opening	*Abroad:* Mode 4 and air transport desirable but probably infeasible. *Home:* Desirable and feasible to open telecom, and so on, on an MFN basis.	*Abroad:* Cooperation on temporary migration and liberalizing air transport is desirable and may be feasible (for example, with the United Kingdom). *Home:* Preferential opening not necessarily desirable.	*Home and abroad:* Reciprocally liberalizing professional, road, and air transport is desirable and may be feasible.
Credibility of reforms	Binding existing openness in financial sectors and precommitting to opening in telecom is feasible and desirable.	May be feasible.	May be feasible.
External assistance	"Aid for trade" is desirable and may be feasible.	Desirable and most likely to be feasible.	Limited feasibility (e.g., South Africa).
Deeper integration	Infeasible in the foreseeable future.	Relatively feasible but not always desirable.	Desirable and feasible for the professional, telecom, and transport sectors. In the financial sector, it is desirable but may not be immediately feasible.

Source: Authors.

Note: The assessment of desirability is based on economic considerations; the assessment of feasibility is based on the authors' view of the broad political environment. COMESA = Common Market for Eastern and Southern Africa; EPA = Economic Partnership Agreement; MFN = Most Favored Nation; SADC = Southern African Development Community; WTO = World Trade Organization.

tional trade negotiations and domestic reform. The aim should be to present donors with a package in which Zambia commits to a program of reform over a certain time period, and donors would commit to provide the requisite technical assistance. This assistance would be consistent with Zambia's broader development priorities, be additional to and build on existing projects and commitments, and be informed by international principles of aid effectiveness.

• The Ministry would engage with domestic stakeholders so that Zambia could commit to the following:

- Eliminate all de jure and de facto impediments to competition, for example, the de facto monopoly in telecommunications, denial of Fifth Freedom rights in aviation, and burdensome licensing in tourism
- Enhance the independence of regulatory authorities in telecommunications, banking, insurance, and transport
- Develop mechanisms to widen access to services, for example, in telecommunications, transport, and financial services

- The Ministry would engage with donors to induce them to commit to the following:
  - Address competition restricting policies that adversely affect Zambia, for example, restrictions on competition in aviation, exemptions from their competition law for export cartels, and highly restrictive immigration regimes
  - Provide technical and financial assistance to strengthen regulatory institutions, for example, in telecommunications, insurance, tourism, and aviation
  - Remedy or develop appropriate regulation, for example, in financial and accounting services (requirements in telecom alone estimated to be $2.7 million)
  - Support schemes to widen access and develop infrastructure, supplementing investment in these areas by the private sector and the government (requirements in telecom alone estimated to be $15 million)

These elements will be mutually reinforcing both substantively, because the ability to use aid fruitfully depends on domestic reforms, and strategically, because the promise of reform makes the demands for assistance less resistible and the promise of assistance could make the demands for reform less resistible.

Cooperation on Temporary Migration: A Priority in the EPA or Bilateral Context

Negotiations on the "temporary presence of natural persons" (mode 4) under the GATS have not been particularly successful in the past, and prospects in the current round of negotiations are not bright. In fact, negotiations primarily have facilitated exploratory business visits and the movement of high-level personnel within multinational corporations. Zambia and other developing countries continue to be disappointed by the dearth of commitments in their area of comparative advantage—that is, the movement of skilled and unskilled individuals unrelated to a commercial presence abroad (foreign direct investment).

Facilitating the temporary movement of both the skilled and unskilled is accomplished more easily in a bilateral than a multilateral context.

Zambia faces contrasting challenges: obtaining greater freedom for the movement of the unskilled and ensuring that the movement of the skilled remains temporary to avoid the adverse effects of brain drain. It may be able to promote more migration of the unskilled if it takes measures, in cooperation with the receiving countries, to ensure that such migration is temporary. Bilateral agreements along these lines have been successfully implemented between the Caribbean and Canada, Ecuador and Spain, and Poland and Germany. Zambia would agree to help with the selection and screening of migrants, provide necessary predeparture training, and cooperate to ensure timely return. Aversion to unskilled immigration in the receiving countries may be reduced through agreements that ensure temporariness.

Temporary migration of the skilled cannot be achieved unilaterally by Zambia and requires cooperation with destination countries in the framework of a bilateral agreement. Today, most temporary migration schemes in the Organisation for Economic Co-operation and Development (OECD) countries are stepping stones to permanent migration. The exceptions are certain managed migration schemes, such as the agreement between Poland and the Netherlands on the temporary movement of nurses and the Seasonal Agricultural Worker's Scheme implemented by the United Kingdom for temporary visits by university students in agriculture. In some cases, receiving countries find it difficult to implement temporariness of the skilled even when it is the socially preferred outcome. In these cases, sending countries such as Zambia can help ensure temporariness through a bilateral treaty clearly ruling out permanent residence. In cases in which highly skilled professions require long and extensive training periods, the receiving countries prefer permanent over temporary migration. Ensuring temporariness here is more difficult, and Zambia must rely on the goodwill of the receiving countries to repatriate its skilled personnel.

Facilitating the temporary movement of both the skilled and unskilled is accomplished more easily in a bilateral than a multilateral context. Existing international agreements on labor mobility, such as the WTO's GATS, have failed to do better because they primarily seek to induce host countries to make commitments to allow entry. Such an approach is currently ill-suited to unskilled migration because provisions are lacking for source countries like Zambia to undertake binding commitments on screening, selection, and facilitating repatriation. The approach is ill-suited for skilled migrations because it does not enable host countries to undertake binding commitments to ensure temporariness of skilled personnel from countries like Zambia. In the absence of a dramatic change in the multilateral framework, a development-friendly approach to manage migration is more easily developed in a bilateral context, for example, with the United Kingdom or as part of the EPA.[11]

Deeper Integration: A Priority in the Regional COMESA and SADC Contexts

Regional agreements in services have followed mechanically the precedent of regional agreements in goods, and the framework of the GATS or NAFTA, and have focused on the elimination of explicit barriers to the entry of service providers. Preferential liberalization in services is difficult because the required legislative changes are usually easier to accomplish on a nonpreferential basis. Furthermore, as noted above, services markets are ideally opened on an MFN or nonpreferential basis. But perhaps the greatest cost of the existing approach is that it may have diverted attention and negotiating resources away from an area of much greater benefit in the regional context: cooperation on infrastructure services and regulation. Such cooperation is more feasible and more desirable in the regional context with proximate countries at a similar level of development than in the multilateral or EPA context.

The priorities are cooperation on telecommunication and transport infrastructure, liberalization of air and road transport, development of regionally appropriate professional standards in areas like accountancy, and enforcement of competition policy. Significant benefits likely would arise from cooperation in financial services, but the prospects for substantial cooperation in this area do not seem to be bright.[12]

Communications: Zambia has a stake in regional cooperation because of shared infrastructure

Currently, Zambia relies on expensive satellite communications for connectivity with the rest of the world and suffers from a lack of adequate and cost-effective international bandwidth. To bridge the connectivity gap in the region, a new regional submarine cable system EASSy is being planned. To gain open, fair, and competitive access to the proposed regional infrastructure needed for the development of Zambia's Internet and telecommunications sectors, cooperation at the regional level is required to facilitate cost-based and cross-border interconnection and pricing agreements. The EASSy fiber-optic cable project offers Zambia the possibility of gaining access to a terrestrial broadband network via its neighbors Malawi and Zimbabwe. Zambia is actively participating in this regional infrastructure initiative, and Zamtel is planning to make an equity investment in the EASSy consortium to build the submarine cable.

Access to the EASSy landing points is envisaged through two links: Lusaka-Lilongwe and Lusaka-Harare. For Zambia to gain efficient, fair, and competitive access to the cable through these intermediary countries, an increased degree of regulatory cooperation will be necessary. In particular, Zambia and its neighbors will need to renegotiate and revise existing cross-border interconnection and pricing agreements. A key difficulty for Zambia, however, is that the enforcement of such agreements is beyond the jurisdiction of national regulators. Thus a strong case can be made for the development of regional interconnection guidelines, the creation of a regional clearing house for interconnection, and the enforcement of regional competition and dispute settlement frameworks. Existing regional initiatives, for example, those under COMESA, could be leveraged to reach this goal. "Policy Guidelines for Interconnection for COMESA Countries" stress that the principles of domestic interconnection should apply at the regional and international levels. If a regional body is empowered to ensure the enforcement of these guidelines, fair and competitively priced access to the EASSy cable for Zambia and other landlocked countries could be safeguarded.

Road and air transport: Steps toward the creation of a regional market
In road transport, it is natural for Zambia to cooperate at the regional level.[13] In air transport, Zambia has a stake in the liberalization of intercontinental routes and regional traffic, but the latter may be more feasible in the current political context. A liberalized air transport market at the regional level would be beneficial for at least two reasons: the development of tourism requires efficient and economical regional connections so that tour operators can bundle Zambia's safari parks with neighboring countries' beaches and other attractions; and a liberalized regional market can reduce the costs of intercontinental transport by facilitating the emergence of a more efficient hub-and-spoke model, from which Zambia is likely to benefit regardless of whether it is the hub or at the end of a spoke.

In air and road transport, the first priority must be to get rid of explicit barriers. In road transport, an additional dimension is analogous to telecommunications: countries must have access at a reasonable cost to the regional road network, which requires regulatory harmonization and the removal of implicit barriers (Buys, Deichmann, and Wheeler 2006).

Liberalization of regional transport markets has stalled
In air transport, as set out above, the YD has yet to be enforced by Zambia or its neighbors. Similarly, movement toward liberalization in COMESA has been slow. As a consequence, Zambia's international air transport remains based primarily on the relatively restrictive BASAs, and evidence suggests that Zambia and South

Africa have denied Fifth Freedom rights to other countries. It would be in Zambia's best interests to push for the full implementation of YD and for liberalization within COMESA, and to negotiate, as far as possible, BASAs with other countries under similar conditions (no capacity constraints, up to Fifth Freedom).

There is an irony in road transport services: significant progress has been made in dealing with implicit barriers to trade, but little progress has been made in addressing the explicit barriers to trade, although the latter are mainly stroke-of-the-pen reforms. Today, bilateral agreements continue to govern international road transport operations in SADC countries. The so-called third-country rule is critical and would allow carriers of one Member State to carry freight on a defined route between two other Member States or between a Member State and a non-member state, irrespective of whether the carrier's vehicle traverses the territory of its home state. Only two countries allow the third-country rule, and, even then, only on a reciprocal basis. States have conditioned their accession to the liberalizing agreement, which was drafted for negotiation in 2002, on the achievement of harmonization and standardization in several areas of operation.

Existing initiatives to remove regulatory barriers to trade in road transport services must be strengthened

Minimum design standards for the Regional Trunk Road Network (RTRN) and standardized road traffic markings were adopted in 2003. These measures, coupled with the implementation of road sector reforms in 9 out of the 12 continental SADC states, are expected to form the foundation for the development of an integrated regional road transport market. Efforts have been made to standardize *axle load limits*, but progress has been slow. For example, Zambia and Angola have lower limits for the tandem axle, which negatively affects some cross-border operations. The SADC Protocol on Transport, Communications, and Meteorology (in Articles 6.4, 6.5, and 6.6) requires Member States to adopt harmonized standards for vehicle safety and equipment. Differences in such standards compromise the efficiency of cross-border operations because operators are forced to use different configurations for different markets.

The SADC Protocol on Transport advocates the recovery of the costs of transport infrastructure by imposing *road user charges*. The region has different sources of road financing arrangements in place, including road or bridge tolls (Mozambique, South Africa, Zimbabwe), fuel levies (all states), fixed charges per unit of weight and distance (SADC states that are also members of COMESA), and other taxes. The differences continue to have a negative effect on the smooth flow of traffic across borders within the region. SADC with EU support is currently reviewing the charges, with a focus on the RTRN, with the intention of helping countries harmonize these charges.

Differences in *third-party insurance* regimes result in an increase in transport operating costs and risks in three respects: increased paperwork, contribution to delays at borders, and the need for drivers to carry cash and the associated risks of doing so. Currently, three main systems of third-party liability insurance are used for cross-border transport in the region, namely, cash payments, fuel levy, and the Yellow Card system. Regional efforts are focused on linking the fuel levy regime used in the South African Customs Union (SACU) States to the Yellow Card under COMESA.

In 1999, SADC adopted the SADC *Drivers License* as an Annex to the SADC Protocol on Transport, Communications, and Meteorology. The license is part of several proposals to harmonize the way in which drivers are trained, examined, and licensed across the region. Standardized manuals on these areas were adopted in 2004. Since the adoption of the Annex on the Drivers License, the following SADC States now issue the SADC drivers license: Angola, Botswana, Lesotho, Malawi, Mauritius, Namibia, South Africa, Swaziland, and Zambia.

Accounting and other professional services: Developing regionally appropriate standards

Because the needs of regional countries are similar, appropriate standards for professional services like accounting are best developed at a regional level, with regionally agreed qualification requirements and regionally administered examinations, and only supplementary national elements. In accounting, although international standards remain appropriate in specific cases (for example, for firms that operate internationally or that wish to list on the Lusaka Stock Exchange), a regional accounting standard would offer a credible alternative for cases in which an international standard is more burdensome than necessary, as is the case for SMEs. The development of such a standard presents Zambia and other countries in the region with an opportunity to address the need for a balance between stringency and access, between existing integration and local appropriateness, and between rules and discretion. The lower tier standard is best determined at a regional level, because of the following:

• The needs of SMEs in countries of the region are similar. The country-specific content is not expected to be large because there is a high universal content to accounting and auditing needs. Hence, horizontal differences between countries can be addressed through country-specific content pertaining to law and taxation. In this respect, developing supplementary local content in the syllabus should be encouraged, given that local law was not previously being taught. Malawi and Botswana, for example, have U.K.-based accountancy examinations but with local law and tax replacing the British modules.

- There is more scope to draw on regional expertise and less duplication of effort, and less scope for regulatory capture at the regional level. In contrast, if this lower-tier standard is developed at a national level, it would lead to an unnecessary duplication of efforts in skill-scarce countries. Credibility could be undermined if there is inadequate capacity to design, promote, and implement national standards, or if it allows undue influence by local vested interests. Concerns were expressed by some stakeholders in Zambia that any problem experienced in the examination and administration of the proposed new local qualification (ZICA) would erode the reputation of the Zambian profession, which currently is high thanks to success in the U.K.-based examinations.
- It will be possible to maintain at least a regionally integrated market. In contrast, setting heterogeneous standards in the region would segment a market that has been quite integrated so far, at least on the regulatory dimension because inherited standards are regionally recognized. (Increasing evidence suggests barriers to international mobility are being created in Zambia and other countries through the application of economic needs tests implemented through visas or work permits.) Segmentation could impose a significant cost for smaller countries in terms of competition and diversity of services.
- A framework for regional cooperation already exists in the form of the ECSAFA. ZICA is a member of ECSAFA and is one of the institutes involved in the development of the ECSAFA Guide on Accounting for SMEs, which is about to be issued. This regional effort should be useful unless and until the IASB issues an acceptable standard for SMEs. Zambia could use the ECSAFA regional structure to obtain a mining accounting standard similar to the one in use in Tanzania. In November 2005, the ECSAFA region developed common training standards for accounting technicians.

Competition policy: Regional cooperation can help overcome the limitations of national bodies

The Zambian Competition Commission (ZCC) cannot on its own ensure competitive conditions. For example, South Africa is a significant investor across southern Africa and "with $373 million invested in more than 300 projects" it is now the largest foreign investor in Zambia (Goering 2006). For the most part, South African investment has been welcome. This investment, however, has led to concerns that South African companies may abuse their market power, either unilaterally or collectively to the detriment of local producers and consumers. The ZCC is not able to deal effectively with accusations against South African companies of anticompetitive behavior in Zambia for four reasons: (1) it often does not have the jurisdiction to deal with companies that operate in Zambia but are not locally incorporated, or for some other reason, do not come under Zambian

Competition law; (2) it does not have the ability to enforce its decisions, even where it does have jurisdiction to issue judgments; (3) the ZCC is often unable to obtain the information necessary to investigate the activities of a foreign company from the home jurisdiction of that company; and (4) it is evident that the Commission, despite its competent and motivated staff, lacks the resources to conduct the detailed empirical investigations required to effectively address allegations of anticompetitive behavior.

One possibility would be for Zambia to condition opening its market to South African firms on a commitment by the South African authorities to investigate anticompetitive behavior by South African companies in Zambia, where the local authorities are not competent to do so (Hoekman and Saggi 2007). In principle, it would be in South Africa's interest to provide such reassurance. An analysis of South Africa's Competition Act reveals, however, the limits of the jurisdiction of the South African Competition Authority. The structure and text of South Africa's Competition Act suggest that it only applies to behavior that has an effect on the South African economy. Section 3 states that the Act "applies to all economic activity, *within*, or having an effect within, the Republic" (own italics). The italicized *within* suggests that the Act may extend to anticompetitive behavior that is planned in South Africa but has no effect there. Section 3 must be read in the context of Section 2, however, which states that the purpose of the Act is to "promote and maintain competition in the Republic." Reading Section 3 in light of Section 2 suggests that the Act is not intended to capture conduct that has no effect on the South African economy. Therefore, from a legal perspective, it seems that South African authorities do not have jurisdiction over the actions of South African firms in neighboring countries that are planned in South Africa. The jurisdiction issue would extend to all aspects of the Commission's work, including the initiation and investigative powers.

Potential for cooperation exists, but it will be difficult to accomplish

Despite its limitations, the South African Act does allow for limited cooperation in particular instances. In light of the current wording of the Act, South Africa's agencies can help foreign agencies investigate behavior that has a South African as well as regional impact. For example, the alleged predatory pricing by South African Airlines on bilateral routes could be investigated. This assistance would consist of an agreement between South Africa's Competition Authority and the neighboring country's authority to consider requests to investigate anticompetitive conduct (known as positive comity). Although no such agreement currently exists that would oblige the South African authorities to initiate such an investigation, the Act does not preclude responding to such a request.

A second form of cooperation is over information. Today, South African Competition Authorities can share information only if the companies concerned agree to this (see Section 15(3)(g) of the Competition Commission Rules regulating the functions of the competition commission). For this reason, the South African Competition Commission has reportedly turned down requests from the ZCC for confidential information stemming from domestic investigations.

A third form of cooperation is achieved through technical assistance. South African Competition Agencies are not restricted legally from providing technical assistance. South Africa's own Commission, however, is relatively young and currently overstretched. These factors pose considerable constraints on its ability to offer assistance to others.

In the longer term, serious consideration should be given to the formation of a regional competition agency to which national competition agencies could forbear jurisdiction in particular circumstances, in a fashion similar to the European Commission. The immediate candidate for such a treaty would be the SACU, in which the economies are already more closely integrated. Extending the scope to other countries may not be easy to achieve within a short period and would require considerable negotiation. Particular areas of concern include the difficulty associated with forbearance rules and the establishment of a regional legal institution as an appeal mechanism.

Notes

1. In preparation of this report, it was established that Zambia has only limited capacity for the export of business-process outsourcing and accounting services.

2. Of the nine banks that failed, three had been set up in the 1980s, Meridien BIAO Bank Zambia, African Commercial Bank, and Manifold Investment Bank. The rest had been established in the 1990s.

3. Suppose a policy change today leads to an increase in total income of 100. It is easier to give 50 to the rich and 50 to the poor today (a Pareto improvement) than to give all 100 to the rich today and then take away 50 from them tomorrow to give to the poor (not a Pareto improvement tomorrow).

4. The Fifth Freedom of the Air grants an aircraft registered in state A the right to pick up traffic in state B destined for state C or put down traffic in state B originating in state C. But it is required that the flight should originate or terminate in state A.

5. Our measurements of business climate and infrastructure are elaborated in endnote 8.

6. An estimated 90 percent of the workforce works in the informal economy.

7. This assessment of the accounting sector is based on research and analysis undertaken for the project by Ndung'u Gathinji.

8. For the purpose of our tourism sectoral report, we focused on one aspect of the business climate: how difficult it is to start and operate a business in Zambia. We used several measures from the World Bank's Doing Business database. As an indicator of infrastructure, we used the percentage of paved roads.

9. In South Africa, incumbent banks have been accused of erecting barriers in the payments system against smaller banks wishing to introduce new technologies (World Bank 2004a).

10. Conceptually, the world trading system faces a classic conflict between efficiency and distribution. Further most-favored-nation (MFN) liberalization would lead to a more efficient allocation of global resources, but it would have an adverse distributional effect on those who have preferential access to markets today. The additional twist is that those who would lose (the small and poor countries) have a say in the creation of more efficient arrangements.

11. The Ministry of Health in Zambia has been working on a possible agreement with the United Kingdom on the temporary migration of health workers.

12. COMESA has not experienced substantial progress in terms of financial integration. The treaty calls for the integration of financial structures and, since 1999, member states have been working to harmonize their regulatory frameworks. The COMESA Bankers Association has been established to exchange information and to strengthen correspondent relationships among banks. Regional integration has not proceeded smoothly despite regulatory cooperation at the highest levels. In addition, countries that were part of both COMESA and SADC are experiencing political problems and issues stemming from incompatible and overlapping legal obligations. For more on this, please see "Regional Financial Sector Integration in Southern Africa: Issues and Opportunities" (World Bank 2006b).

13. This assessment of the road transport sector is based on analysis and research conducted by Gael Raballand, Bo Giersing, and Charles Kunaka for the project.

References

Ajwad, I., J. Balat, and G. Porto. 2005. "Zambia: Trade and Poverty." Report for the Zambia Diagnostic Trade Integration Study.

Arnold, J., B. Javorcik, and A. Mattoo. 2006. "The Productivity Effects of Services Liberalization: Evidence from the Czech Republic." Unpublished paper, World Bank, Washington, DC.

Arnold, J., A. Mattoo, A., and G. Narciso. 2006. "Services Inputs and Firm Productivity in Sub-Saharan Africa: Evidence from Firm-Level Data." World Bank Policy Research Paper , World Bank, Washington, DC.

Beck, Thorsten, Asli Demirguc-Kunt, and Maria Soledad Martinez Peria. 2005. "Reaching Out: Access to and Use of Banking Services across Countries." World Bank Policy Research Paper 3754, World Bank, Washington, DC.

Brambilla, Irene, and Guido Porto. 2005. "Farm productivity and market structure: Evidence from Cotton Reforms in Zambia." Yale Working Papers on Economic Applications and Policy No. 5, Yale University, New Haven, CT.

Buys, Piet, Uwe Deichmann, and David Wheeler. 2006. "Road Network Upgrading and Overland Trade Expansion in Sub-Saharan Africa." Policy Research Working Paper 4097, World Bank, Washington, DC.

Eifert, Benn, Alan Gelb, and Vijaya Ramachandran. 2005. "Business Environment and Comparative Advantage in Africa: Evidence from the Investment Climate Data." Working Paper 56, Center for Global Development, Washington, DC.

Eschenbach, Felix, and Bernard Hoekman. 2006. "Services Policy Reform and Economic Growth in Transition Economies, 1990–2004." Weltwirtschaftliches Archiv, forthcoming.

Fink, C., A. Mattoo, and I.C. Neagu. 2002. "Assessing the Impact of Communication Costs on International Trade." *Journal of International Economics* 67: 428–45.

Goering, Laurie. 2006. "South Africa Trading Up the Continent." *Chicago Tribune*, April 20.

Hoekman, Bernard, and Petros Mavroidis. 2003. "Economic Development, Competition Policy and the WTO." *Journal of World Trade* 37 (1): 1–28.

Hoekman, Bernard, and Kamal Saggi. 2007. "Tariff Bindings and Bilateral Cooperation on Export Cartels." *Journal of Development Economics* 83 (1): 141–56.

IMF (International Monetary Fund). 1999. "Zambia: Statistical Appendix." International Monetary Fund, Washington, DC.

Konan, Denise, and Keith Maskus. 2006. "Quantifying the Impact of Services Liberalization in a Developing Country." *Journal of Development Economics* 81 (1): 142–62.

Lawson, Cina, and Natalie Meyenn. 2000. "Bringing Cellular Phone Services to Rural Areas." World Bank Viewpoint Note Series 205, World Bank, Washington, DC.

Mattoo, Aaditya, Randeep Rathindran, and Arvind Subramanian. 2006. "Measuring Services Trade Liberalization and its Impact on Economic Growth: An Illustration." *Journal of Economic Integration* 21: 64–98.

Ndulo, M., P. Mlewa, and I. Sambondu. 2000, April. "Measures Affecting Trade in Services in Zambia." CAPAS.

OED (Operations Evaluation Department). 2004, May 6. "Review of Bank Lending for Lines of Credit." World Bank, Washington, DC.

Onumah, Gideon. 2005. "Feasibility of Introducing an All-Inclusive Financial Product in Zambia to Improve Access to Rural Finance." National Resources Institute, Chatham, Kent, United Kingdom.

Schmukler, S., and J.C. Gozzi. 2006. "Innovative Experiences in Access to Finance: Market Friendly Roles for the Visible Hand?" World Bank, Washington, DC.

Simumba, T. 2006, June. "Zambia Services Trade Capacity Study." Report for the International Trade Centre, World Bank and USAID, Washington, DC.

Winters, L. Alan, Niel McCulloch, and Andrew McKay. 2004. "Trade Liberalization and Poverty: The Evidence So Far." *Journal of Economic Literature* 42 (1): 72–115.

World Bank. 2002. "Investment Climate Survey Data for Zambia." World Bank, Washington, DC. http://www.enterprisesurveys.org/.

———. 2003a. "Republic of Zambia: Implementation Completion Report on a Credit for an Enterprise Development Project." World Bank, Washington, DC.

———. 2003b. "Zambia: The Challenge of Competitiveness and Diversification." World Bank, Washington, DC.

———. 2004a. "South Africa: Technology and Access to Financial Services: Lessons from Experience." World Bank, Washington, DC.

———. 2004b. "Zambia: An Assessment of the Investment Climate." World Bank, Washington, DC.

———. 2004c. "Zambia Country Economic Memorandum, Vols. 1–2." World Bank, Washington, DC.

———. 2005. "Zambia Diagnostic Trade Integration Study." World Bank, Washington, DC.

———. 2006a. "Regional Financial Sector Integration in Southern Africa: Issues and Opportunities." World Bank, Washington, DC.

———. 2006b. "The Role of Postal Networks in Expanding Access to Financial Services." World Bank, Washington, DC.

Annex 1. List of Meeting Participants

The following participants attended meetings during the mission in Lusaka, March 10–31, 2006.

General

Hon. Dipak Patel	-	Minister of Commerce, Trade, and Industry
David Chilipamushi	-	Permanent Secretary, Ministry of Commerce, Trade, and Industry
Dorothy Tembo	-	Director, Foreign Trade, Ministry of Commerce, Trade, and Industry
Mwila Mukosa-Daka	-	Economist, Multilateral Trade, MCTI
Chawe Mpande Chuulu	-	Program Manager, Regional Assessment of Trade in Services in the COMESA Region Project, COMESA Secretariat
Prof. Manenga Ndulo	-	Economics Department, University of Zambia
Ms. Chuulu	-	Deputy Director, Economics and Statistics, Central Statistical Office
Kellyford Nkalamo	-	Director, Balance of Payments and Debt, Bank of Zambia
Chalimba Phiri	-	Acting Director General, Zambian Investment Centre
Glyne Michelo	-	Export Board of Zambia

Accounting

Vickson Ncube	-	Chief Executive Officer, ZICA
F. M. Banda	-	Chairman, ZICA and Finance Director, National Airports Authority
Dr. Y. G. Rao	-	Executive Director, ZCAS
George Sokota	-	Chairman, ZCAS and Senior Partner, Deloitte
Hastings Mtine	-	Senior Partner, KPMG
Hakainde Hichilema	-	MD, Grant Thornton
Mary Ncube	-	Sole Practitioner, MTN
Chisanga Chungu	-	Partner, Deloitte
Anne Chifungula	-	Auditor-General
Mike Goma	-	Acting Accountant-General
Diego Casilli	-	Chairman, Zambia Associations of Manufacturers
Brian K. Tembo	-	Lusaka Stock Exchange (LUSE)
Celine Meene Nair	-	Lusaka Stock Exchange (LUSE)

Hakainde Hichilema	-	MD, Grant Thornton
Daisy Kopolo	-	Manager, ACCA
B. Msiska	-	Commissioner-General, Zambian Revenue Authority
Richard Mazombwe	-	PricewaterhouseCoopers
Rodgers Chibuye	-	Director, ZAMIM
Mr. Milinga	-	Principal, ZAMIM
D. C. Mulenga	-	Registrar, ZAMIM
Larry Kalala	-	MD, Stanbic Bank

Finance

Chisha Mwanakatwe	-	Director, Bank Supervision, Bank of Zambia
Edna Mudenda	-	Director, Non-Bank Financial Institutions
Benjamin Musuku	-	Special Assistant to the Governor, Bank of Zambia
Dr. Denny Kalyalya	-	Deputy Governor - Operations, Bank of Zambia
Danies Chisenda	-	Principal Economist, Ministry of Finance and National Planning
Felix Nkulukusa	-	Senior Economist, Tax Policy Unit, Ministry of Finance and National Planning
John Janes	-	MD, Hurford Investments Ltd. (former MD Standard Chartered Bank)
Sherry Thole	-	MD, Intermarket Discount House and Chairperson, Bankers' Association of Zambia
Weby Mate	-	Executive Secretary, Association of Microfinance Institutions of Zambia
Irene Mutalima	-	MD, Cetzam
Chrispin Chikwashi	-	Chief Executive, African Banking Corporation
David King	-	MD, Finance Bank
B. H. Mufalali	-	Area Manager, ZAMPOST
Reginald Mfula	-	MD, National Savings and Credit Bank

Telecommunications

Dr. Evans Chibiliti	-	Deputy Secretary to the Cabinet, Cabinet Office, Office of the President
Ambassador Bob Samakai	-	Permanent Secretary, Ministry of Communications and Transport
Dr. Mambwe	-	Deputy Permanent Secretary, Ministry of Communications and Transport

Shuller Habeenzu	-	Communications Authority of Zambia
Patrick Mutimushi	-	Communications Authority of Zambia
David Mwanza	-	Regional Director, Zamtel
Raphael Maseko	-	Acting Managing Director, Zamnet
Mike Blackburn	-	Chairman, MTN
Jerome Kawesha	-	Government Carrier and Services Manager, Celtel

Migration

Josiah Ogina	-	International Organization for Migration (IOM) Resident Representative in Lusaka
M. Kapihya	-	Director Human Resources, Ministry of Health
Jere Mwila	-	Ministry of Health

Air Transport

David Zulu	-	Senior Transport Economist, Ministry of Communications and Transport
Mr. Maeti	-	Transport Economist, COMESA
Luke Mbewe	-	Chief Executive, Zambian Export Growers Association
George Lewis	-	MAC2000 Corp, Ltd.
Chileshe Kapwepwe	-	MD, National Airports Corporation
Ms. Manatunga	-	Country Commercial Manager, British Airways
Richard Jeffrey	-	Charter airline operator
Don McDonald	-	CEO, Zambia Airways
Lilian Dring	-	Country Manager, South African Airways

Tourism

David Thompson	-	Deputy Chairman, Tourism Council of Zambia and Manager of the Lusaka Hotel
Adam Pope	-	Luangwa Safari Association
J.J. Sikazwe	-	Chairman, Tourism Council of Zambia
Charity Lumpa	-	MD, Zambian National Tourism Board
David Bennet	-	Wilderness Safari
Adam Elliot	-	Star of Africa
Tom Mushenge	-	Acting Director General, Zambia Wildlife Authority (ZAWA)

Annex 2. Schedule of Specific Commitments

Table A-2.1. Zambia—Schedule of Specific Commitments

Modes of supply: (1) Cross-border (2) Consumption abroad (3) Commercial presence (4) Presence of natural persons

Sector or subsector	Limitations on market access	Limitations on national treatment	Additional commitments
I. HORIZONTAL COMMITMENTS			
ALL SECTORS INCLUDED IN THIS SCHEDULE	(4) Unbound except for measures concerning the entry and temporary stay of natural persons employed in management and expert jobs for the implementation of foreign investment. The employment of such persons shall be agreed on by the contracting parties and approved by the Ministry of Home Affairs. Enterprises must provide for training in higher skills for Zambians to enable them to assume specialized roles.	(3) With permission from the Bank of Zambia, a foreign-controlled company can obtain loans or overdrafts of up to one-third of the value of its paid up capital. (4) Unbound except for measures concerning the categories of persons referred to in the market access column.	
II. SECTOR-SPECIFIC COMMITMENTS			
1. BUSINESS SERVICES			
A. Professional Services			
b) Accountancy (862)	(1) None (2) None (3) None (4) Unbound except as indicated in the horizontal section	(1) None (2) None (3) None (4) Unbound except as indicated in the horizontal section	

(Table continues on the following page.)

Table A-2.1. (continued)

Sector or subsector	Limitations on market access	Limitations on national treatment	Additional commitments
h) Medical and dental services (9312)	(1) None (2) None (3) None (4) Unbound except as indicated in the horizontal section	(1) None (2) None (3) None (4) Unbound except as indicated in the horizontal section	
j) Services provided by midwives, nurses, physiotherapists, and para-medical personnel (93191)	(1) None (2) None (3) None (4) Unbound except as indicated in the horizontal section	(1) None (2) None (3) None (4) Unbound except as indicated in the horizontal section	
F. Other Business Services			
e) Technical testing and analysis services (8676)	(1) None (2) None (3) None (4) Unbound except as indicated in the horizontal section	(1) None (2) None (3) None (4) Unbound except as indicated in the horizontal section	
h) Services incidental to mining, exploration (883 + 5115)	(1) None (2) None (3) None (4) Unbound except as indicated in the horizontal section	(1) None (2) None (3) None (4) Unbound except as indicated in the horizontal section	

Sector		
3. CONSTRUCTION AND RELATED ENGINEERING SERVICES	(1) None (2) None (3) None (4) Unbound except as indicated in the horizontal section	(1) None (2) None (3) None (4) Unbound except as indicated in the horizontal section
8. HEALTH-RELATED AND SOCIAL SERVICES		
A. Hospital Services (9311)	(1) None (2) None (3) None (4) Unbound except as indicated in the horizontal section	(1) None (2) None (3) None (4) Unbound except as indicated in the horizontal section
B. Other Human Health Services (9319) (other than 93191)	(1) None (2) None (3) None (4) Unbound except as indicated in the horizontal section	(1) None (2) None (3) None (4) Unbound except as indicated in the horizontal section
9. TOURISM AND TRAVEL-RELATED SERVICES	(1) None (2) None (3) None (4) Unbound except as indicated in the horizontal section	(1) None (2) None (3) None (4) Unbound except as indicated in the horizontal section

Source: Authors.

2

SERVICES IN THE ZAMBIAN ECONOMY

Jens Arnold and Aaditya Mattoo

This chapter describes the critical role services play in the Zambian economy and the potential role of services trade. We highlight the existing openness and the few remaining restrictions to trade, and then argue that openness has not produced the anticipated benefits in terms of enhanced services exports or wider access to services for the Zambian people.

Why do services matter and what is the role of services trade?

Services matter in Zambia because they make a large direct contribution to national income and a powerful indirect contribution through their impact on the performance of other sectors of the economy.

Services Dominate the Zambian Economy

Nearly 64 percent of Zambia's GDP is now generated in services, as compared with 56 percent a decade earlier and 47 percent in other Sub-Saharan African countries, excluding South Africa.[1] As Zambia has sought to reduce its reliance on copper, nearly 90 percent of the country's economic growth in the period from 1965 to 2002 and half of its GDP growth during the period from 2000 to 2004 has come from the services sector, which is significantly greater than contributions from the manufacturing and mining sectors.

Figure 2.1. Postindependence Growth by Broad Sector

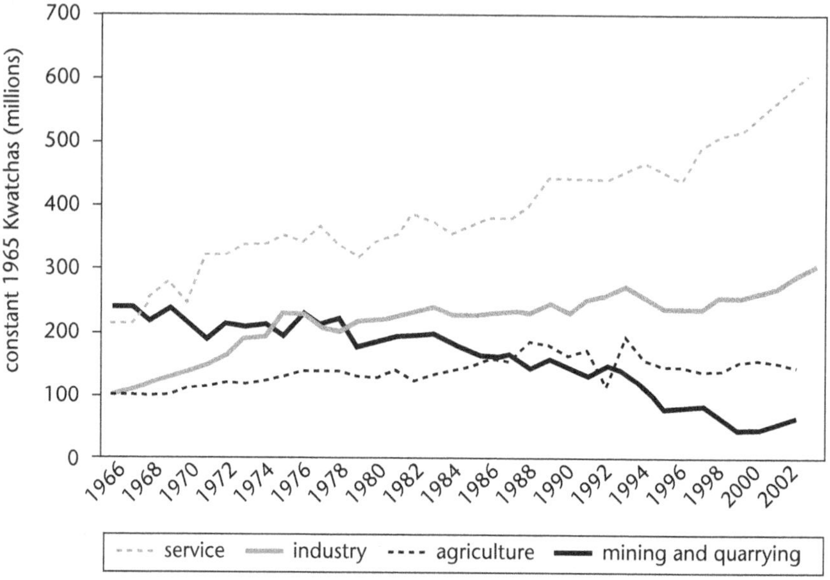

Source: World Bank 2004a.

The performance of services, however, has been impressive only relative to the poor performance of other sectors of the economy. The average annual growth of the services sector has been just 3 percent in the period from 1965 to 2002 compared with the overall GDP growth of 1.4 percent. Within services sectors, the largest contributors to growth have been community and social services, real estate and business services, and wholesale and retail trade, which tend to be "employers of last resort," rather than sectors like tourism, transport and communications, and finance and insurance, which tend to reflect broader economic dynamism.

Although the increase in copper production since 2000 and high copper prices in world markets have been helpful for growth in recent years, diversifying its export structure is crucial for Zambia. Nontraditional exports, defined as all exports except basic metals, have been growing strongly at an average annual increase of 16 percent over the last three years. Measured exports of services grew at about the same rate and currently constitute about 13 percent of Zambian exports. Tourism exports are perceived to have grown substantially over recent years, but reliable statistics are not available. Despite this increase, Zambia has not as yet realized the development potential of its services sectors.

**Figure 2.2. Value Added by Broad Sector and the
Contribution of Different Services Sectors**

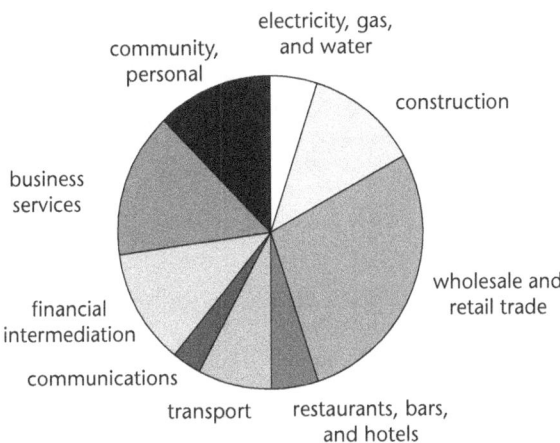

Source: Zambia Central Statistical Office 2005 data.

Services Matter...

Apart from their direct contribution to GDP, services affect the other sectors of
the economy and the productive potential of Zambians. Widening access to services like finance, communication, and transport, as well as education and health,
must be a critical dimension of any growth enhancement and poverty reduction
program. It could, of course, be argued that the poor in Zambia have less of everything, and that we should not care in particular about the dearth of certain services. Inadequate access to services not only hurts households in their role as consumers, but also perpetuates poverty by undermining the productivity of farms

Table 2.1. Sources of Growth in Zambia, 1965–2002

	Average GDP shares[a] A	Period average growth rates[b] B	Weighted average growth rates[c] C	Sources of growth[d] D
GRP at factor cost	100	1.04	1.4	100.0
A. Agriculture, forestry, fishing	16	1.9	0.2	11.3
B. Mining and quarrying	17	−3.2	−0.7	−48.9
C. Industry	24	3.3	0.7	48.4
1. Manufacturing	16	4.0	0.5	38.3
2. Gas, electricity, water	3	9.1	0.2	12.1
3. Construction	5	−1.0	0.0	−2.1
D. Services	43	3.0	1.2	89.2
Services				
1. Wholesale and retail trade	11	0.9	0.2	12.2
2. Hotels and restaurants	2	7.1	0.1	7.5
3. Transport and communications	5	1.4	0.1	4.1
4. Finance and insurance	5	1.6	0.0	3.2
5. Real estate and business	7	7.5	0.4	30.8
6. Community and social services	14	3.9	0.4	31.4

Source: World Bank 2004a.

a. Calculated from the average of constant price data from four base years, 1965, 1970, 1977, and 1994. Total may not sum perfectly due to rounding up.

b. Calculated as the average of annual growth rates.

c. Calculated from the average of annual growth rates weighted by annual shares.

d. Shares are calculated from figures in column C.

and firms, and the ability of Zambia to benefit from internal and external trade. Limited access to services cannot be accepted as one more aspect of the low levels of consumption in Zambia, because it is access to these services that can help break the poverty trap. Although these effects are hard to quantify, there are strong intuitive reasons to believe that improved access to services can have a profound effect on overall economic performance.

for the operations of firms...

The World Bank's Investment Climate Surveys (2002) reveal that a large proportion of Zambian firms identify inadequacies in services as a major or severe obstacle to their operations and this proportion is higher than in other comparator countries, both within and outside the region (see table 2.2).

Figure 2.3. Zambia: Metal Exports and Nontraditional Exports

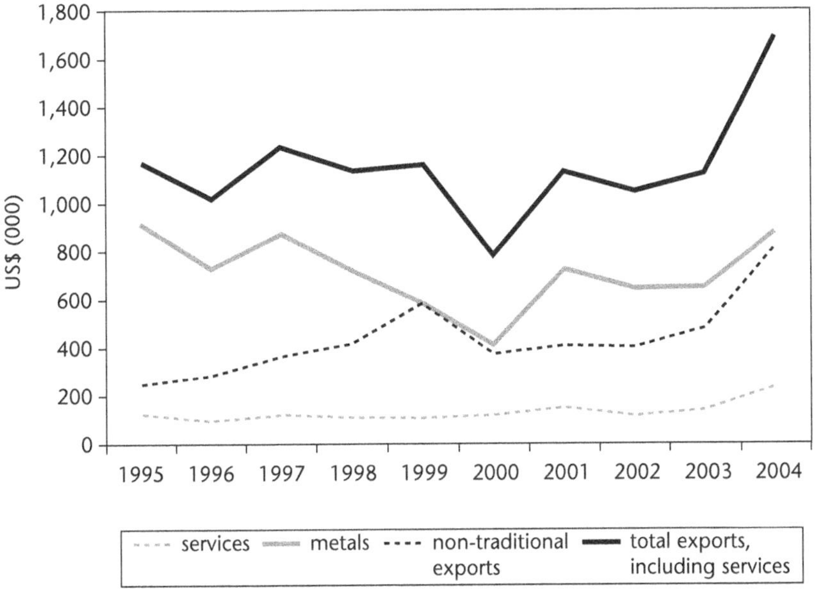

Source: Authors' calculations based on UN Comtrade database and Bank of Zambia data.

When looking at information about the cost structures of firms included in the Investment Climate Surveys, a recent study found that the share of indirect costs in Zambian firms—a large part of which is attributable to services inputs into production—is on average 22 percent of gross value added, which is more than twice the share of labor costs (Eifert, Gelb, and Ramachandran 2005). In fact, Zambia has the second-highest share of indirect costs among the countries analyzed. In other words, a reduction in the prices of services is likely to have a bigger effect on competitiveness than a reduction in labor costs.

Table 2.2. Services as a Constraint to the Operation of Firms (percent of firms evaluating constraint as "major" or "very severe")

	Zambia	Kenya	Uganda	Tanzania	China	Turkey
Cost of financing	82.1	73.3	60.3	56.2	21.6	28.2
Access to financing	54.1	44.1	45.0	47.1	24.1	17.3
Telecommunications	32.9	44.1	5.2	11.6	16.5	10.9
Transportation	30.4	37.4	22.9	22.5	19.4	8.4

Source: World Bank 2002.

Figure 2.4. Cost Structures: Firm-Level Average by Country

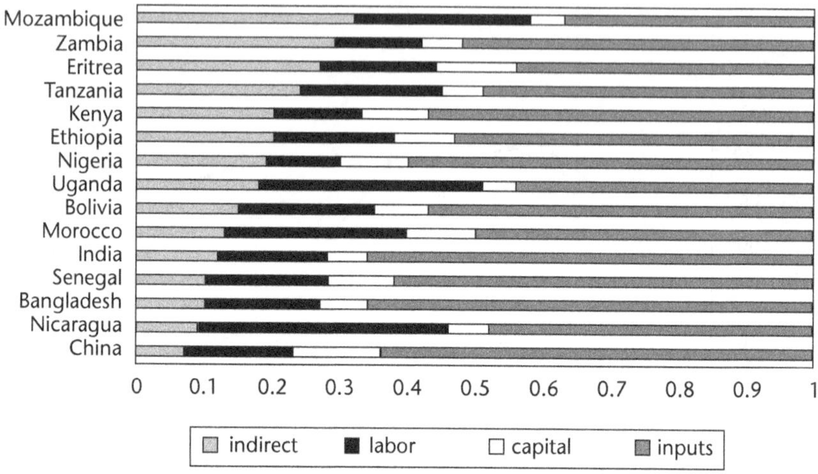

Source: Eifert, Gelb, and Ramachandran 2005.

Table 2.3 shows that interest rates average 28 percent, which is high even after accounting for inflation. And inequality exists across size groups: medium-size firms paid an average of 37 percent interest, while large firms paid just over 20 percent. Moreover, as the World Bank's Assessment of the Investment Climate notes, kwacha-denominated rates often exceed 50 percent per year (World Bank 2004b). Aside from trading firms seeking short-term financing, no legitimate business can sustain this cost of finance. Without financing, businesses cannot develop, modernize, or compete with other firms from neighboring countries where financing is accessible.

On average, the survey finds that banks in Zambia finance 16 percent of firms' working capital and 18 percent of investment requirements. In Kenya, the corresponding numbers are 25 percent and 27.4 percent. Considerable inequality also exists across firm size: small firms have the lowest access to bank loans (less than 20 percent have a loan), and of these, 93 percent must provide collateral averaging more than 400 percent of the loan value. Surprisingly, two-thirds of the overdraft facilities in the sample are secured by fixed assets. The lack of a robust microfinance market structure makes it virtually impossible for small businesses to access finance.

In addition to these financial costs, telecommunications and transport problems were ranked high on the list of business constraints. In telecommunications, Zambian firms have to wait an average 132 days for a new phone line, whereas firms in Uganda or Tanzania can have a new line connected in 33 and 23 days, respectively. Inadequate roads cause frequent disruptions and delays.

Table 2.3. Use and Cost of Loans

	Sample	Small	Medium	Large	Non-exporter	Exporter	Domestic	Foreign
Bank Loan								
% firms with loan	31	20	33	49	27	44	34	26
% loans collateral required	87	93	94	78	92	77	87	90
Value of collateral, % of loan	324	402	481	158	398	159	292	468
Interest rate %	28	31	37	20	33	18	30	21
Overdraft Facilities								
% with overdraft	47	38	51	62	45	53	48	47
% collateral required for overdraft	82	67	100	82	76	100	81	82
Interest rate %	45	45	47	45	46	41	40	49

Source: Authors' compilation; World Bank 2002.

Note: small = 10–49 employees, medium = 50–99 employees; large = more than 100 employees.

Thus, the emerging picture illustrates that access to services is a business impediment. Most firms are finding it difficult to operate under the current situation, let alone to invest more and expand their businesses. Furthermore, the constraints appear to be more severe and widespread than in most African countries.

for the productivity of firms...

Not surprisingly, the burden of high indirect costs of Zambian firms translates into a low productivity in international comparison. Figure 2.5 shows how the productivity of Zambian firms compares with other African countries, as well as Bolivia, Bangladesh, Nicaragua, India, and China (which is used as the benchmark). Zambian firms are clearly the lowest performers of the countries analyzed, with only about one-quarter of the average productivity of Chinese firms.

Empirical research at the World Bank has demonstrated the link between the state of local services industries and the productivity of African firms. Using a large panel data set of firms from 10 Sub-Saharan African countries, including Zambia, Arnold, Mattoo, and Narciso (2006) analyze the relationship between measures of local services performance and the productivity of firms in downstream industries. The study uses detailed firm-level data from the World Bank's Investment Climate Surveys, which contain sufficient information to carefully estimate and analyze total factor productivity for 1,185 firms.

Using subjective and objective measures of services performance and availability, the analysis demonstrates how productivity differences are related to the performance of and access to services of the telecommunications, financial, and electricity sectors. Even after controlling for systematic differences between countries

Figure 2.5. The Productivity of Zambian Firms in International Comparison

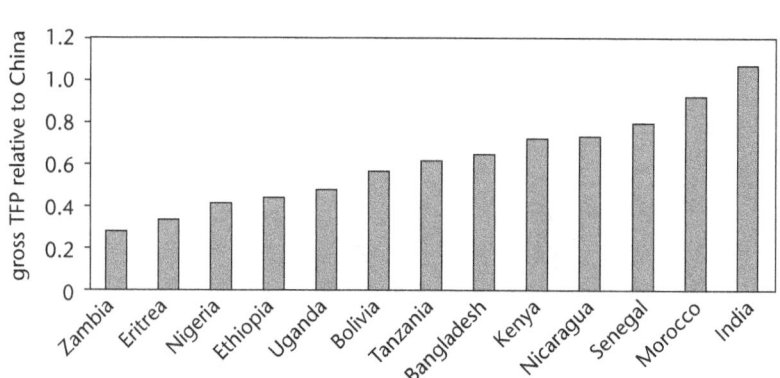

Source: Eifert, Gelb, and Ramachandran 2005.

and industries, differences in firms' export and ownership status, age, size, and location, the paper detects a strong and statistically significant relationship between firm performance and the development of services sectors. The estimates predict that if Zambian firms were to enjoy the access to telecommunications services that South African firms currently have, they could be 13 percent more productive. Similarly, access to banking services of the average level experienced in South Africa could boost the productivity of Zambian firms by almost 6 percent. The result that services sectors affect productivity in downstream sectors is consistent with similar evidence from other countries.[2]

The performance of firms, and hence their growth prospects, is systematically related to the state of locally available services inputs. If, for instance, phone communications and electricity provision become more reliable, disruptions to production will be limited and operating costs in downstream economic activities will decrease. Similarly, if savings are allocated efficiently to the private sector by a well-functioning banking sector, then firms will be able to make use of profitable investment opportunities. Moreover, efficient service providers will introduce new services that help downstream firms operate more efficiently. Examples include innovative financial instruments, multimodal transport services, or digital value-added services in telecommunications. The availability of such services may allow manufacturers to introduce productivity-enhancing changes to their operations, such as receiving production orders online or coordinating with their suppliers by electronic means.

Firm performance plays an important role in the private sector's ability to contribute to poverty reduction. A healthy and growing manufacturing sector can offer employment opportunities and generate linkages to agriculture by sourcing raw materials. Formal employment reduces households' dependence on agriculture and increases public sector revenues by increasing the tax base.

farms...

Agriculture is the main source of income for an overwhelming number of Zambians. Currently, however, the country is using only 14 percent of its cultivable land and an even lower fraction of its water resources (World Bank 2005). Given the small domestic market, however, the best opportunities to expand current production levels exist in export markets. As the World Bank's 2005 Diagnostic Trade Integration Study (DTIS) notes, demand is not a constraint on the rapid expansion of agricultural production, particularly given that Zambia's trade arrangements provide ample export opportunities for many agricultural and agroprocessing products in regional and international markets. It is more likely that supply-side problems are preventing Zambia from meeting its full potential as a producer and exporter of agricultural goods.

Many farmers in Zambia have yet to make the step from subsistence farming to cash crop production. Low productivity is often a problem for making this step, which can have important implications for poverty reduction. Simulations at the World Bank have shown that farmers growing cotton as a cash crop instead of engaging in subsistence farming can increase their income by 20 to 24 percent, if one assumes that the farmers give up subsistence farming to produce cash crops, and by up to 68 percent, if one assumes that the farmers have enough time and land to do subsistence farming on the side. For maize, these income increases are estimated at 55 percent and 100 percent, respectively (Ajwad, Balat, and Porto 2005). Other studies with similar conclusions include Hertel, Keeney, Ivanic, and Winters (2006).

Cotton is Zambia's largest cash crop for smallholders, followed by maize, which can be planted for domestic consumption and as a cash crop. Brambilla and Porto (2006) collected detailed data on farm productivity in a number of Zambian districts for maize and cotton farms. When juxtaposing district-level averages of farm yields with services performance indicators from the Investment Climate Surveys, a significant correlation between farm productivity and the local performance of telecommunications, availability of transport, and the cost of obtaining finance becomes apparent (see table 2.4). In those districts where access to these services is better, cotton and maize farmers tend to enjoy higher yields per hectare.

Regarding farm productivity in the cotton sector, the rank of Zambian districts according to cotton yields per hectare is 90 percent correlated to the rank of the same districts according to the reliability of transport services, and it is 90 percent

Table 2.4. Indicators of Weak Services Performance and Agricultural Productivity Are Negatively Correlated (Spearman rank correlation between farm yields per hectare and services performance in Zambian districts)

	Maize	Cotton
Local availability of phone line (no. of days to get a new landline connection)	−0.77**	−0.90**
Local availability of reliable transport services (no. of days per year with transport failures)	−0.4	−0.90**
Local cost of finance (perceived difficulty of local firms)	−0.15	−0.87*

Source: Authors' calculation; Brambilla and Porto 2006; World Bank 2002.

Note: The districts taken into account are Chingola, Choma, Kafue, Kalulushi, Kazangula, Kitwe, Livingstone, Mazabuka, and Monze for maize, and Choma, Kafue, Kazungula, Mazabuka, and Monze for cotton.

*, ** The hypothesis of independence between the two rank orderings can be rejected at the 90 percent and 95 percent confidence levels, respectively.

correlated to the rank of these districts according to the reliability of telecommunications services. When ordering the districts according to the perceptions of local nonagricultural firms about the difficulties arising from the cost of getting credit, the correlation with the rank according to farm productivity is negative (–87 percent). In other words, those districts where accessing credit at reasonable cost is more difficult are precisely those where farm yields are low.

In the production of maize, a similar relationship between farm productivity and local service performance emerges. The rank according to farm productivity and the rank according to cost of credit are negatively correlated at 68 percent, while the rank according to the reliability of telecommunications services is correlated at 77 percent.[3]

The productivity of cotton production is directly relevant for Zambia's export performance in agricultural goods. In 2001, cotton accounted for almost 20 percent of Zambia's total agricultural exports, most of which was exported to South Africa and the European Union. Moreover, downstream activities such as the production of cotton and poly-cotton yarn account for more than 90 percent of Zambia's textile exports. Approximately 24,000 people were directly engaged in the manufacture of textiles in Zambia, and the wages earned in the sector contributed to the welfare of some 156,000 people (World Bank 2005).

and their ability to take advantage of new opportunities that arise from trade liberalization.

Zambian firms and farms can benefit from access to export markets and compete with imports only if they have access to efficient and competitively priced transport, distribution, and other services. In fact, Sub-Saharan African exporters like Zambia now pay transport costs that are at least five times higher than the tariffs they face in industrial country markets. The contraction in manufacturing output in Zambia and the return of many farmers to subsistence agriculture after trade liberalization in the 1990s was accentuated by their limited access to credit, transport, and distribution networks. Today, the growing stake of certain Zambian regions in horticulture exports is affected by the state of road transport, on which farmers must rely to reach the airport at Johannesburg.

The high level of indirect costs attributable to the high prices of services inputs undermines the competitiveness of Zambian firms in export markets, as demonstrated by Eifert, Gelb, and Ramachandran (2005). They note that countries with lower per capita income tend to have a lower overall price level because the prices of services that are not tradable across borders tend to be lower. Looking at the individual country deviations from this generally upward-sloping relationship between GDP and price levels—referred to as the Balassa curve—they find that most successful exporters have a lower price level than predicted, while negligible exporters tend to have higher price levels than predicted. Of the 42 countries they analyze, Zambia has the second highest upward deviation from the predicted pattern (top panel of figure 2.6), which may explain its poor export performance (bottom panel of figure 2.6).

Reform of services policy has an impact not only on overall export performance but also on the composition of exports. Although the profound effect that transport costs have on trade and the distribution of economic activity across regions is well documented, the impact of communication costs on trade costs has received less attention. One recent study finds that international variations in communication costs have a significant influence on trade patterns (Fink, Mattoo, and Neagu 2002). More interesting, lower communication costs can shift a country's comparative advantage toward more sophisticated communication-intensive differentiated goods and away from more standardized primary goods. Evidence also suggests that a country's ability to participate in the growing trade in business process outsourced (BPO) services critically depends on the state of the telecommunications services. For example, an outsourcing firm indicated that the high cost of international communication in Zambia deterred them from taking advantage of its stock of skilled accountants.

Openness and foreign participation could, in principle, contribute to the development of Zambia's services sectors and hence overall economic performance

The constraints on the development of Zambia's services sector because of its limited endowments of capital and skills and small market could be alleviated by greater openness. This is particularly the case for producer services, like telecommunications and finance, which are relatively capital and skill intensive and use increasingly sophisticated technology. If the entry of international providers is prevented, Zambia must rely completely on national services providers. If the market is opened, it does not mean that only foreign or entirely foreign suppliers would provide these services. As in mobile telephony, insurance, and aviation, Zambian firms are likely to continue to operate and foreign firms are likely to have Zambian ownership and employees. But the mere fact of being open to foreign entry should, in principle, make these markets more contestable and ensure that the desired quality of services will be provided most efficiently.

Small economies like Zambia's derive another type of benefit from integration. Given the large economies of scale in services industries, from telecommunications to insurance, incentives to invest would be greater if the Zambian market was not segmented from other neighboring markets. For example, all providers, domestic and foreign, would be able to spread, for example, the fixed costs of establishing transmission facilities, over a larger market. The result is that, for any given level of

Figure 2.6. The Balassa-Gap for Select Countries (reflecting the relative cost of services) and Export Performance

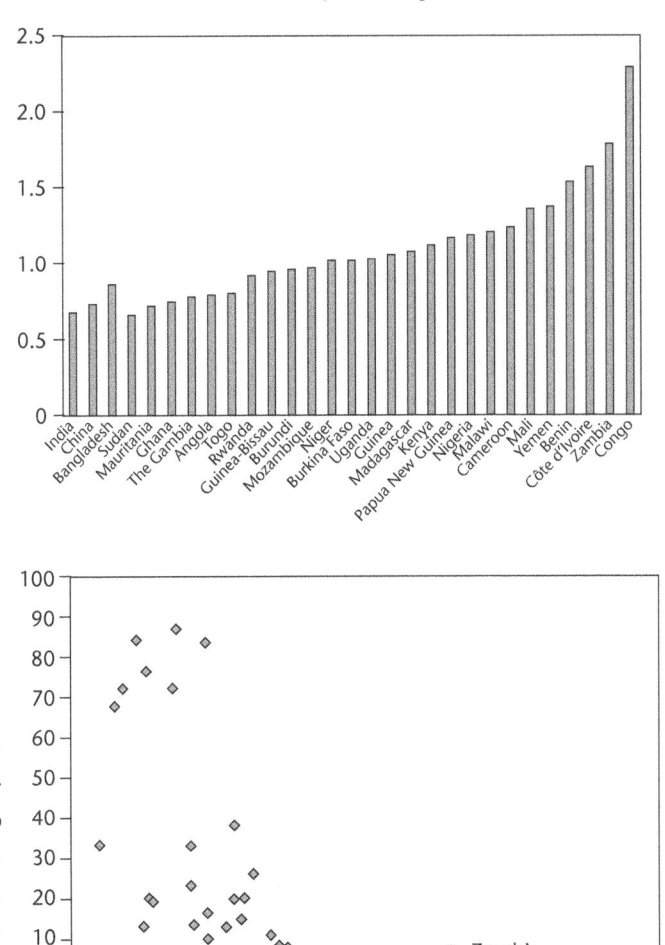

Source: Eifert, Gelb, and Ramachandran 2005.

Note: The Balassa-Gap indicates the deviation of a country's price level from the level predicted by its GDP per capita. A value of 1 implies that a country's cost or price level is as predicted by the regression line relating price and income levels.

scale economies, there would be more entry and hence greater competition in a larger market. To realize the benefits of scale economies and competition, however, the Zambia market would need to be deeply integrated with neighboring markets, which, as we shall read in box 2.1, is often particularly hard to accomplish.

Box 2.1. The Potential Gains from Services Reform: International Evidence

Removing barriers to trade in services in a particular sector is likely to lead to lower prices, improved quality, and greater variety. As in the case of trade in goods, restrictions on trade reduce welfare because they create a wedge between domestic and foreign prices, leading to a loss to consumers that is greater than any benefit to producers and government. Empirical studies generally support this contention. Because many services are inputs into goods production, the inefficient supply of such services acts as a tax on production and prevents the realization of significant gains in productivity. Furthermore, as countries reduce tariffs and other barriers to trade, effective rates of protection for manufacturing industries may become negative if they are confronted with input prices that are higher than they would be if services markets were competitive.

A major benefit of liberalization is likely to be access to a wider variety of services, the production of which is subject to economies of scale. Consumers derive not only a direct benefit from diversity in services such as health care, education, and entertainment, but also an indirect benefit because a wider variety of more specialized producer services, such as telecommunications and finance, can lower the costs of both goods and services production.

Although empirical studies on services have limitations as a result of data weaknesses, recent research suggests that a services policy reform agenda focusing on enhancing competition in services industries can help enhance welfare and boost growth prospects. Estimates of benefits vary for individual countries—from less than 1 percent to more than 50 percent of GDP—depending on the initial levels of protection and the assumed reduction in barriers. Moreover, the gains from liberalizing services may be substantially greater than those from liberalizing trade in goods, because current levels of protection in many countries are higher and because liberalization could create greater spillover benefits. For instance, one model finds that the welfare gains from a 50 percent cut in services sector protection would be five times larger than those from nonservices sector trade liberalization (Konan and Maskus 2006).

Dynamic effects may also be significant. Certain service industries clearly possess growth-generating characteristics. A competitive and well-regulated financial sector leads to the efficient transformation of savings to investment, ensuring that resources are deployed wherever they have the highest returns, and facilitates better risk-sharing in the economy. Improved efficiency in telecommunications generates economywide benefits, because this service is a vital intermediate input and crucial to the dissemination and diffusion of knowledge. Business services such as accounting and legal services are important in reducing transaction costs.

Box 2.1. (continued)

In all such sectors, greater foreign participation and increased competition together imply a larger scale of activity and, hence, greater scope for generating the special growth-enhancing effects. Even without scale effects, the import of foreign factors that characterizes services sector liberalization could still have positive effects because they are likely to bring technology with them. Econometric evidence confirms that openness in services influences long run growth performance. Mattoo, Rathindran, and Subramanian (2006) find that countries that fully liberalized telecommunications and the financial services sectors were associated with an average growth rate 1.5 percentage points above that of other countries. Focusing on a sample of transition economies, Eschenbach and Hoekman (2005) find that services-related policies play an important role in attracting FDI. Controlling for other potential explanatory variables, they too find that improvements in services policies—infrastructure and finance—have a statistically significant positive impact on per capita growth.

Box Figure 1. Greater Reform in Services Is Associated with More Rapid Growth

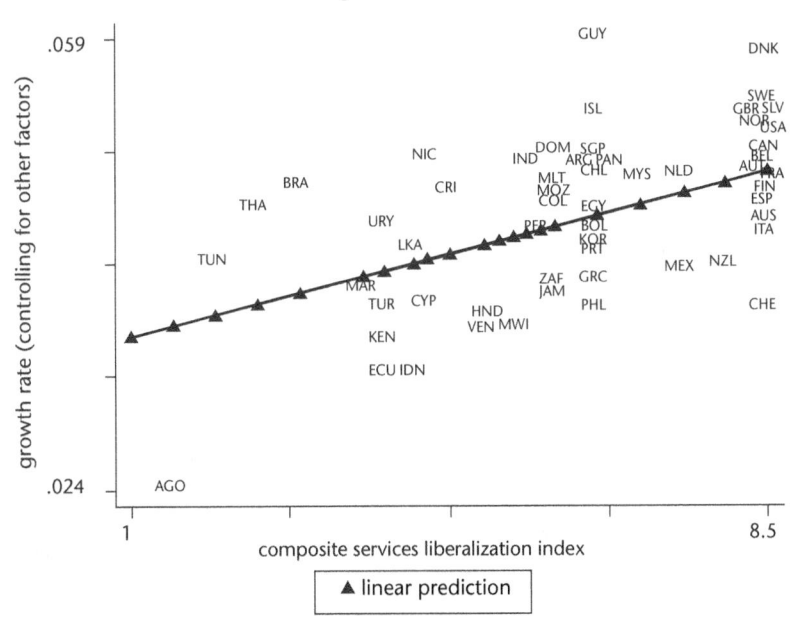

Source: Matoo, Rathindran, and Subramanian 2006.

As we will read below, it would be wrong to assume that these gains can be obtained by a mechanical opening of services markets.

Source: Authors' creation.

Zambia also has a growing stake in exports of tourism services

By virtue of its endowments—of wildlife and the Victoria Falls—the peacefulness of the country, and the friendliness of its people, Zambia undoubtedly has significant potential for tourism. A recent study funded by United Nations Development Fund and the Global Endowment Fund(UNDP/GEF) suggested that better management of Zambia's wildlife resources could potentially generate economic activity of approximately $1 billion a year. Zambia faces significant competition from other countries in the region with similar endowments and its tourism sector must compete for resources with other vital sectors of the economy, but Zambia's advantage in tourism and the advantages of tourism for the economy cannot be doubted.

A closer look at the composition of Zambia's services exports reveals that these exports consist largely of travel services (tourism) and transport. Together these two categories accounted for more than 90 percent of services exports in 2003, while communications and insurance services make up the remaining services export.[4] Zambia's limited capacity to export business process outsourcing and other professional services (including accounting) was confirmed by investigations carried out in the process of preparing this report. On the import side, transportation and travel again account for a significant portion, but construction services and other business services also have shares above 5 percent.

Figure 2.7. The Composition of Zambia's Services Trade

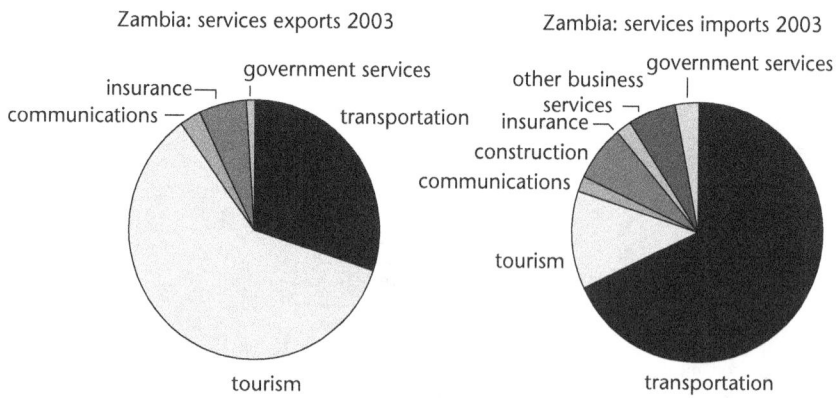

Source: Bank of Zambia.

Despite its natural advantages, Zambia has performed poorly as an exporter of services

Zambia has underperformed even after accounting for its low income

Zambia's relatively large share of services in domestic value added does not translate into strong export performance in services sectors, unlike in a number of developing countries that have become successful services exporters in recent years. In international comparison, Zambia's level of services exports (relative to population size) is low. This pattern continues to be true even after controlling for Zambia's relatively low income per capita. Figure 2.8a plots services exports per capita against income per capita for a cross-section of countries with available data (109 countries in 2003).[5] Across these countries, services export performance rises with income, as can be seen from the positive slope of the regression line in

Figure 2.8. International Comparison: Services Exports per Capita

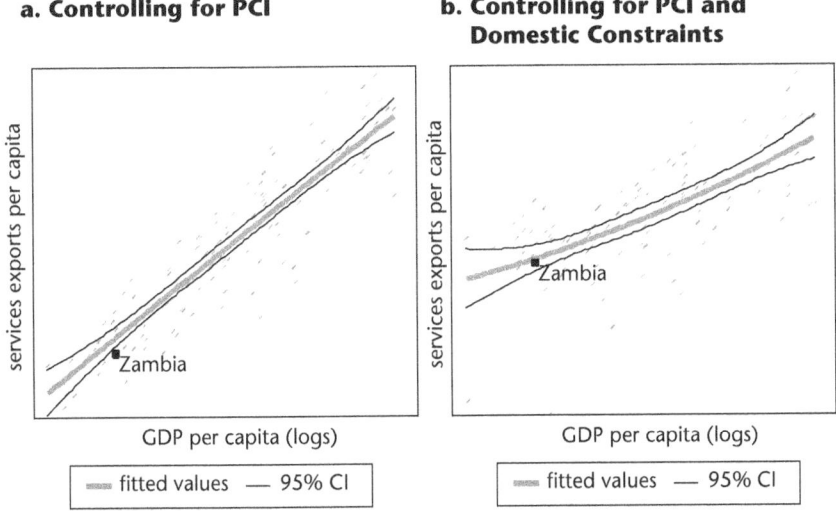

a. Controlling for PCI

b. Controlling for PCI and Domestic Constraints

Source: IMF Balance of Payments, UN Comtrade, and Bank of Zambia. All variables are in logs.

Note: The gray line represents the estimated quadratic regression line, while the black lines are confidence intervals (CIs). The fact that Zambia falls outside the confidence intervals indicates that its services exports per capita are significantly below that expected at its level of income. Figure 2.9b shows the same relationship, but after controlling for the influences of telecommunications infrastructure, financial depth, and a measure of the business climate. This indicates that when these country characteristics are taken into account, Zambia is no longer an outlier. In other words, Zambia's low performance is related to these domestic constraints.

PCI = per capita income.

figure 2.8a. But the graph also shows that, conditional on income levels, Zambia is still underperforming with respect to services exports. This becomes evident from the fact that it is situated below the regression line, outside the confidence interval. This means that Zambia is a statistically significant downward outlier even after accounting for its income level.

...because of weaknesses in the business environment, communications, and finance.

This raises the question about possible reasons why Zambia is underperforming in services exports, which suggests that we look beyond income differences and consider additional variables that may help explain Zambia's low performance compared with other countries. To do this, we switch from the graphic representation to a multivariate regression analysis. The first column of table 2.5 presents the results of a simple regression of services exports (in logarithms) on GDP per capita (also in logarithms) for a cross-section of 109 countries. This is the same approach as the one presented graphically in figure 2.8a. The estimated coefficient on per capita income is highly positive and statistically significant at the 1 percent level (which is the analogue to the upward-sloping regression line in figure 2.8a). Introducing an indicator variable for Zambia into the regression allows us to evaluate empirically the degree to which the country is an outlier from the simple pattern of this regression model. Indeed, we find that the estimated coefficient on this indicator is negative and significant, which is in line with the previous finding that Zambia is located outside the confidence interval around the regression line that was fit to the scatter plot in figure 2.8a.

This model is oversimplified and much more is needed to explain countries' services export performance than just differences in economic development. Although doing full justice to the question of what determines a country's services export performance would be beyond the scope of this report, it is interesting to see how our results regarding Zambia are affected by a simple attempt to introduce further explanatory variables. With services exports often characterized as being particularly reliant on the availability of communications facilities (especially important for cross-border trade), financial services, and the state of the business climate (especially relevant in Zambia's case for investment in tourism capacity), we would like to control at least for these three issues, and we do so in the second column of table 2.5.

The development of communications infrastructure is proxied by teledensity, which is the availability of financial services by the ratio of domestic credit to the private sector as a share of GDP, and the quality of the business climate by the

Table 2.5. Zambia's Services Export Specialization in a Cross-Section of Countries

	Dependent variable: log services exports per Inhabitant in $	
Zambia indicator	-0.300**	-0.032
	[0.139]	[0.235]
Log GDP per capita	1.123***	0.421***
	[0.052]	[0.125]
Log teledensity		0.655***
		[0.110]
Credit to private sector		0.224*
(as % GDP)		[0.127]
Business climate (procedures		-0.452**
required to open a business)		[0.193]
N	108	108
	0.82	0.87

Source: Authors' calculation.

Note: Robust standard errors in brackets are robust and clustered on industries.
*, **, *** indicate statistical significance at the 10, 5, and 1 percent level.

number of procedures required to open a new business.[6] The regression results show that teledensity is positively related to services exports per capita, and the same holds for financial depth. A good business climate (represented by a low number of procedures required) seems to be positively associated with strong services export performance. These three estimated coefficients are statistically significant.

It is remarkable that in this second regression the estimated coefficient on the Zambia indicator is now much smaller than before, and it has ceased to be statistically significant. Once we add telecommunications and financial infrastructure and a measure of the business climate to our model, Zambia is no longer an outlier from the overall pattern observed. In other words, these three variables partly explain the current low level of Zambian services exports.

This conclusion is supported by evidence from the tourism sector, which accounts for a large proportion of services exports. Our preliminary cross-country estimates suggest that Zambia is receiving significantly less tourists than would be warranted by its fundamental endowments, and the country could receive a much larger share of tourism flows (51 percent more tourists, that is, 295,000 per year) if it were to improve its business climate and infrastructure.[7]

Despite openness and significant foreign participation, access to services in Zambia has hardly expanded

Zambian services sectors are mostly open and have significant foreign presence...

A key argument normally advanced for liberalization is that allowing foreign direct investment is critical to improving the state of capital- and technology-intensive services. The sectors covered in this study reveal a high degree of openness with virtually no restrictions on FDI. Furthermore, unlike some other least developed countries whose open markets have been largely ignored by foreign investors, in Zambia (in sectors ranging from banking to mobile telephony), for-

Table 2.6. Services Policy in Zambia: Past and Present

Sector	Situation before the reforms of the 1990s	Major policy changes
Banking	The pre-Independence banks, Barclays Bank (1918), Standard Chartered Bank (1906), and Grindlays (1956), primarily served foreign corporate entities. New foreign banks included Citibank (1979), Meridien Bank (1984), Indo-Zambian Bank (1985), and Union Bank (1991). The state did not nationalize commercial banks but established its own savings institutions, the Zambian National Commercial Bank (1969), the National Savings and Credit Bank (1972), Lima Bank (1987), and the Cooperative Bank (1989). The Development Bank of Zambia was set up by the government in the 1970s to be a development finance institution.	*Liberalization/Competition:* Partial liberalization of interest rates and removal of sectoral credit ceilings late 1980s. From 1991–94 there was a de facto liberalization of licensing, although prudential criteria for new banks were not made explicit until the 1994 act. In addition, there was a de facto reduction in the minimum capital requirement because of high inflation from 1989 until 1994. The business environment for private banks became more attractive with the decontrolling of interest rates in 1992, the removal in 1993 of all restrictions on commercial bank lending and deposit rates, and the remaining foreign exchange regulations in 1994. *Privatization:* No government-owned banks have been privatized. The privatization of Zambia National Commercial Bank is reported to be under way.

eign firms dominate, and in sectors like distribution and tourism, they have a significant share. For example, in banking, six foreign banks own 67 percent of the total assets of the sector, with 76 percent of loans and 64 percent of deposits. In mobile telephony, two foreign-owned cellular companies have 91 percent share of the market, with Celtel alone having 77 percent. In Livingstone National Park, Zambia's main tourist attraction, 76 percent of tourist activity operators, 50 percent of hotels, and 72 percent of lodges are fully or partially foreign owned. (For a full description of the initial state of policy in the early 1990s, the subsequent policy changes, the degree of openness today to cross-border trade and foreign investment, and a summary of the market structure for each sector covered by the report, please see table 2.6.)

(*Text continues on page 90.*)

Openness to services trade today	Market structure today
Mode 1: Capital market liberalized. Cross-border lending and borrowing are permitted by both banks and households. *Mode 3:* Private and foreign ownership is permitted (up to 100 percent). Foreign banks must be licensed to operate in their home country. The Bank of Zambia must be satisfied that foreign banks are adequately supervised by their home regulatory authority. All foreign banks must be incorporated locally (no branches of foreign banks that are not locally incorporated). Banks may not engage in insurance services. National treatment principles are applied (regulatory conditions on foreign banks are no more restrictive than those to which domestically owned banks are subject). There are no restrictions on lending and borrowing rates.	Today, there are 13 commercial banks in total. The six foreign banks own 67 percent of the total assets of the sector, with 76 percent of loans and 64 percent of deposits. Between 1991 and 1994, 10 banking licenses were issued. Between 1995 and 1998, however, nine commercial banks failed and several government-owned financial institutions were allowed to collapse as previously guaranteed subsidies were withdrawn.

(*Table continues on the following page.*)

Table 2.6.   (continued)

Sector	Situation before the reforms of the 1990s	Major policy changes
		Regulatory Reform: The 1994 Banking and Financial Services Act, covering banks and non-bank financial institutions (NBFIs), gives the central bank authority to issue prudential directives, for example, on capital adequacy requirements, restrictions on large loan exposure, and insider lending, and introduces standardized reporting and accounting procedures. The 1996 Bank of Zambia Act established, in principle, the independence of the Bank of Zambia to implement monetary policy and supervisory policies.
Insurance	Before 1992, the only provider was Zambia State Insurance Corporation (ZSIC), which was formed in 1970, when the existing 26 foreign insurers were forced to transfer their assets to the government-owned monopoly.	*Competition:* The sector was opened to competition in 1992. *Privatization:* Zambian State Insurance Company continues to be 100 percent publicly owned. *Regulatory Reform:* The Pensions and Insurance Authority was established after the enactment of the Pensions Scheme Regulation Act No. 28 of 1996 and the Insurance Act No. 27 of 1997 to provide regulation and supervision of pension and insurance schemes. In 2005, regulations were introduced that require life and nonlife insurance companies to be separated.

Openness to services trade today	Market structure today
Mode 1: Cross-border purchasing of insurance services is not permitted. However, if it can be proven that the type of insurance required is not available in Zambia, then special permission may be sought from the Pensions and Insurance Authority to purchase insurance cross-border. This does not apply to reinsurance. Foreign insurers are not allowed to advertise their services in Zambia. Zambian insurance company firms may insure foreign nationals. *Mode 3:* Private and foreign ownership permitted (up to 100 percent). Foreign firms must be incorporated locally to open a branch. Minimum requirements are the following: (1) proof of qualification and experience of principle officer; (2) declaration of minimum capital; (3) evidence of reinsurance program, (4) detailed business plan; (5) ownership structure and biographies, including net worth of key investors; (6) paid up capital of K 1 billion; (7) license fee of K 1,800,000.	Today, ZSIC holds less than a quarter of the market in terms of Gross Written Premium. In December 2004, there were eight insurance companies and one reinsurance company (ZimRe). The market is dominated by locally owned companies, while five foreign- or part foreign-owned companies account for just 17 percent of premium income.

(Table continues on the following page.)

Table 2.6.   (continued)

Sector	Situation before the reforms of the 1990s	Major policy changes
Telecom—Fixed	Before 1994, the public Post and Telecommunications Corporation (PTC) was the exclusive provider of telecom and postal services and also regulated the sector under the 1984 Postal and Telecommunications Act.	*Liberalization/Competition:* The 1994 Telecommunications Act divided PTC into Zamtel and Zampost and, in theory, opened the fixed and mobile sector to private and foreign participation. In 2002, entry into the provision of international services opened, but a license fee was set at $12 million. *Privatization:* Zamtel remains 100 percent publicly owned. There are plans to offer equity to a foreign investor. *Regulatory Reform:* The Communications Authority of Zambia (CAZ) was established in 1995 by the Telecommunications Act No. 23 of 1994. CAZ was created to regulate the provision of telecommunication services in Zambia and is empowered to prescribe rules and regulations for the operations of licensees and suppliers of telecommunications equipment. Zamtel has never been relicensed so it is not subject to the regulations of CAZ.
Telecom—Mobile	Cellular telephony was introduced to Zambia in 1995 by Zamtel.	*Liberalization/Competition:* Licenses issued to competing providers in 1997 (Telecel, now MTN), 1998 (Celtel), and 2001 (Vodacom), although the latter has not begun operations because of disagreements over its spectrum allocation. *Privatization:* Cell-Z remains 100 percent state owned. *Regulatory Reform:* Licensed and regulated by CAZ since 1994.

Openness to services trade today	Market structure today
Mode 1: Call-back services and Voice over Internet Protocol (VoIP) are illegal and there are high access charges for call termination through the incumbent. *Mode 3:* Private and foreign ownership permitted in principle (a policy that at least 30 percent of equity must be domestically owned). Licenses are allocated through competitive tender. The license fee for operating an international gateway, set at $12 million is prohibitively high, effectively precluding competition with Zamtel in the international segment. Firms providing value added services must use existing (Zamtel) basic infrastructure. End-user tariffs are set by Zamtel and are subject to regulatory approval. VoIP and call-back services are illegal.	No foreign investment in the sector. In terms of cross-border supply of services, there are reports of widespread use of call-back services and VoIP services on the international segment.
Mode 1: Call-back services and VoIP are illegal and there are high access charges for call termination through the incumbent. *Mode 3:* Private and foreign-owned firms are allowed to bid for competitively tendered licenses (a policy that at least 30 percent of equity must be domestically owned). Currently, four licenses have been allocated. All firms (foreign and domestic) must use Zamtel's international gateway. End-user tariffs are market determined.	Two foreign-owned cellular companies have 91 percent share of the market, with Celtel alone having 77 percent. As with fixed-line international calls, there are reports of widespread use of call-back services and VoIP.

(Table continues on the following page.)

Table 2.6. (continued)

Sector	Situation before the reforms of the 1990s	Major policy changes
Internet	The first Internet services were introduced by Zamnet in 1994.	*Liberalization/Competition:* Licensing liberalized under the 1994 Act. *Privatization:* Zamtel remains 100 percent state owned. *Regulatory Reform:* Internet Service Providers (ISPs) licensed and regulated by CAZ since 1994.
Air Transport	Until 1994, Zambia Airways was the only airline operating and was the only designated carrier in bilateral air services agreements (BASAs). Roam Air, a charter company, ran flights between Lusaka and the Copperbelt and was owned by KCCM and Meridien.	*Liberalization/Competition:* The government announced its intention to liberalize the sector in 1991. However, no legislation was passed. After 1994, BASAs were renegotiated and no longer specified a single carrier. Licenses were issued to new airlines, such as AeroZambia and Zambian Express. The main BASAs are with Tanzania (1977), Angola (1991), the United Kingdom (2004), South Africa (2001), Kenya (2000), Malawi (1995), and Zimbabwe (1995). *Privatization:* Zambia Airways, the national carrier, was privatized and liquidated in 1994. *Regulation:* No change since the Civil Aviation Department was created before Independence by the Civil Aviation Act in 1954.
Accounting	In the 1960s and 1970s, the accountancy profession represented by a predominantly expatriate organization, the Zambian Association of Accountants. There is no history of public providers.	*Liberalization/Competition:* Historically, there have been no legal restrictions on entry. *Regulatory Reform:* The Accountants' Act of 1982 created the Zambian Institute of Certified Accountants (now Chartered). It is responsible for education, training, and examination; establishing and

Openness to services trade today	Market structure today
Mode 1: ISPs have a right to their own international gateway for data but not for voice. *Mode 3:* No restrictions on foreign investment. The ISP entry license fee is K 20,000 plus a 5 percent annual regulatory charge. This annual charge is high by regional standards and may act as a deterrent to entry.	Coppernet set up in 1996 and Zamtel launched its Internet service in 1997. MicroLink and U UNet joined in 2001. Foreign ownership is confined to part foreign-owned Microlink, which controls 3 percent of the market.
Mode 1: Committed to fifth freedom liberalization according to the Yamoussoukro Decision, which became fully binding in 2002, and to Common Market for Eastern and Southern Africa (COMESA) through the COMESA Legal Notice No. 2. In practice, denial of fifth freedom rights under the BASA continues in both Zambia and other countries. *Mode 3:* No formal ownership restrictions. Airlines must be incorporated and have their principle place of business in Zambia to be a designated carrier. There are no formal restrictions on foreign ownership, but the directorship of the company must be 50 percent Zambian, according to the Department of Civil Aviation in Lusaka.	The domestic and regional air traffic markets are currently served by two fully Zambian-owned carriers and carriers of neighboring countries (Kenya, Ethiopia, and South Africa). On the intercontinental route, the only carrier is British Airways.
Mode 3: No restrictions on foreign presence. *Mode 4:* Restrictions through economic means tests implemented through visa and work permit requirements.	Of the nine accounting firms that have three or more partners, seven were linked to international networks.

(Table continues on the following page.)

Table 2.6.   (continued)

Sector	Situation before the reforms of the 1990s	Major policy changes
		maintaining professional standards; and registration and licensing. An indigenous technician qualification was introduced in the late 1990s. In 1994, amendments to the Act created three categories of membership: Associate, Licentiate, and Technician. Accountants from Asia (India, Pakistan, Bangladesh, and Sri Lanka) and Africa (Kenya and Tanzania) were relegated to the nonvoting status, while accountants holding qualifications from the United Kingdom and Ireland, the United States, Australia and New Zealand, Canada, and Zimbabwe hold full voting rights.
Tourism	A number of hotels, lodges, and camps were owned by the government, mainly through the National Hotels Corporation, within the umbrella Zambia Industrial and Mining Corporation (ZIMCO) parastatal structure.	*Liberalization/Competition:* Concessions for the management of protected areas: Liuwa (2004, African Parks, [Zimbabwe?]), Kasanka (1990 and 2003, Kasanka Trust, United Kingdom). Currently under consideration for public-private partnerships: Isangano, Mweru-wa-ntipa, Lusenga Plains, Sioma Ngwezi, Lukusuzi, and Nyika. *Privatization:* Four hotels in 1996, two hotels in 1998, five lodges and camps in 1999. *Regulatory Reform:* The Zambia Wildlife Act of 1998 transformed the Department of National Parks and Wildlife Services into a semiautonomous corporate body—Zambian Wildlife Authority (ZAWA). A new Tourism and Hospitality Bill aiming to simplify and rationalize the licensing framework in the sector is under discussion.

Openness to services trade today	Market structure today
Mode 3: No restrictions on foreign investment. *Mode 4:* Limitations of the number of authorized intracorporate transferees.	The formal tourism sector is largely foreign owned in terms of the value of assets, although numerically there are more Zambian-owned entities. In Livingstone, Zambia's main tourist destination, 76 percent of tourist activity operators, 50 percent of hotels, and 72 percent of lodges are fully or partially foreign owned.

(Table continues on the following page.)

Table 2.6. (continued)

Sector	Situation before the reforms of the 1990s	Major policy changes
Distribution	The Agricultural Rural Marketing Board (ARMB), the Grain Marketing Board, and Producer Marketing Cooperatives were introduced soon after independence as a way of bringing more rural people into mainstream markets. The two boards were merged in the National Agriculture Marketing Board (NAMBOARD) in 1969 to become a sole marketing agent for maize and other designated crops and inputs.	*Liberalization/Competition:* In 1989, NAMBOARD was dismantled so that, in principal, private agents were allowed to purchase and market maize and fertilizer. In 1992, mealie meal and fertilizer subsidies were removed. In 1993, decontrol of maize producer prices and elimination of maize transport subsidies took effect.

Source: Authors' compilation from World Bank documents.

Figure 2.9 shows the distribution of FDI inflows into Zambia across broad economic sectors and the division of the services share across different services sectors. As can be seen from the figure, services account for approximately 52 percent of the FDI inflows in 2001, of which almost half went toward financial services.

Figure 2.9. The Distribution of FDI Inflows by Broad Sectors and across Services Sectors in 2001

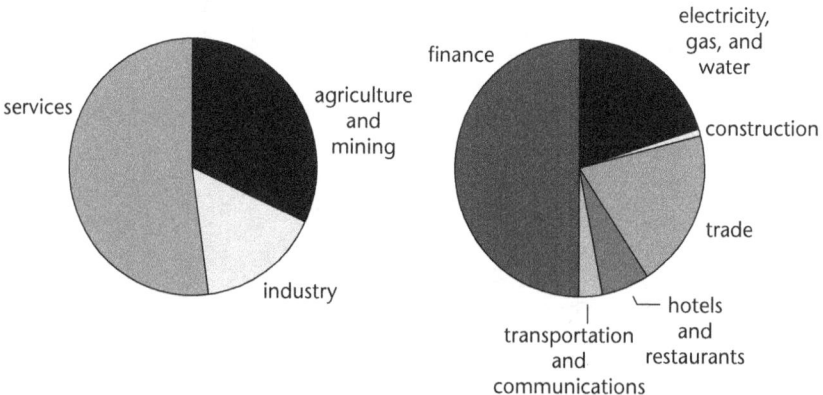

Source: Bank of Zambia.

Openness to services trade today	Market structure today
Mode 3: No restrictions on foreign investment.	The overwhelming majority of formal retail sector is foreign owned. The formal sector represents around 40 percent of the overall retail sector.

and in some areas Zambia has already benefited from openness...

Mobile telephony was opened to international competition in 1995 and has since seen a 300,000-person increase in the number of subscribers, whereas fixed-line telephony, which has remained a de facto monopoly, saw an increase over the same period of less than 20,000 subscribers. In tourism, although there is some concern about the generous tax incentives Sun International was granted, its investments (a total of $120 million in two hotels with 385 rooms) have created 350 permanent jobs, supported by 500 or more casual and contract workers, and significantly boosted economic activity in Livingstone and the neighboring area (Mosi-oa-Tunya National Park and the rapids). In air transport, the recent entry of a new domestic carrier has led to the Lusaka-Johannesburg flight being available for $100, one-third of the price the incumbent was charging. In insurance, since the liberalization of the sector in 1992, nonlife premium rates have dropped; for example, motor vehicle insurance premium rates fell from 10 to 16 percent of the value of the car to 6 percent of the value.

but in others, despite openness and foreign investment, access to services remains low.

To put the state of access to services in Zambia into an international context, we graph the performance of a cross-section of countries with available data (approximately 110 countries) against per capita GDP and fit a regression line to the points, analogous to the analysis earlier in this section.

Not surprisingly, per capita incomes play a significant role in access to services, as can be seen from the generally upward-sloping regression lines. But it also becomes clear from this exercise that, even after controlling for differences in income, Zambia is still lagging behind other countries in a number of sectors. Regarding teledensity, both for land lines and overall phone lines, Zambia is a statistically significant downward outlier with respect to the pattern observed around the world. If Zambia were to follow the pattern of the average country in this sample, then given its income level, it would have a higher teledensity (see figure 2.10). This picture is confirmed by a comparison with other countries in the region—out of 31 Sub-Saharan African countries with available data for 2003, Zambia ranks twentieth. Neighboring Botswana has more than 12 times more phone lines per inhabitant than Zambia.

Looking at access to financial services in figure 2.11, it becomes evident that Zambia's number of bank branches (relative to population size) is in line with the level enjoyed by other countries of similar income (Beck, Demirguc-Kunt, and Peria 2005). When controlling for population density (not reported here), Zambia's relative performance is even more positive. When it comes to the provision of credit, however, Zambia is clearly underperforming. In other words, Zambia's banks are not less present than in other comparable countries, but they seem to lend less. In fact, credit to the private sector by banks represented only 8 percent of GDP in 2005, one of the lowest ratios in Sub-Saharan Africa.

Figure 2.10. International Comparison:
Access to Telecommunications Services

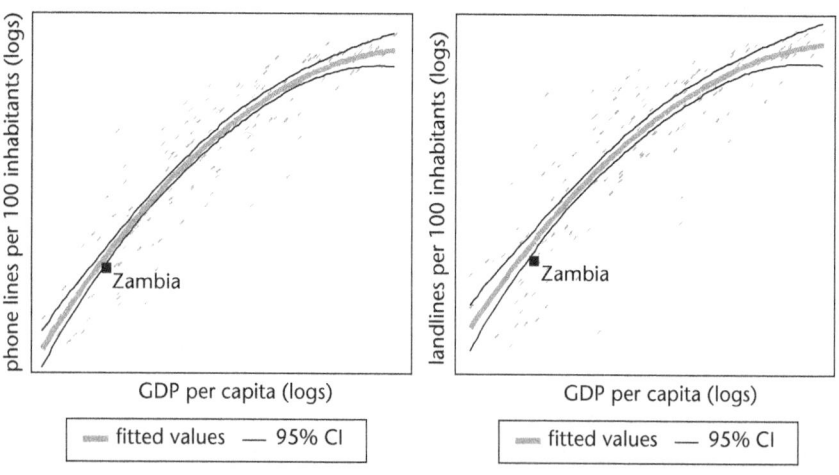

Source: World Bank DDP 2003.

**Figure 2.11. International Comparison:
Access to Financial Services**

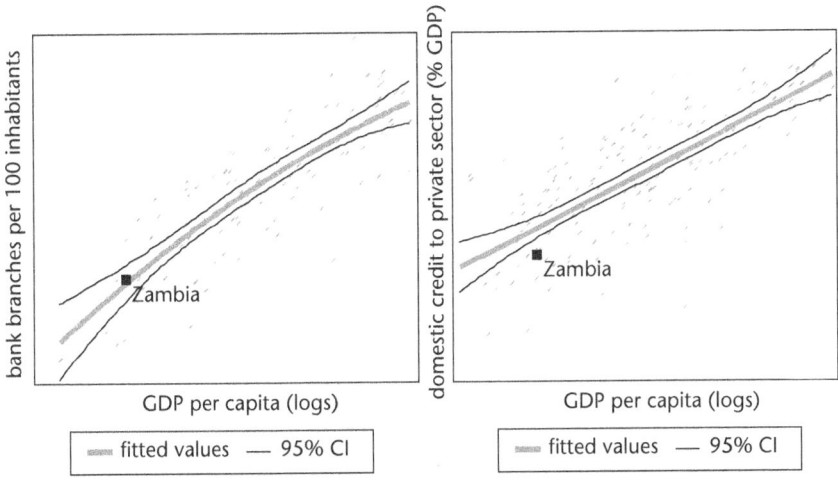

Source: Beck, Demirguc-Kunt, and Peria 2005; World Bank DDP 2003.

In comparison with other countries in the region, Zambian firms have to do more to obtain credit. Figure 2.12 uses data from the World Bank Investment Climate Surveys and shows the amount of collateral that Zambian firms have to pledge before getting a bank loan (expressed as a percentage of the value of the loan). In other countries in the region, the average required collateral to secure a bank loan ranges between 100 and 200 percent of the value of the loan, but Zambian firms have to pledge an average of more than 300 percent of the loan as collateral.

Zambia also displays lower access to air transportation services than other countries of similar income. This is measured by the number of air passengers per inhabitant and is depicted in figure 2.13.

Access to basic health and education services is another area in which Zambia is performing less well than its income level would predict. In education, the underperformance is not attributable to the number of teachers; however, in terms of enrollment in primary and secondary education, Zambia's performance is low (see figure 2.14). The same holds true for access to medical services (measured by the number of physicians) and access to clean drinking water (see figure 2.15).

Access is also unequal...

Access is not just low, it is also extremely unequal. Teledensity covers less than half of the regions outside the four major provinces (figure 2.16). Nearly 80 percent of

**Figure 2.12. Collateral Required to Obtain a Loan
                (in % of loan value)**

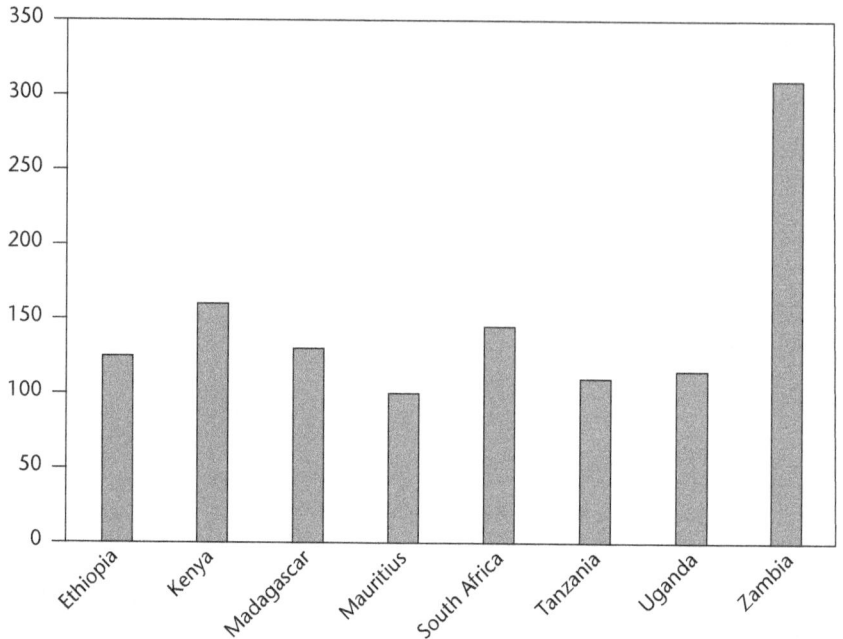

Source: World Bank 2002.

**Figure 2.13. International Comparison:
                Access to Air Transport Services**

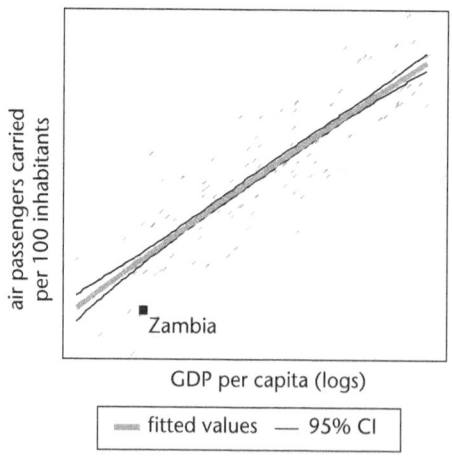

Source: World Bank DDP 2003.

**Figure 2.14. International Comparison:
Access to Education Services**

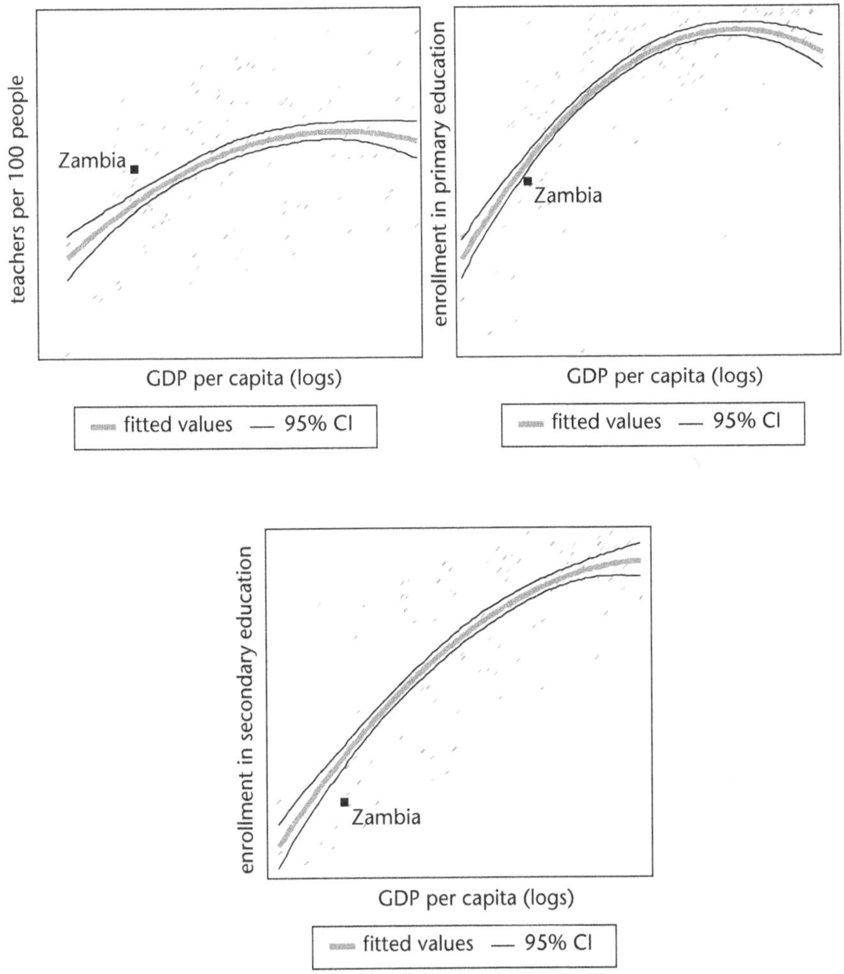

Source: World Bank DDP 2003.

fixed lines are located in Lusaka and the Copperbelt, where only 30 percent of the population lives. Only 0.30 percent of Zambia's rural households, accounting for 65 percent of Zambia's population, own a telephone. Less than 0.50 percent of Zambians have access to the Internet and three-quarters of users are in Lusaka and a handful of large towns.

As far as financial services are concerned, of Zambia's 72 districts, 32 do not have banks or any other financial institutions. In fact, only 8 percent of Zambia's

**Figure 2.15. International Comparison:
Access to Health Services**

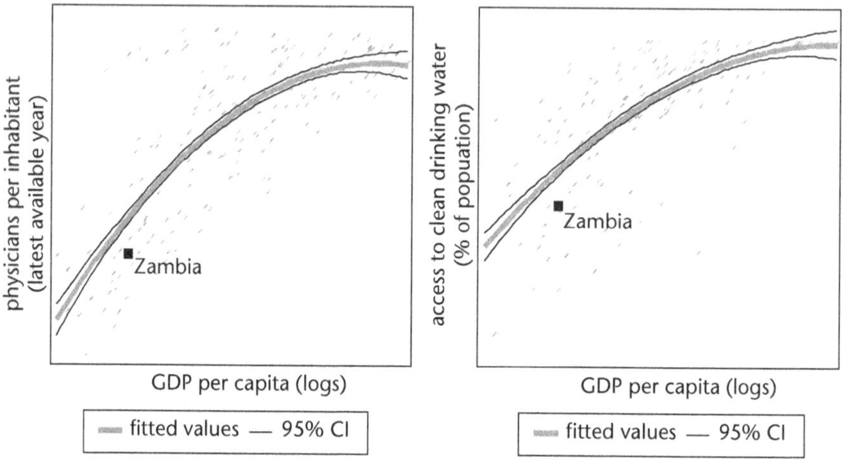

Source: World Bank DDP 2003.

adult population had a bank account in 2005. On average, firms outside of Lusaka, Ndola, and Livingston had to give 65 percent more collateral (relative to the size of the loan) than firms in those three major centers. Moreover, the average interest rate paid by firms outside those major centers was 6 percent higher than in Lusaka, Livingston, or Ndola.

Regional location is not the only dimension along which differences in access to services exist. Firm size also seems to play an important role. The average small and medium-size firms in the Investment Climate Surveys considered getting finance a major obstacle, whereas large firms with turnover greater than $1.5 million considered it only a minor issue. As pointed out in the Zambia DTIS (World Bank 2005), the levels of interest rates on kwacha have essentially made kwacha lending for the long term impossible. For those companies that can borrow in foreign exchange, however, the interest rates are well in line with other emerging economies.

No interest at all is paid on small savings accounts denominated in kwacha and only large firms receive positive interest rates on their deposits. To open a savings account, five of the 13 banks require customers to have a minimum balance of between $156 and $313 or more. In five other banks, the minimum balance to open an account is lower (in the range of $16 to $78). In the context of Zambia, however, where 58 percent of the population lives on less than $1 a day, these minimum balances prevent most people from having access to basic banking services.

Figure 2.16. Regional Disparities in Teledensity

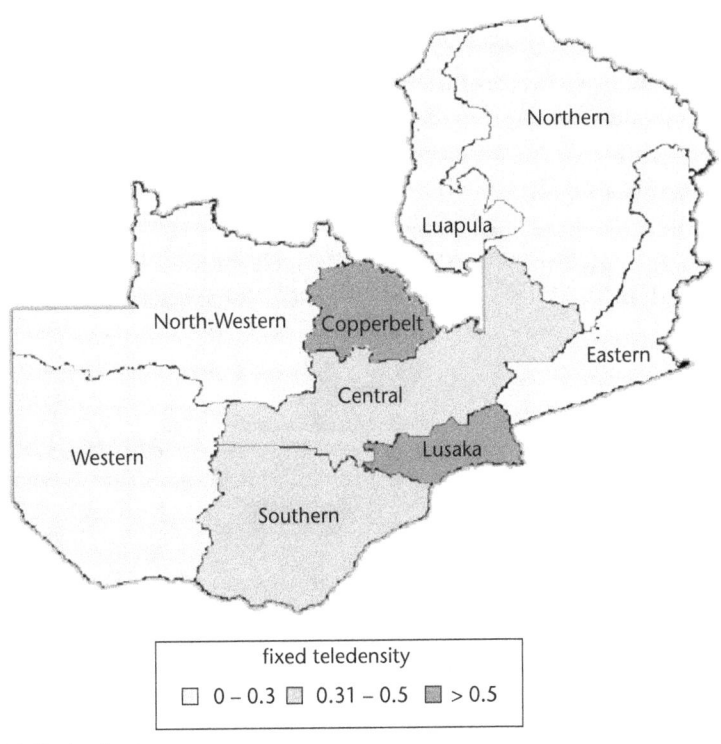

fixed teledensity

☐ 0 – 0.3   ☐ 0.31 – 0.5   ▣ > 0.5

Source: World Bank estimates.

Thus, with the exception of high-income households, public servants, and employees of large companies, most Zambians do not have access to products offered by banks.

and in some areas, access has actually deteriorated after liberalization.
The number of fixed telephone lines per 1,000 inhabitants has dropped from 7.95 in 1995 to 7.84 in 2005. Over that period, the total fixed-line telecommunications network grew from 76,000 lines to just 90,000, while Uganda has seen an increase from 20,000 lines in 1998 to 1.4 million today. Credit to the private sector by banks represented only 8 percent of GDP in 2005, which is lower than the level registered in 1990. The number of rural branches of banks actually declined in the last decade by 15 percent to 65. Although international air traffic grew by 7.1 percent per year on average between 1995 and 2004, domestic traffic decreased at an average 5.3 percent per year. In 2005, five weekly cargo freighters operated to

Lusaka with a total dedicated capacity of 175 to 250 tons; by early 2006, the number of flights had declined to two per week with a total of about 80 to 100 tons capacity. In other services like health and education, too, the picture is of stagnant or declining access to services. Between 1990 and 2000, public expenditure on education as a percentage of GDP declined from 2.4 percent to 2.0 percent, while the net primary enrollment ratio fell from 79 percent to 68 percent. As an indicator of the effect of this decline, youth literacy rates fell from 81.2 percent to 69.4 percent over the same period.[8]

As the rest of this report will argue, failures to implement the appropriate accompanying policies and deeper regional integration are likely to be at the root of some of the access deficiencies documented in this chapter.

Notes

1. Data supplied to the team from the Zambia Central Statistical Office in Lusaka.
2. Arnold, Javorcik, and Mattoo (2007) find that liberalization and foreign presence in services sectors is associated with productivity improvements in downstream manufacturing industries in the Czech Republic.
3. In all of these cases, statistical tests can reject with at least 90 percent certainty that the two rank orderings are uncorrelated.
4. Regarding the remaining components of Zambia's services exports, it should be noted that not all of these represent genuine trade flows. In communication services, exports mainly consist of settlement charges for call termination within the country, and the value of these are artificially inflated because prices for call termination are high because of a lack of competition in Zambia and because of a substitution of outgoing international traffic for incoming traffic. In insurance services, exports are measured as the difference between premia and claims.
5. Both variables are expressed in natural logarithms. Thus, the slope of the regression line can be interpreted as an elasticity.
6. The latter information is available for a large number of countries from the World Bank's Doing Business database.
7. For the purpose of our tourism sector report, we focused on one aspect of the business climate: how difficult it is to start and operate a business in Zambia. We used several measures from the World Bank's Doing Business database. As an indicator of infrastructure we used the percentage of paved roads.
8. Youth literacy rate here is the percentage of 15 to 24 year olds able to read and write to the standard as defined by the United Nations Development Report.

References

Ajwad, I., J. Balat, and G. Porto. 2005. "Zambia: Trade and Poverty, December 2004." Report for the Zambia Diagnostic Trade Integration Study, 2005.

Arnold, J., B. Javorcik, and A. Mattoo. 2007. "The Productivity Effects of Services Liberalization: Evidence from the Czech Republic." World Bank Policy Research Paper 4109. World Bank, Washington, DC.

Arnold, J., A. Mattoo, and G. Narciso. 2006. "Services Matter for Productivity: Firm-level Evidence from Sub-Saharan Africa." World Bank Policy Research Paper 4048. World Bank, Washington, DC.

Beck, Thorsten, Asli Demirguc-Kunt, and Maria Soledad Martinez Peria. 2005. "Reaching Out: Access to and use of banking services across countries." World Bank Policy Research Paper 3754, World Bank, Washington, DC.

Brambilla, Irene, and Guido G. Porto. 2006. "Farm Productivity and Market Structure: Evidence from Cotton Reforms in Zambia." World Bank Policy Research Paper 3904, World Bank, Washington, DC.

Eifert, Benn, Alan Gelb, and Vijaya Ramachandran. 2005. "Business Environment and Comparative Advantage in Africa: Evidence from the Investment Climate Data." Working Paper 56, Center for Global Development, Washington, DC.

Eschenbach, Felix, and Bernard Hoekman. 2005. "Services Policy Reform and Economic Growth in Transition Economies, 1990–2004." World Bank Policy Research Working Paper 3663, World Bank, Washington, DC.

Fink, C., A. Mattoo, and I.C. Neagu. 2002. "Assessing the Impact of Communication Costs on International Trade." *Journal of International Economics* 67: 428–445.

Hertel, T., Roman Keeney, Maros Ivanic, and L. Alan Winters. 2006. "Distributional Effects of WTO Agricultural Reforms in Rich and Poor Countries." Policy Research Working Paper 4060, World Bank, Washington DC.

Konan, Denise, and Keith Maskus. 2006. "Quantifying the Impact of Services Liberalization in a Developing Country." *Journal of Development Economics* 81 (1).

Mattoo, Aaditya, Randeep Rathindran, and Arvind Subramanian. 2006. "Measuring Services Trade Liberalization and its Impact on Economic Growth: An Illustration." *Journal of Economic Integration* 21: 64–98.

World Bank. 2002. Investment Climate Survey data for Zambia. World Bank, Washington, DC. http://www.enterprisesurveys.org/.

———. 2004a. "Zambia Country Economic Memorandum." World Bank, Washington, DC.

———. 2004b. "An Assessment of the Investment Climate in Zambia." World Bank, Washington, DC.

———. 2005. "Zambia Diagnostic Trade Integration Study" (June). World Bank, Washington, DC.

3

TELECOMMUNICATIONS: THE PERSISTENCE OF MONOPOLY

Jens Arnold, Boutheina Guermazi, and Aaditya Mattoo

Overview

Zambia's telecommunications market is characterized by unusually high prices of international calls, unusually low and unequal access to services, and sluggish growth of the network. The cost of an international call to the United States is four times that in Ghana, while the teledensity of three lines per 100 people is less than half of the regional average in Sub-Saharan Africa. The fixed-line network has grown from 76,000 in 1995 to 90,000 in 2005, while Uganda has seen an increase from 20,000 lines in 1998 to 1.4 million today. Nearly 80 percent of fixed lines are located in Lusaka and the Copperbelt, where 30 percent of the population lives, and only 0.3 percent of Zambia's rural households, accounting for 65 percent of Zambia's population, own a telephone. Less than 0.5 percent of Zambians have access to the Internet and three-quarters of users are in Lusaka and a handful of large towns. The poor state of telecommunications in Zambia deprives business of efficient international connectivity, leaves small farmers at the mercy of middlemen, and excludes most Zambians from the information and communication technology revolution.

Zamtel's monopoly in the international segment and the inability of the regulator to ensure a level playing field have negative effects on competition in all market segments. Profits from the international segment have not found their

---

We thank Mavis Ampah, David Satola, and Charles Kenny for comments on earlier drafts.

way to finance the expansion of the rural network; rather, they cross-subsidize services for urban households that are already in possession of a phone line and for government departments that do not pay their bills. At the same time, Zamtel's monopoly inflicts losses on mobile service providers that must use its gateway, depriving them of resources that could have been invested in the expansion of their networks. Discriminatory practices in Internet access undermine the growth of other dynamic firms.

The case for introducing meaningful competition is overwhelming, based on international experience and evidence specific to Zambia. Our estimates suggest that competition could provide another 30,000 Zambians with access to fixed-line telephones, and the gains in mobile access could be comparable. A reformed Zamtel could flourish in a competitive environment, whereas an unreformed Zamtel is unlikely to survive even with a monopoly on the international gateway. Tariff rebalancing and commercialization of Zamtel must be priorities. Competition need not compromise any of the government's objectives, and aggregate fiscal revenues derived from the telecommunications sector are likely to increase.

Competition will require significant regulatory and legal improvements, given that strong regulation is a precondition for the creation of competitive markets. The enforcement capacity and regulatory independence of the Communications Authority of Zambia (CAZ) are vital, particularly to devise and enforce a cost-based interconnection regime that reflects new market conditions. The Ministry of Communications and Transport needs to have the technical capacity to oversee the development of the sector. Zamtel must be issued a proper license to bring it under the ambit of the regulatory regime. The division of power between the regulator and the competition authority needs to be clarified.

Even an efficient, competitive market will not deliver socially desirable levels of access to telecommunications services, so it must be a policy priority to institute an effective and efficient universal access policy. Fortunately, evidence from other countries reveals that universal access policies are most successful when implemented in competitive markets, using instruments that harness competition, rather than those that distort the market through a reversion to monopolistic practices. Resources for potential subsidies (from donors, the Government of Zambia [GoZ] budget, and contributions from information and communications technology [ICT] service providers) must go into a central, independent universal access fund that is managed on a nondiscriminatory, transparent basis and distributed according to clear criteria and procedures. Allocation of the funds is best achieved through minimum-subsidy auctions, in which all potential providers are invited to bid for the minimum subsidy amount necessary to connect a locality. The GoZ is already exploring options to expand access to rural communities through private-public partnerships and is finalizing a universal access policy and strategy.

Regarding the sequencing of the reform process, Zambia's first and immediate steps should be to make the regulator independent, to begin tariff rebalancing by Zamtel, and to allow competition in the international gateway to the currently licensed operators. It should initiate three processes that will take no more than one year to implement: enhancing the regulatory capacity of CAZ, restructuring Zamtel so that it can operate on a commercial basis, and instituting a meaningful universal access policy. At the end of the year, Zambia should allow free entry into the international segment to new providers that currently are not present in the market, and let the market determine the number of providers. The issue of the incumbent's ownership can be addressed later, as long as it can be induced to follow commercial objectives and to restructure in the proposed time frame.

Zambia should precommit under the GATS to eliminate all impediments to competition in all segments of the telecommunication market at the end of the year. WTO commitments constitute legally binding obligations on members, enforceable through the WTO's binding dispute settlement process. The experience of other countries demonstrates that binding commitments to liberalization at a precise point in the future lends credibility to reform programs and urgency to the efforts of the incumbents and regulators to prepare for openness. Zambia could also subscribe to the WTO Reference Paper on regulatory principles for telecommunications. The draft Electronic Communications Act of Zambia reflects many of the requirements that would be expected to be seen in a WTO-compliant legal framework.

Through regional cooperation, Zambia can gain fair, efficient, and competitively priced access to regional infrastructure that is essential to the development of the country's Internet and telecommunication sectors. Currently, Zambia relies on expensive satellite communications for connectivity with the rest of the world and suffers from a lack of adequate and cost-effective international bandwidth. The East African Submarine Cable System (EASSy) fiber-optic submarine cable offers Zambia a chance to reduce significantly its international communication costs. As a landlocked country, Zambia must access the fiber-optic cable via its neighbors Malawi and Zimbabwe, a situation that will demand cooperation on regulation as well as a revision of existing cross-border interconnection and pricing agreements. A key difficulty for Zambia, however, is that the enforcement of such agreements and the resolution of disputes is beyond the jurisdiction of national regulators. Zambia would benefit from, and should push for, the development of regional interconnection guidelines, such as those put forward by Common Market for Eastern and Southern Africa (COMESA); the creation of a regional dispute resolution mechanism; and full participation in regional regulatory collaboration to enforce such guidelines.

Through international engagement, Zambia can mobilize financial and technical support for regulatory improvements and universal access policies, and

lend credibility to its reform program. The four key elements of an "aid-for-services trade reform" package would include the following:

- Zambia's commitment to eliminate all de jure and de facto impediments to competition in all segments of the telecommunications market
- Zambia's commitment to enhance the independence of CAZ to guarantee a level playing field and to create an entity that oversees the design and implementation of universal access policies
- Donor commitments to provide technical and financial assistance to improve regulatory institutions, especially the capacity to ensure interconnection and guarantee competitive conditions (estimated requirements: $2.7 million)
- Donor commitments to help institute policies that promote universal access and the development of a national telecommunications backbone and to supplement investment in these areas by the private sector and the government (estimated requirements: $15 million)

The state of telecommunications in Zambia

In 1994, the GoZ initiated reforms of the telecommunications sector following the adoption of the newly developed Telecommunications Act. The reforms resulted in the introduction of competition in mobile and Internet services. Zambia initially made faster progress in telecommunications than other countries in the region, but the momentum declined. Today, Zambia has fallen behind regional standards in terms of providing access to telecommunication services to its citizens and businesses, and in terms of competitive prices for key services.

Limited Access and Slow Growth of Telecommunications Services

With only three lines per 100 people, Zambia's teledensity remains well below the regional average of 5.86 lines in Sub-Saharan Africa, as well as below the rates of its neighboring countries. The fixed-line network has grown by only 18 percent over the last 10 years—from about 76,000 in 1995 to 90,000 in 2005 for a population of 11 million people. Uganda, in contrast, has seen an increase from 20,000 lines in 1998 to 1.4 million subscribers in 2006.

Although the Zambian fixed-line network extends to all the nine provinces of the country, access is limited and quality of service is variable. Zambia lacks a modern national backbone, and a number of the provinces are connected via satellite networks or analog backbones, several of which are so outdated that support from manufacturers has been discontinued. Zamtel, the incumbent fixed-line operator, has little capital for new investments; the percentage of revenues

Box 3.1. The Early History of Telecommunications in Zambia

The first manual telephone exchange in Zambia, then Northern Rhodesia, was installed in Livingstone in 1913. A second telephone exchange in Ndola and trunk services between Zambia and South Africa were installed in the early 1930s. By the late 1950s, telephone subscribers were able to place calls between the main urban centers without operator assistance, which was approximately the same time that these services were introduced in Britain. A microwave link between Livingstone and Kabwe was commissioned in 1967, followed by the Lusaka–Livingstone link in 1974. Over the next 10 years, these links were extended to other major towns.

Until 1994, telecommunications services were provided by the public Post and Telecommunications Corporation (PTC). The Telecommunications Act of 1994 split PTC into two autonomous entities: Zambia Postal Services Corporation (Zampost, an autonomous entity wholly owned by the government) and Zambia Telecommunications Company Limited (Zamtel, a limited liability company, with the government as sole shareholder). The Act also created the Communications Authority of Zambia (CAZ) as the regulator for the sector. The first Internet services were introduced by Zamnet in 1994. Cellular telephony was introduced to Zambia in 1995 by Zamtel, with competing providers entering in 1997 (Telecel, now MTN) and 1998 (Celtel).

Box Figure 1. Chronology of Sector Reform

The Telecommunications Act of 1994 led to the increase of private participation and significant liberalization in some segments of the sector

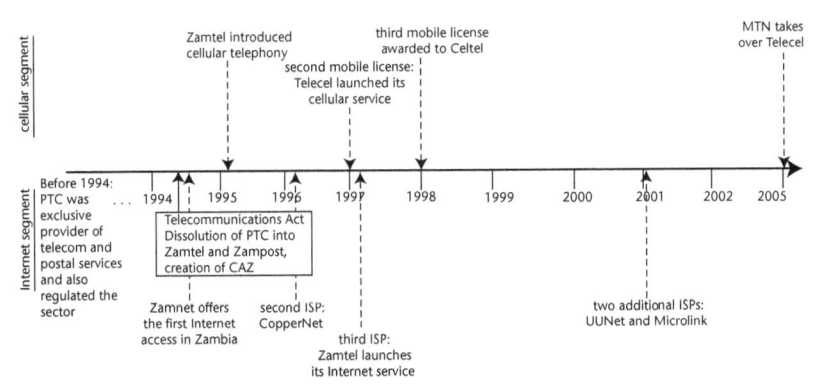

going into new investment has been reduced from about 25 percent in 1995 to below 10 percent.

Zambia also has low Internet penetration, largely because of the poor fixed-line infrastructure. With only 52,000 users, just 0.48 percent of Zambians have

Figure 3.1. Access to Telecommunications Services

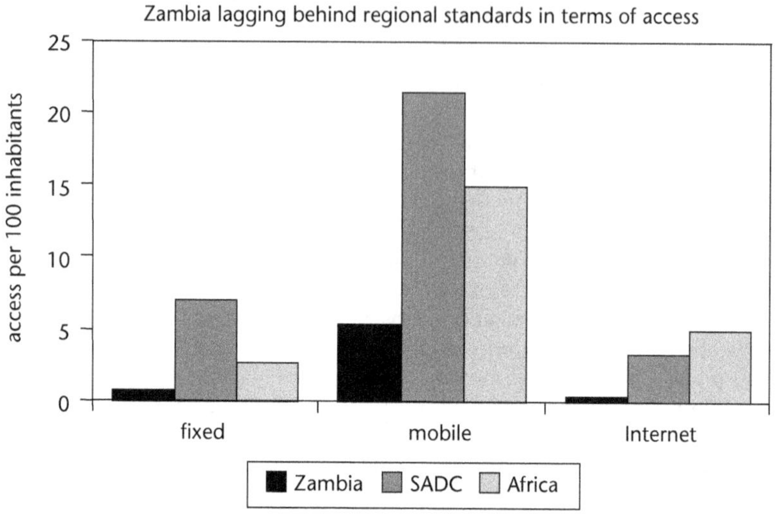

Zambia lagging behind regional standards in terms of access

Source: World Bank analysis based on the ITU World Telecommunications Database 2006.

access to the Internet. Because of the limited points of presence (POPs) in other parts of the country, 75 percent of Internet users are concentrated in Lusaka and a handful of other larger towns. Botswana, Namibia, and Zimbabwe each have Internet penetration rates that are more than five times as high.

The country displays a marked disparity of access to telecommunications among rural and urban areas. About 78 percent of fixed lines are in Lusaka and the Copperbelt, where 30 percent of the population live. Provision of ICT services in Zambia is concentrated in areas along the line of rail. However, about 65 percent of Zambia's population live in rural areas, and only 0.3 percent of rural households own a telephone. In addition, access to public pay phones is limited compared with other countries in the region.

High international call prices

International call prices in Zambia are well above regional and global standards (see figure 3.2). A call from Zambia to the United States now costs $1.15 per minute after a 40 percent price drop in early 2006, compared with below $1.00 per minute for the region. For an individual or firm in Zambia, 13 hours of communications to the United States amount to the entire annual GDP per capita.

The fact that Zamtel was recently able to reduce its prices substantially shows how far pricing decisions are detached from actual costs. South Africa, for example, is able to provide calls to the United States at about one-fifth of the price at which this service is available in Zambia. Not surprisingly, outgoing international call minutes per subscriber are much lower than for other countries in the region. For Zambia, this number is less than half of the average of Angola, Botswana, Malawi, Namibia, Mozambique, and Zimbabwe. Of these countries, only Mozambique is at a similarly low level. Between 1990 and 2004, total outgoing traffic in Zambia grew by about 35 percent, while in Botswana the volume grew by 300 percent in the same period.

Some argue that high international revenues are needed to promote the expansion of the current network and increase Zambia's comparatively low teledensity. However, network expansion has been progressing at a slow pace despite high revenues in the international segment.

The poor state of telecommunications services penalizes other sectors

In the current situation, few Zambian households have access to telecommunication services, and Zambian businesses are handicapped by the high cost of international communication. In the Investment Climate Surveys undertaken by the World Bank in many countries around the world, companies were asked to rate the seriousness of various barriers to doing business. The global average for the percentage of firms that listed telecommunications as a significant barrier was 9.8 percent. For Zambia, that same number was 33 percent.

Today, telecommunications are a vital intermediate input and are instrumental to disseminate and diffuse knowledge; the spread of the Internet and the dynamism that it has lent to economies around the world bears testimony to the

Figure 3.2. High International Call Prices Compared with Selected Countries in Africa and Middle East

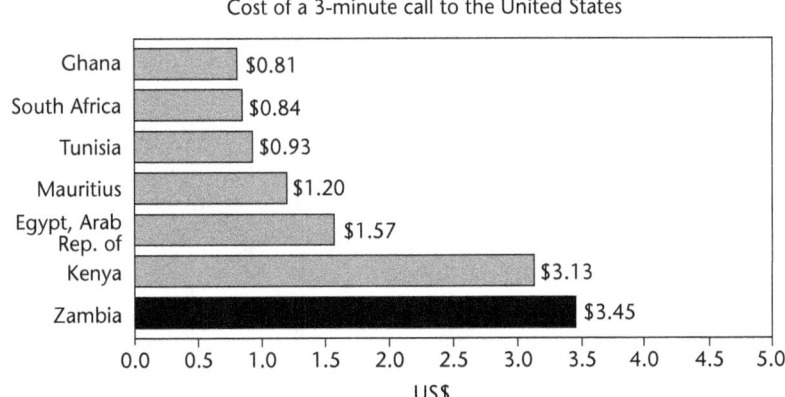

Cost of a 3-minute call to the United States

Source: Compiled from the Web sites of operators in these countries (2006).

importance of telecommunications services. It is difficult to think of any manu-facturing or service activity that does not rely on communication services. Com-munication is important for learning about sourcing alternatives and price devel-opments, for coordinating with the customer, and for exploring new market opportunities. Insufficiently developed or insufficiently competitive telecommu-nications services will immediately translate into a competitive disadvantage for current or potential exporters in relation to their foreign competitors, especially if potential competitors have cheaper and more reliable access to telecommunica-tions services. Under current conditions, the state of the telecommunications sec-tor places Zambian firms at a disadvantage compared with international competitors.

Even in agriculture, the importance of telecommunications services cannot be underestimated. Interviews with associations engaged in the organization of smallholder farmers' cooperatives in Zambia revealed that an important problem facing smallholders is the lack of knowledge about current market conditions and prices. If farmers are able to bridge the knowledge gap with respect to markets, they can receive better and more stable prices for their produce, and they would no longer be at the mercy of intermediaries who often do not have their best inter-ests at heart. There is also an indirect effect: interviews with banks in Zambia revealed that the poor state of the telecommunications infrastructure was a major constraint on their ability to extend services to rural areas.

A recent study of the World Bank analyzes the relationship between telecom-munications services and the productivity of firms in Sub-Saharan African countries (Arnold, Mattoo, and Narciso 2006). The study uses detailed firm-level data from the World Bank's Investment Climate surveys for 10 African countries. The survey data contain subjective and objective measures of telecommunications performance and availability at the level of each firm. The study estimates productivity for 1,185 firms, and shows how productivity differ-ences are related to the performance of telecommunications services available in the same region of the country. The regression analysis controls for systematic differences between countries and industries, and accounts for differences in firms' export and ownership status, age, size, and location. Even after control-ling for these other determinants, the analysis detects a strong and statistically significant relationship between firm performance and the state of telecommu-nications services.

The poor state of telecommunications in Zambia deprives business of vital low-cost international connectedness, leaves small farmers at the mercy of inter-mediaries, and excludes most Zambians from the information and communica-tion technology revolution.

Why has telecommunications performance been below par?

Market Structure and Regulatory Environment

A key aspect of the Zambian telecommunications market is the perpetuation of Zamtel's de facto monopoly in the international gateway market (IGW). Although, in theory, entry into the provision of international services has been open since 2002, the license fee of operating an international gateway, set at $12 million is prohibitively high, effectively precluding competition in the international segment.

A second aspect is that the regulatory environment in the telecommunications sector is not well defined. The incumbent fixed-line operator is operating under a deemed license, which places its operations largely out of the scope of regulatory authorities. Moreover, the public sector faces a conflict of interest because of its dual role as regulator and owner of the incumbent operator Zamtel, which is operating in all segments of the market. Table 3.1 describes the current market structure in the three segments of Zambia's telecommunications sector.

In this section, we demonstrate how these aspects of the Zambian market lead to distorted competition in all segments of the market.

Table 3.1. The Market Players

Operator	Service	Ownership	Market share (%)[a]	Subscriber base (2006)	Growth (2003/02)
ZAMTEL	PSTN	Domestic Public	—	84,956	1.5
CELTEL	MOBILE	Majority foreign owned	77	800,000	24.8
MTN	MOBILE	Foreign owned	14	90,000	−0.2
ZAMTEL/CELL Z	MOBILE	Domestic Public	9	57,000	1,752.5
VODACOM	MOBILE	Foreign owned	—	—	—
ZAMNET	INTERNET	Domestic	33	3,529	0.9
ZAMTEL	INTERNET	Domestic Public	33	3,983	26.0
COPPERNET	INTERNET	Domestic	29	3,913	97.6
MICROLINK	INTERNET	Majority foreign owned	3	329	—
UUNET	INTERNET	Majority foreign owned	2	221	—

Source: Interviews with operators in Zambia (2006).

a. Market share within the respective market segment.

Fixed-line services

First consider international services: all international traffic has to be routed through Zamtel's gateway. Interconnection fees paid by the cellular providers are set at 80 percent of the incumbent's retail price, which leaves no room for competition on prices. With supply constraints, the result is high prices and low quality of service because of congestion. Hence, under a de facto monopoly on international traffic, the fixed-line incumbent operator operates a high-margin, low-volume, low-quality business.

Monopoly profits originating in the international segment allow the incumbent operator to cross-subsidize local calls and fixed-line subscriptions. The current rates for local fixed-line calls and the monthly subscription rate are not enough to cover the costs of offering these services. The cost of a residential connection and monthly residential tariff for a fixed telephone is among the lowest in Southern African Development Community (SADC) countries (see figure 3.3). Zamtel's de facto monopoly in this segment will remain in place as long as the monopoly in the international gateway generates sufficient profits to continue the cross-subsidies. Prospects for profitable entry are even made more challenging because the fixed-line market is becoming increasingly less attractive than broadband and wireless where most of the investment is going.

Another problem is that the incumbent finds it difficult to enforce the payment of current charges and outstanding debts with the public administration, which weakens its financial health. In a newspaper interview in March 2006, Zamtel put its outstanding debt at $62 million, more than four months' worth of the company's revenues. It has been argued that the high revenues from the IGW are needed to keep the incumbent alive. In reality, however, with a more solid business model, Zamtel would be able to enforce its claims and become profitable. The inability of Zamtel to enforce bill payment by the public sector amounts to a redistribution of resources toward public sector entities and away from the large number of Zambians who could benefit from access to telecommunications services under a fully competitive scenario.

The status quo is thus beneficial for urban households that are already in possession of a phone line and for government departments that do not pay their bills. The result is that Zamtel's profits from the international segment are not invested in the expansion of the network. At the same time, the low monthly subscription fee discourages private sector participation in network expansion and limits the extension of benefits of a residential fixed line to more households. This situation precludes many households, especially those in rural areas, from obtaining a phone line leading to an extremely low fixed-line penetration. In other words, the effect of the status quo, that is, the monopoly in the IGW, is equivalent to a redistribution from (on average poorer) rural households to (on average wealthier) urban households.

**Figure 3.3. Zambia Has One of the Lowest Residential Connection
and Local Call Rates in the SADC Region**

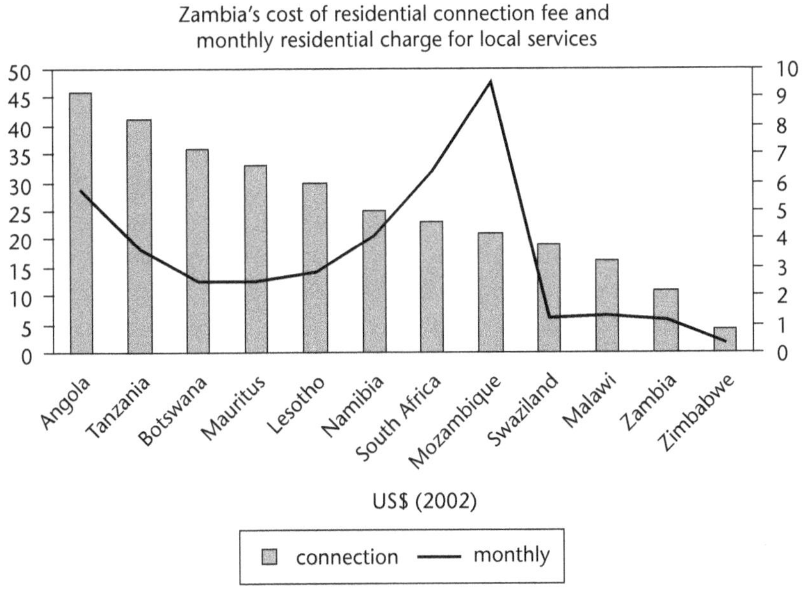

Zambia's cost of residential connection fee and
monthly residential charge for local services

US$ (2002)

□ connection —— monthly

Source: World Bank analysis based on ITU World Telecommunication Indicators Database 2006.

Cellular mobile segment

Under the current situation, the two independent cellular providers have to route their international traffic through the incumbent's gateway. On outgoing international calls, the two mobile operators not associated with the incumbent are charged 80 percent of the incumbent's retail price as an interconnection fee for the delivery of the call. The remaining margin is insufficient to cover the mobile operators' costs associated with administration (for example, the cost of distributing prepaid scratch cards with airtime) and with delivery of the call to the international gateway. The Mobile Telecommunications Network Zambia (MTN), for example, which is passing on a 10 percent discount of Zamtel's international rates to their customers, claims that they are making an annual loss of $50,000 by providing international calls. Whether or not Zamtel's profits from its international gateway monopoly are being invested in the expansion of the network, the losses that this monopoly is inflicting on other firms seem to be depriving them of resources that they could have invested in the expansion of their networks.

On inbound international traffic, the low quality and high rates of noncompletion are a constraint to business. It is not straightforward to quantify the income the cellular providers lose because of the de facto monopoly in the IGW. On the basis of accounting figures and international comparisons, however, a first-order approximation can be made on the basis of three plausible scenarios. It seems reasonable to assume that the mobile providers could make a margin of $0.35 per minute on outgoing international calls if they had their own gateway and prices were to drop by about 50 percent. The current level of profits generated from that segment is zero, or possibly even negative. For inbound international calls, MTN currently receives $0.14 from Zamtel, but the expected margin there is $0.05. Hence, the operators expect an increase of $0.36 on incoming calls. To quantify the additional profits that the two independent providers could get if they were allowed to operate IGWs, we consider the following three scenarios:

Scenario 1. Current call volumes remain unchanged despite a 50 percent reduction of call charges: MTN and Celtel together could have additional profits of approximately $3.5 million per year.

Scenario 2. Given that the high call charges currently cause some substitution of outbound minutes for inbound minutes, a 50 percent price reduction might bring down the ratio of inbound to outbound call minutes from the current level of 8:1. Supposing this ratio goes down to a level of 4:1,[1] MTN and Celtel together could have additional profits of approximately $4.8 million per year.

Scenario 3. If the inbound to outbound ratio drops down to 4:1, and lower prices, better quality, and lower noncompletion rates cause outbound traffic to grow by around 15 percent: MTN and Celtel together could have additional profits of approximately $5.3 million per year.

These numbers should be interpreted with care as they rely on estimates by the current providers. They do illustrate, however, that substantial additional gains would be possible for the two independent cellular providers on the sole basis of traffic generated by their phone lines. Under the current situation, competition is distorted by the fact that Zamtel receives a substantial part of the revenue generated by its competitors.

Apart from the international segment, the current situation distorts competition because Zamtel operates both the fixed-line network and a mobile operator, Cell-Z. In countries where the calling party bears the entire cost of the phone call, calls from a fixed line to a mobile phone are generally charged significantly higher rates than those to another landline. In Zambia, however, an exception to this practice is made for calls from a landline to Cell-Z, which are billed by Zamtel at the same rate as calls to a landline. Survey results indicate that, as a result, some private companies and civil service sectors allow Cell-Z mobile phones to be called from office phones, but not other cell phones, which gives Cell-Z an unfair competitive edge (Mulavu, Kanyanga, Imasiku, and Mwenda 2005). This practice is possible only because Zamtel is simultaneously present in the fixed and mobile segments, and it is not subject to adequate regulatory supervision. With competition distorted in this way, cellular tariffs in Zambia are higher than in many other countries in the region (see figure 3.4).

As the Zambia Competition Commission notes, "there is need to separate the telecommunications essential infrastructure from the fixed telephony, the Internet service provision, as well as the impending GSM services. The position of Zamtel means it has the power to prevent, restrict or distort competitor access to this essential infrastructure that was built with public funds" (2003). The same study stresses the need to enhance competition to attract investment into the sector: "Deficiencies in access to essential wholesale services in a strategic industry provided by a vertically integrated firm with substantial market power to competitors in upstream or downstream markets should be addressed if at all investment would be attracted in the sector" (2003).

Internet access

The Internet access segment, although in principle open to competition, is suffering from the lack of a level playing field because of the dominant position of the incumbent fixed-line operator. Internet access in Zambia is achieved mainly through dial-up connections, using the fixed-line telephone network controlled

Figure 3.4. Mobile Rates Are Higher in Zambia

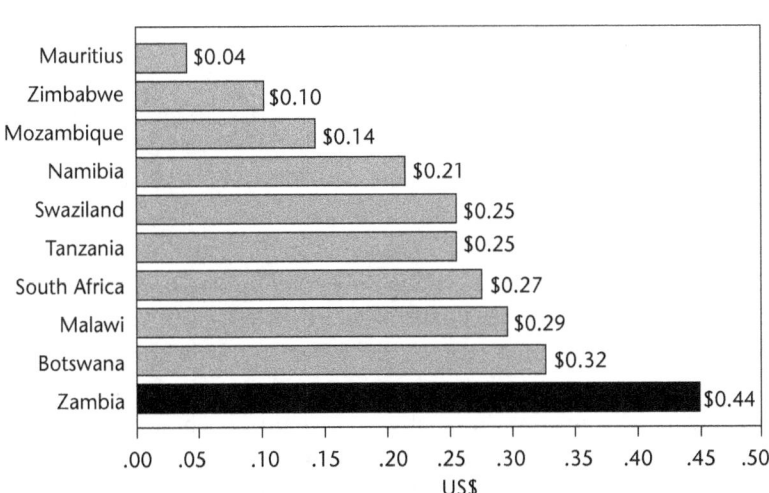

Source: World Bank analysis based on ITU World Telecommunication Indicators Database 2006.

by Zamtel. By controlling the landline infrastructure, the incumbent is able to offer better access conditions to its own Internet subsidiary than to competitors. Zamtel has set up so-called virtual local access points, which allow customers outside Lusaka to access the Internet at local call rates, but these rates are available only to customers of Zamtel Online. Customers of other Internet service providers (ISPs) have to pay long-distance telephone charges to access the Internet if they are located outside the capital.

The distortion created by this unequal access is demonstrated by using the example of a customer located in Mpika in the Northern Province, who uses the Internet for an average of 70 minutes per day. As a customer of the independent ISP Zamnet, the customer would pay a subscription charge of kwacha (K) 105,750 a month to the ISP, and additionally face call charges of K 2,467,500. The same customer could access Zamtel Online for call charges of K 593,500 because of the virtual local access point. In other words, the total monthly cost of using the incumbent's subsidiary is less than 25 percent of the cost of using one of Zamtel's competitors for this customer, and this difference is only due to the call charges made by Zamtel, which are beyond the control of competitive ISPs. For customers outside the capital, competition is thus largely nonexistent.

Recently, Zamtel began to offer asymmetric digital subscriber line (ADSL) broadband connections to customers, and currently, Zamtel is the only provider of this service. Provision of ADSL consists of using spare capacity in the local loop with digital subscriber line (DSL) modems at both ends, which allows data handling at a much faster rate than a normal modem can provide. To offer this service, ISPs need access to the local loop on an unbundled basis. This would require a detailed negotiated line-sharing arrangement with Zamtel against the payment of rental charges for using the local loop.

In the absence of a clear policy and regulatory framework on local loop unbundling (LLU), requests by competitive ISPs to access the local loop on an unbundled basis currently have not been answered. As a result, Zamtel is the only provider of broadband Internet at this time, and other ISPs feel that their inability to offer faster Internet connections is eroding their customer base. However, there is more than one reasonable regulatory approach to this issue. There is a trade-off between allowing competition on existing infrastructure, which will bring competition faster but presents a number of regulatory challenges, and strengthening the incentives to invest in alternative access technologies, which have the long-term benefits of competition in access technologies. In either event, the current regulatory uncertainty is hampering the development of broadband Internet in Zambia, and it is essential for regulatory authorities to define their position with respect to the strategy to promote broadband access in Zambia. Only in a clearly defined environment will private actors be able to make the necessary investments.

As depicted in figure 3.5 the de facto monopoly in the international gateway prevents a level playing field in other segments.

The benefits of liberalization and sector reform in Zambia

The Benefits of Competitive Markets: Evidence from Other Countries

Telecommunications markets worldwide have undergone tremendous changes in the last two decades. Developed and developing countries alike have moved away from monopoly toward a competitive market structure across all segments of the sector. According to the International Telecommunication Union (ITU), basic

Figure 3.5. The International Gateway Monopoly and Weak Regulation Adversely Affect Competition in Other Segments

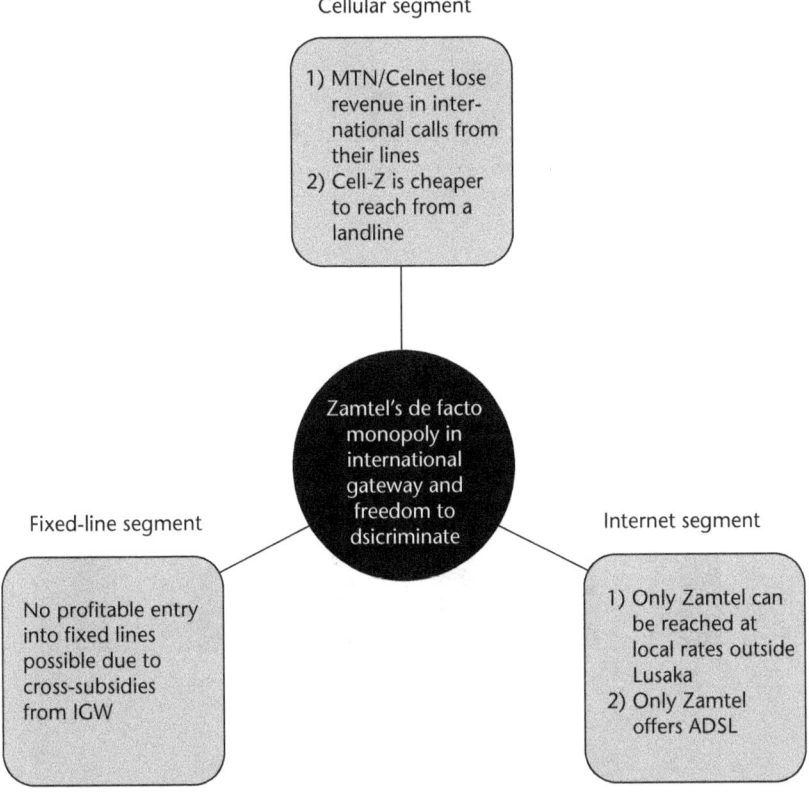

Source: Authors.

services are now provided under competitive conditions in 54 percent of countries worldwide (ITU 2005). However, some important regional differences remain.

Considerable evidence has accumulated, demonstrating the huge potential benefits of competition on several dimensions. Competition has drastically reduced prices for communications services, improved access, promoted investment in communications infrastructure and in the provision of new services, and

Figure 3.6. Variations in the Level of Competition by Segment and by Market

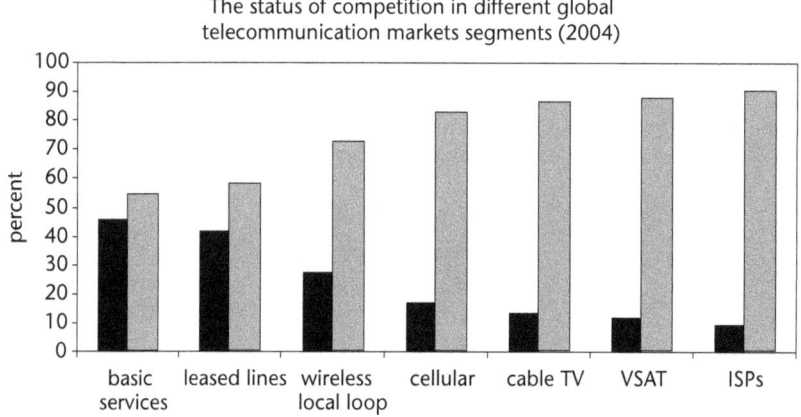

The status of competition in different global telecommunication markets segments (2004)

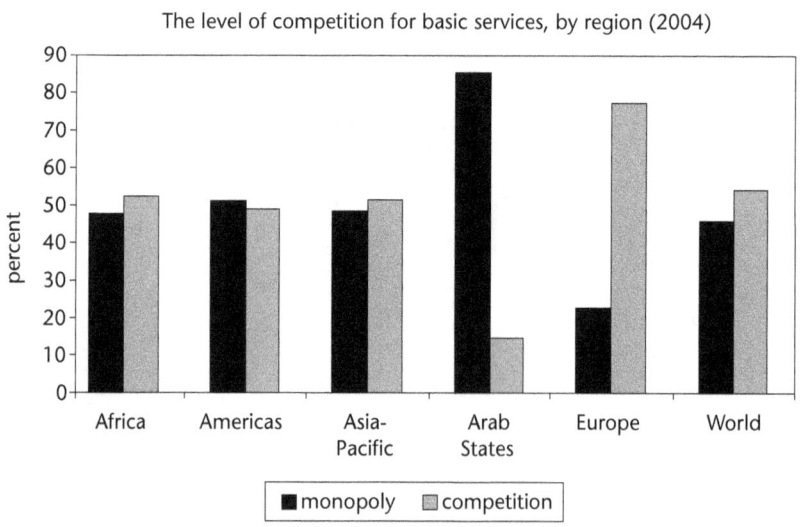

The level of competition for basic services, by region (2004)

Source: ITU World Telecommunication Regulatory Database.

caused significant positive spillover effects to other sectors of the economy. This section will describe some of this evidence.

Lower call tariffs

Data from other countries show that, on average, full competition is associated with prices at about 50 percent of the average in partially competitive markets (Rossoto, Wellenius, Lewin, and Gomez 2004). Figure 3.7 depicts the relationship between call prices and competition for all countries with available data.

In Africa, countries that introduced full competition saw prices decrease much more than others. In Uganda, for example, competition reduced the lowest available price for a call to the United States from $1.32 to $0.83 within only two years. Similarly, in Ghana, these prices declined from $3.85 in 1990 to $1.25 in 1995 and $0.25 in 2005.

Increased penetration of communication services

A study undertaken at the World Bank analyzes the impact of policy reform in basic telecommunications on sectoral performance using a new panel data set for 86 developing countries across Africa, Asia, the Middle East, Latin America, and the Caribbean in the period from 1985 to 1999 (Fink, Mattoo, and Neagu 2002). The study found that both privatization and competition can independently lead

Figure 3.7. International Calls Are Lower with Competition

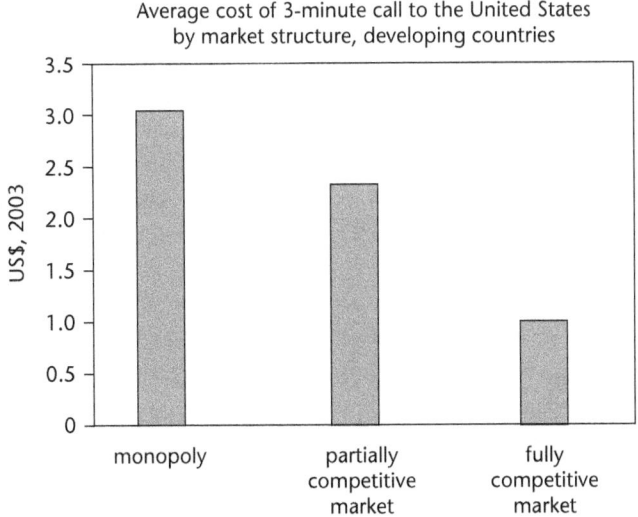

Average cost of 3-minute call to the United States
by market structure, developing countries

Source: Based on Rossoto, Wellenius, Lewin, and Gomez 2004.

Figure 3.8. The Introduction of Competition Often Marks the Start of a Significant Increase in Fixed-Line Penetration

Fixed line penetration and competition
(1980 level = 100)

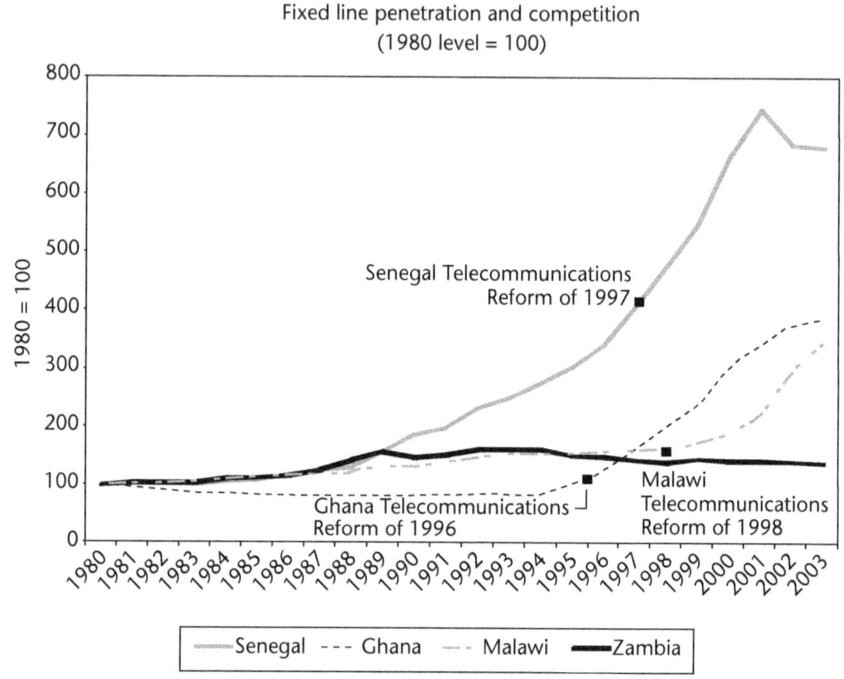

Source: World Bank WDI Database 2006.

to significant improvements in penetration. But a comprehensive reform pro-gram, involving policies and the support of an independent regulator, produced the largest gains: an 8 percent higher level of mainlines and a 21 percent higher level of labor productivity compared with years of partial and no reform.

Case evidence from African countries confirms this picture. Figure 3.8 depicts the development of fixed-line penetration around the respective year in which the major step toward full competition was undertaken for Ghana, Senegal, and Malawi. To make the developments comparable, the graph takes each country's 1980 level of mainlines per inhabitant as the starting point and marks the time of major procompetitive reforms. The introduction of competition usually consti-tutes the starting point of a significant increase in fixed-line penetration. The example of Mauritania, described in box 3.2, demonstrates the benefits of telecommunications reform in more detail.

Investment

A competitive environment in which providers compete for the provision of serv-ices to customers can provide incentives for investment into telecommunications

Box 3.2. The Case for Reform: A Comparison of Mauritania and Ethiopia

Mauritania embarked on an ambitious reform of its telecommunications sector in 1998. The World Bank Group supported the reform process through financing consultancy services, transaction advisors, and capacity-building efforts. These helped to set up a sound legal and regulatory framework, establish a fully operational and effective regulatory agency, open the market to competition, and privatize the incumbent operator. The reform program brought major benefits to users by improving access to services and lowering prices. Overall teledensity jumped from 0.6 percent in 1998 to 11.07 percent in September 2003. A credible and transparent sectoral framework attracted record levels of private investment and rapid rollout: proceeds from the sale of two mobile licenses totaled $56 million, while the two operators launched services in a record six months. Privatization proceeds from the fixed-line operator amounted to an additional $48 million (equivalent to $4,065 per line), of which more than $32 million was injected as fresh capital into the company through a capital increase. The macroeconomic impact of the reform goes well beyond these one-time revenues: the continuous development of the sector has led to higher fiscal revenues, the creation of a large number of new jobs, and increased global competitiveness.

Conversely, Ethiopia has not undertaken any substantial reform of its telecommunications sector. Its current policy of maintaining a monopoly in the provision of all telecommunications infrastructure and services has cost the nation in inefficiency and opportunity costs. The government has yet to articulate a sector reform strategy and liberalization timetable. The lack of reform has manifested itself in poor sector growth and performance. In fact, whereas telecom penetration in Mauritania increased from 0.41 in 1995 to 11.07 in September 2003 as a result of sector reform (moving the country from 27th to the 10th, out of 48 Sub-Saharan African countries), in Ethiopia, where sector reform has been lagging, the increase was only from 0.25 to 0.61 over the same period (moving the country from 39th to 48th place).

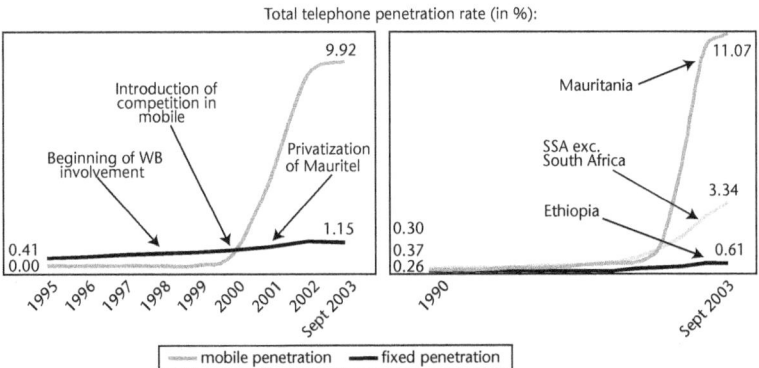

The Rewards of Liberalization: Evidence from Mauritania

Ethiopia vis-à-vis Mauritania: The Cost of Not Reforming

Source: Guislain et al. 2005.

Note: WBG GICT analysis based on ITU World Telecommunications Indicators Database 2006, World Bank WDI Database, and Middle East and Africa Wireless Analyst for 2003 Data on Mobile.

infrastructure. Investment reduces costs, increases the subscriber base, and gives providers a competitive edge in relation to their competitors. The absence of effective competition can dilute the incentives to undertake infrastructure investments. This is consistent with evidence from the Ugandan telecommunications reform, following which the telecommunications sector saw a total of $203 million of new investment by the incumbent and the private operators.

In the Caribbean, liberalization and the introduction of competition enabled one new entrant alone to invest more than $750 million, while increasing geographic service coverage by more than 90 percent and reducing service prices by as much as 59 percent. In another example, a new entrant in Morocco was able to increase investment by nearly 230 percent under four years of policy liberalization, while contributing to an increase in telephony penetration (fixed plus mobile) from 6 percent under the monopoly in 1999 to 45 percent in 2005 (WSIS 2006).

The Benefits of Competitive Markets: Estimates for Zambia

The dismantling of the de facto monopoly is expected to spur strong growth of the telecommunications sector in Zambia, as has been the case with the introduction of competition in other countries. Based on the regression analysis outlined in box 3.3, it is predicted that the introduction of full competition would generate a 33 percent increase in fixed-line penetration, equivalent to almost 30,000 additional fixed lines. Leveling the playing field in the mobile segment and remedying the regulatory imperfections associated with the current monopoly in one segment of the industry could improve mobile penetration by 21 percent, which is equivalent to more than 28,000 new mobile lines. Similarly, the number of Internet users could increase by 24 percent of the current level. These improvements in access to telecommunications services could have a large impact on the Zambian economy and could generate significant tax revenues.

Addressing concerns raised by liberalization

The benefits of liberalization, as set out in the sections above, are compelling. Against these reasons, however, the concerns of several stakeholders must be weighed regarding the removal of the international de facto monopoly. The incumbent operator Zamtel is unsure about its role in a competitive environment, and concerns have been expressed about empowerment, fiscal revenue, and security. At the same time, regulatory inadequacies will have to be dealt with to achieve a successful reform. Finally, the success of universal access policies will depend critically on the reform of the sector and on the institution of complementary policies.

Box 3.3. Estimated Gains from Full Competition in Telecommunications Services in Zambia

On the basis of the relationship between telephone and Internet penetration and the state of competition across a large number of countries, we can make some first-order estimates of how access to communications services in Zambia might evolve if full competition were introduced in the sector. This box presents some rough estimates of the gains from removing the remaining barriers to full competition.

Using data on 152 countries, we estimate the relationship between performance of a country's telecommunications system and its progress in introducing competition. The state of competition is assessed on the basis of information from the International Telecommunications Union (ITU), which lists the state of competition separately for fixed calls, cellular telephony, and international communications. To quantify these assessments, we attach a score of 0 to countries with monopolies in a given subsector, 1 for partial competition or duopolies, and 2 for full competition, and regress the landline teledensity, mobile teledensity, and Internet usage on these competition indicators, controlling additionally for differences in per capita income. The regression results presented in the table below reveal a significant positive relationship between competition and access to communications services.

Box Table 1. The Relationship between Competition and Access to Communication Services

	(1) Mainline teledensity (Fixed Phones/ 100 people)	(2) Mobile teledensity (Cell Phones/ 100 people)	(3) Internet Usage (per 100 people)
Log GDP per capita	8.887***	12.059***	6.031***
	(0.480)	(0.803)	(0.440)
Fixed-Line competition	3.533***		
	(1.049)		
Mobile competition		5.674***	
		(2.350)	
Overall index telecommunications			1.523***
			(0.342)
Observations	152	148	141
Adjusted R-squared	0.75	0.62	0.67

Standard errors in parentheses. * indicates statistical significance at the 10% level, ** at the 5% level, and *** at the 1% level.

(Box continues on the following page.)

Box 3.3 (continued)

Using the relationships identified in this analysis and following Kenny (2006), we can make a projection of how teledensity would respond to further progress with regard to competition in the Zambian telecommunications sector. The ITU currently classifies Zambia as a de facto monopoly in fixed lines, whereas in mobile services, the market structure is considered as partial competition in ITU terms, because of regulatory imperfections and impediments to competition stemming from other segments of the telecommunications market.

Box Table 2. Projected Access Figures under Full Competition

	Fixed	Mobile	Internet
Percentage increase in density moving to full competition	33 %	21 %	24 %
Number of lines added	29,181	28,584	12,336

Our projections indicate that moving from monopoly to full competition will increase Zambian teledensity in landlines by 33 percent of its current value, which corresponds to an additional 29,181 lines in service. In mobile services, a removal of all remaining impediments to a fully competitive market would increase mobile phone penetration by 21 percent, equivalent to 28,584 additional mobile lines. Finally, a fully competitive telecommunications sector would increase the number of Internet subscribers in Zambia by roughly a quarter, which is equivalent to more than 12 thousand additional users.

Source: ITU 2005; ITU World Telecommunication Indicators Database 2006.

Addressing Zamtel's Concerns: The Future Role of the Incumbent

In many countries, concerns over the financial viability of the incumbent have proven the main reason for resisting a full liberalization agenda. The concern is that liberalization could result in a drastic reduction of revenues and profits to the incumbent, threatening its financial sustainability and leading to employment losses. However, Zamtel's financial viability will not be at risk if appropriate action is taken. In many countries, the incumbent provider has continued to play an essential role in the sector (India and Uganda provide two examples of this). Conversely, if no action is taken, the company's sustainability is at risk regardless of whether or not competition is allowed. Addressing Zamtel's concerns needs to be placed in the context of a fast-changing market and technological developments that gradually move away from traditional circuit-switched telephony toward an environment that embraces IP-enabled (or packet-switched) technologies for the communications sector.

A joint delegation from the Ministry of Communications and Transport and the Ministry of Commerce, Trade, and Industry, which visited countries that have successfully introduced competition in the sector, recommended that "Zamtel should urgently rebalance its tariffs and commercialise immediately."[2] These recommendations are fleshed out below.

Tariff rebalancing

Balancing international and local tariffs is necessary to ensure that Zamtel is equipped to face competition. Under the current situation, the pricing structure does not reflect the true costs of individual services. As noted above, the cost of a residential connection and monthly residential tariff for a fixed-line telephone is among the lowest in SADC countries. If Zamtel is to be confronted with competition in the international segment, then local and rental charges will need to be revised to reflect costs, so that these services can be provided through profitable operations without the need for cross-subsidies.

A comparison among the prices charged for local, national, and international communications is revealing. Zamtel's ratio of international call tariffs to local call tariffs is approximately 50:1 for a call to the United States. For major European operators, this ratio tends to be in the range of 4 to 10. As an example from a prior successful rebalancing of tariffs, table 3.2 illustrates the level of this ratio for the Mauritanian incumbent Mauritel at different points in time (see box 3.2 for a description of the Mauritanian case).

Tariff rebalancing is likely to face some political opposition from its present beneficiaries, who enjoy the current rates for monthly subscription and local costs below cost-recovery levels. Unlike in other countries, however, a rise in local call rates originating from a landline is not going to hurt the poor in particular, because most of the low-income population has no access to a landline under present conditions. Local calls originating from a cellular phone are already quite high in Zambia, and they are more likely to be reduced by competition than to be increased. In the current situation, the only group that may face short-term price increases of subscription charges and local tariffs are urban households in possession of a fixed telephone line.

Two other arguments should help strengthen the case for tariff rebalancing: that the status quo is not sustainable, and that the change may actually be profitable.

Table 3.2. Ratio of International to Local Tariffs

British Telecom	4.20
Deutsche Telecom	4.20
France Télécom	4.20
Telecom Denmark	4.60
Telefónica de España	8.25
Telecom Italia	5.00
Koninklijke PTT Nederland (KPN)	4.50
Portugal Telecom	11.30
Mauritania: Mauritel	
1999	60.00
2004	6.24
Target for 2010	4.26

Source: World Bank interviews with operators (2004).

The long-term implications of a loss of the international gateway monopoly for Zamtel must be seen in the context of global trends in international service delivery and the global pressure to reduce international prices closer to cost. An increasing amount of (particularly international) traffic is diverting away from public switched telephone networks (PSTNs) to other competing networks, including IP-based networks. Globally, in 2003, there were slightly fewer than 170 billion minutes of international voice traffic, of which 85 percent traveled over traditional switched networks and about 15 percent was routed using VoIP (voice over Internet protocol; see figure 3.9). In 2004/05, estimated VoIP use reached 35 percent. In other words, even without reform, the current reliance on monopoly rents in the international segment is likely to become unsustainable. It is better for Zamtel to react early than to react too late.

A move to a fully competitive telecommunications sector would certainly change the revenue structure of the industry, but it need not threaten the sustainability of the incumbent. All segments of the sector are likely to experience significant growth and operate with higher efficiency, with beneficial effects for all players in the sector. For example, the number of outgoing international call minutes from Zambia could easily double. In the current situation, Zambia has eight minutes of incoming international calls for each minute of outgoing calls, a ratio that could easily be reduced with more competitive prices. In addition, demand will increase as prices diminish. The key lesson learned from other countries in this regard is that the fear of financial "discomfort" of the incumbent is unjustified, and this should not be a reason for continuing to rely on outdated models and non-cost-based pricing structures.

Figure 3.9. Percentage of International Traffic Traveling over IP

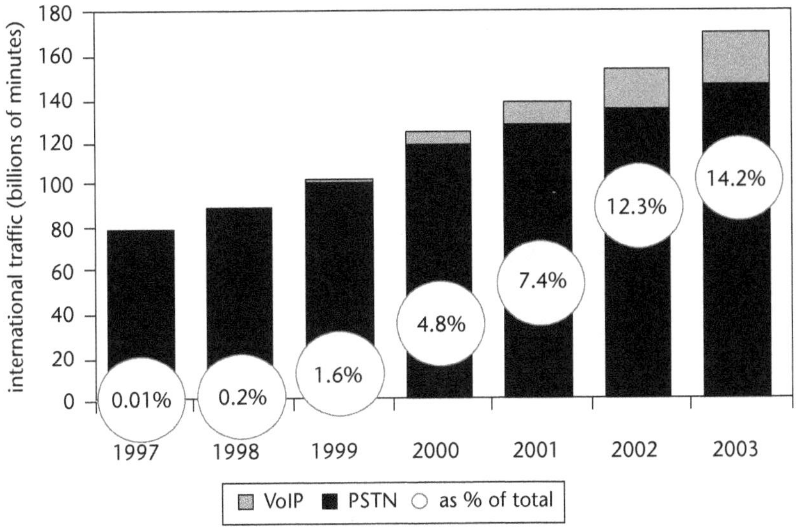

Source: ITU 2005.

Restructuring Zamtel

The restructuring of Zamtel is necessary not only to enable it to compete on the international market, but also to face challenges posed by a convergence of networks and services. In addition, because of its current financial situation, Zamtel is facing serious liquidity problems caused by a low bill recovery ratio, high payroll expenses, deferred maintenance expenses, and past underinvestment. All of these factors can jeopardize the company's long-term viability, even without competition, unless the company is restructured. Zamtel's situation is similar to that of other incumbents that failed to improve their performance and embrace a new business model to meet increasing competition.

Although reform is generally seen as a necessity to improve the viability of the public incumbent, countries have adopted different approaches with respect to the question of private participation in the incumbent operator. Many governments have come to acknowledge the benefits of private sector participation in the incumbent, because this can have a strong impact on network growth. Depending on whether there is enough interest from the private sector and sufficient political will to undertake radical reform, however, privatization may or may not be an option in the short term for many countries. In either event, the benefits of privatization hinge crucially on the introduction of competition in the sector.

Figure 3.10. Percentage of Countries with Fully or Partially Privatized Incumbents

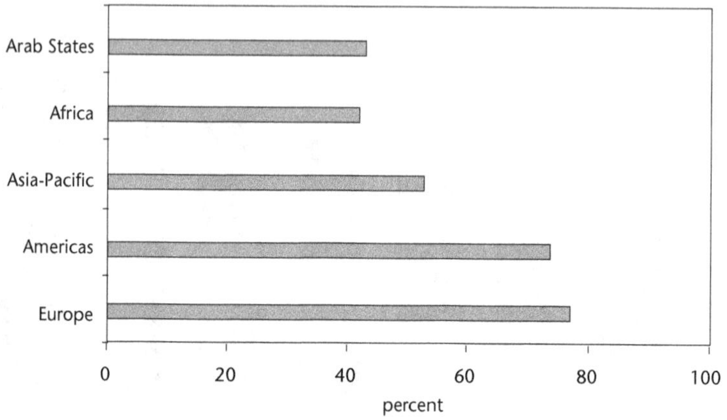

Source: ITU World Telecommunication Indicators Database 2006.

The alternative governance models are outlined in table 3.3. Under private law, the immediate benefits include ensuring commercial freedom of Zamtel to obtain additional funding for investment outside of government sources and to enhance the commercial incentives to supply services to meet demand. This is key to reducing political influence on Zamtel and to enhancing the company's financial performance by recovering outstanding government debts and adopting prepaid services. The staff need to be trained in new technical and commercial skills. The corporatization stage may involve the introduction of a contractor to manage the business through performance contracts. Other possibilities include entering into a joint venture or build-operate-transfer schemes geared toward specific upgrades, replacements, or rollout objectives.

Improving the performance of Zamtel may have some social costs in terms of employment within the company. The overall employment impact of reform is likely to be positive, because competing providers will increase their workforce and other businesses are able to benefit from more competitive telecommunications services. It is, however, possible that the new employment opportunities arising in the sector may be less attractive to current Zamtel staff than the protected status of a public sector employee. This concern is even more relevant if labor market rigidities imply that many new jobs will take the form of contractual, temporary employment. Unless the labor market is sufficiently flexible, firms may avoid formal employment to retain sufficient flexibility to adjust to market conditions. The best way to address this issue is to ensure sufficient flexibility of the labor market, which would prevent a diversion into informal employment.

Table 3.3. Alternative Governance Models

Administration	Commercialization	Corporatization	Privatization
Telecom operator owned by the government as a department, entity, or public agency	Introduction of commercial objectives and practices into the management and operations of a state-owned enterprise	The transformation of a state-owned enterprise into a public corporation governed under company law	The transfer of ownership and or assets or activities from the public to the private sector
PUBLIC LAW		**PRIVATE LAW**	
PUBLIC OWNERSHIP			**PRIVATE OWNERSHIP**

Source: Authors.

Nonetheless, reform of the incumbent can involve a carefully designed package of support to ease the social costs of transition.

Addressing Potential Concerns of the Government

Three types of concerns may need to be addressed: fiscal revenues, empowerment, and national security.

Fiscal revenues

Concerns have been expressed about the fiscal impact of abolishing Zamtel's monopoly over the international gateway. To evaluate these concerns, one must take a closer look at the tax structure in the telecommunications sector. Profits made in the telecommunications sector are subject to a 35 percent corporate tax, except for those operators that are currently benefiting from tax breaks because of their investment in infrastructure. Additionally, excise tax is levied on all revenues of the sector. From a fiscal point of view, the best scenario is one that maximizes the overall profits and revenues of the telecommunications industry.

Currently, Zamtel is making monopoly profits in the international segment. Because these profits are likely to decrease under competition, the tax basis could be negatively affected. At the same time, however, competition would improve the overall financial health of Zamtel and increase its profitability in other segments, with a positive impact on the tax basis, provided that the restructuring of the company and the rebalancing of the tariff structure are successfully implemented. Furthermore, the overall volume of the sector is likely to grow in a competitive setting, and this growth could generate additional revenues from Zamtel and from other providers.

Taxable telecommunications revenues will increase if the sector starts to grow, and there is clearly scope for growth in the current situation. The current ratio of inbound to outbound international minutes is extremely high for Zambia (around 8:1), which is a sign of evasion of the high current charges. If this ratio were reduced, more minutes of international traffic would be subject to taxation in Zambia.

The calculations presented in box 3.3 predict sectoral growth in terms of phone lines and Internet users in the transition to full competition. According to these calculations, Zambia is expected to gain almost 30,000 new fixed lines and a similar number of mobile lines, in addition to 12,000 new Internet users. This will have a significant positive impact on tax revenues.

According to projections by the mobile operators, who are currently taking a loss on the provision of international calls because of the high interconnection charges, there would be a significant increase in the international call volume if these operators had their own international gateways. Both of the current mobile operators expect market prices to fall by around 40 percent to 50 percent, and thus they will trigger a rapid expansion of outgoing call minutes. Under this scenario, and despite lower prices, Celtel could easily have a revenue increase of about $500,000 on international calls originating from Celtel lines, while MTN could have more than $100,000 of additional revenue. This revenue is over and above the currently generated revenue, 80 percent of which the mobile providers must pass on to Zamtel under the current monopoly situation.

Empowerment

Perhaps one of the most empowering attributes of a competitive international communications market is its potential to bring affordable communications to a large number of Zambians. To maximize the benefit to the people, an appropriate policy and regulatory framework must be established to ensure that the benefits of a liberalized international market are passed on to the end user.

It is also questionable whether empowerment goals would be served by ensuring at least partial Zambian ownership of telecommunications firms. A number of other countries have implemented targeted interventions to ensure national ownership of telecommunications and ICT investments. The government will need to proceed cautiously to balance ownership restrictions with the need for creating a favorable environment for competition and growth.

Many countries have eased foreign ownership restrictions to attract foreign investment, particularly because public sector financing has shrunk since the 1980s, and the private sector, both domestic and foreign, has had to assume responsibility for financing development in the ICT sector. FDI has facilitated the growth and development of the telecommunications sector in many countries. Particularly for developing countries, FDI has improved the access to capital needed for network build-out and updating, and facilitated the transfer of technology and know-how. These two combined can have a large positive impact on productivity, coverage, and quality of telecommunications services. Governments have realized that any restriction they place on investment (be it foreign or domestic) raises the cost of financing and hampers continued investment inflows.[3] In the light of urgently needed capital in the Zambian telecommunications sector, the GoZ will need to assess carefully the merits of any foreign ownership restrictions in the sector.

National security

If the public sector relinquishes control of the international gateway, it may raise security concerns. But these concerns are best dealt with by using the latest technological developments in security devices and imposing proper license obligations and conditions on the incumbent and new entrants. In particular, with the convergence of networks and services, the government needs to devise appropriate cyber-security programs to deal with the challenges posed by the information society without compromising consumer privacy. Addressing these challenges does not, however, create a need to delay liberalization of the sector.

Addressing Regulatory Inadequacies

In telecommunications, the benefits of competition are not realized by a mechanical opening up of market segments, and the gains from liberalization can be undermined by a flawed reform program. Telecommunications is a sector in which competition can work well and bring tremendous benefits, but it is not one in which competition will emerge naturally. The functioning of competition in interconnected networks hinges crucially on the regulator's ability to enforce interconnection between networks at cost-based fees, to facilitate new entry, and to ensure a level playing field among large and small operators, incumbent and entrepreneurs alike. Thus, it is essential for Zambia to address current regulatory inadequacies to benefit from the full potential of competition.

Implementing a cost-based interconnection regime

The main problem with the current interconnection regime in Zambia is that interconnection charges bear little relation to costs. Interconnection charges that are well above costs hurt the development of the sector and prevent mobile operators from offering lower rates to the consumer. This explains, to a large extent, why the prices of cellular service in Zambia remain among the highest in the subregion, despite competition and growth of the subscriber base. An overview of telecommunications service prices is given in table 3.4.

Interconnection charges reflect the distortions created by Zamtel's monopoly rather than true costs. For example, Zamtel protects its mobile subsidiary Cell-Z by setting the interconnection charges. Calls from Cell-Z to Zamtel are cheaper than from the independent mobile operator, reflecting the preferential interconnection charge for Cell-Z calls to the Zamtel network. A statutory instrument (SI) has been issued under the current legal framework to address the failure of operators to enter into interconnection agreements.[4] Despite this SI, an interconnection agreement has not been reached between Zamtel and Celtel, and a dispute may well arise between Celtel and MTN after the expiration of their current agreement.

In principle, major operators should be required to interconnect with each other, and with new entrants, on equitable and transparent terms, and at interconnection prices that closely reflect the true underlying costs of such interconnection. Procedures for negotiation and dispute resolution should be transparent and expedited. When appropriate, interconnection arrangements should favor the rapid introduction of new networks and operators, and should provide incentives for faster rollout of new services.

In practice, however, calculating cost-based interconnection is not always straightforward and is already a source of tension between Zamtel and the mobile operators. The tension seems to be centered around what types of costs should be recovered in interconnection. Both Zamtel and CAZ seem to favor a fully allocated cost approach. Under this approach, the total costs for providing service, including historical and depreciated investment costs, is divided by the volume of service provided. This method has been criticized on the grounds that it does not provide a reliable method to measure cost because it is based on historical accounting of costs and thus might reflect operational or technological inefficiencies of the incumbent. Mobile operators favor a different costing method that focuses on forward-looking approaches rather than on historic approaches. In other words, interconnection costs should anticipate actual and future costs using current technology and best performance standards rather than rely on costs incurred in the past. The forward-looking approaches better reflect the working of competitive markets.

The failure of CAZ to resolve the controversy has resulted in interconnection payments being suspended between operators. Mobile operators have decided not to pay Zamtel any interconnection charges. This is putting further strain on Zamtel's financial situation. In a market in which mobile operators are becoming the dominant players—with a high mobile to fixed-line ratio—fixed-line operators are losing their bargaining powers to enforce the payment of interconnection charges. The capacity of CAZ to devise and enforce a cost-based interconnection that reflects new market conditions needs to be significantly strengthened.

**Table 3.4. Phone Charges in Zambia (as of February 2005,
in US$)**

	Peak	Off-peak
PSTN to Cell-Z	0.26	
Cell Z to PSTN	0.38	0.19
MTN to other mobile	0.44	0.33
MTN to MTN	0.28	0.15
Celtel to other mobile	0.44	0.33
Celtel to Celtel	0.28	0.17
Celtel to PSTN	0.50	0.50

Source: Interviews with operators in Zambia (2006).

Improving capacity at policy and regulatory institutions

The Ministry of Communications and Transport plays a critical role in driving the reform agenda. Unfortunately, the capacity to play a proactive role in driving sector development is constrained. The Ministry needs to have the technical capacity to develop implementation strategies as well as monitoring and evaluation instruments to ensure the development of the sector.

The enforcement capacity and regulatory independence of CAZ needs to be improved. CAZ was created by the Telecommunications Act of 1994. The Act mandated the regulator to promote competition among providers of telecommunications services and infrastructure to ensure that the benefits of this sector accrue to the citizens of Zambia and its economy and to take reasonable steps to extend the provision of services in rural and urban areas (Republic of Zambia 1994). These objectives will not be achieved, however, unless the regulator is fully independent. CAZ should have the power to issue and enforce regulations without requiring the approval of the Ministry of Communications and Transport and without the intervention of any of the operators. In addition, the skill base in the Communications Authority needs to be strengthened to allow adequate monitoring and enforcement of the sector regulations.

Adopting a procompetitive licensing regime

Opportunities to obtain licenses or other authorization to construct and operate telecommunications networks should be as open, technology neutral, and streamlined as possible. In particular, smaller operators that are prepared to construct systems to serve villages or regions that have not been adequately covered by existing networks should be able to introduce their services with a minimum of restrictions and delays.

Zamtel must be issued a proper license to bring it under the ambit of the regulatory regime to ensure a level playing field with all players in the market. In addition, a new license should be drafted for the international gateway. The international license should clearly stipulate the license fee and conditions (for example, the carrying of the licensee's end-user traffic only, the possibility of direct negotiations of commercial arrangements with foreign operators, and the possibility to carry transit traffic over licensee's network). Because of the change in the licensing regime under the draft Electronic Communications Act (2006), it is important that the law is passed as soon as possible to ensure regulatory certainty. Adequate support is needed to ensure that relicensing of the mobile operators under the new act strikes the right balance between the need to preserve investor confidence and the need to preserve the flexibility of the regulatory process to accommodate market and policy developments (Guermazi and Neto 2005).

Strengthening competition policy

Accelerating market opening requires improving Zambia's arrangement to monitor and enforce fair competition. This becomes especially important to deal with the vertical integration of Zamtel. As outlined above, mobile competitors claim that Cell-Z services offerings are below cost and they are only sustainable through cross-subsidies from monopoly markets. Similarly, independent ISPs complain about favorable pricing for the incumbent's Internet subsidiary through the creation of virtual exchange points for its own traffic, while other ISPs need to pay long-distance charges. In fact, currently, all Internet access calls to Zamtel Online are metered as local calls regardless of their origin, while independent ISPs cannot offer this convenience.

Measures such as mandatory structural separation of the vertically integrated incumbent may be needed. In fact, Zambia's Competition Commission (ZCC) called for the legal separation of Cell-Z from Zamtel in March 2004. According to the ZCC, "the players in the sector must have the same terms and conditions with Government, CAZ and Zamtel, in order for each market participant to have a fair chance to exploit their distinctive competencies on a level playing field." Moreover, a clear definition of significant market power along with a clear regime for regulating operators with such power needs to be established.

The division of power between the regulator and the competition authority needs to be clarified. The general trend in other countries has been for the sector regulator to take the lead in enforcing economic regulation if the sector is at an early stage of development. Implementing the basic elements necessary to ensure a competitive environment, such as drafting interconnection rules and creating a licensing framework, requires a high degree of sectoral expertise. Once there is full competition and the market has developed, the competition commission would tend to play a more significant role in enforcing competition law, working in tandem with the sector regulator.

Addressing distributional concerns and meeting universal service objectives
A key argument presented by opponents of full competition is that the surplus revenues from the operation of the IGW are important for network rollout and expansion. However, a review of Zamtel's performance over the last few years clearly demonstrates that these monopoly rents have hardly contributed to network expansion. Telephone ownership is still restricted to 0.3 percent of rural households. Furthermore, in a converged environment in which access needs to be measured not only in terms of the ability to make a phone call but also in terms of the possibility to run applications that require adequate bandwidth, the issue of universal access is necessarily linked to having an adequate backbone infrastructure. Here, again, the current infrastructure in Zambia is woefully inadequate.

Whether the challenge in bridging the access gap is connectivity to rural areas or building up the backbone, evidence from around the world demonstrates that the up-front investment needed may be too high to be justified on purely commercial grounds. The role for complementary government initiatives that fill the access gap is especially evident in areas that require significant investment, involve high operating costs, and feature limited or uncertain demand (Navas-Sabater, Dymond, and Juntunen 2002). Following are a variety of solutions being explored by CAZ for universal access. These solutions are based on successful experiments in other countries and may also be relevant for Zambia's backbone needs.

Bringing connectivity "beyond the market"
In Zambia, the fixed-line network has grown by only 18 percent during the last 10 years—from about 76,000 in 1995 to 90,000 in 2005 for a population of 11 million people. This is far below the network expansion achieved in other countries in that same time frame. Moreover, the gap in access to telecommunications between rural and urban areas remains large, with 78 percent of fixed lines located in Lusaka and Copperbelt where 30 percent of the population lives. Telephone ownership is still restricted to 0.3 percent of rural households.

In other countries with competitive markets, policies aimed at improving access beyond the level that the market alone would deliver have led to substantial network growth, without hampering competition and without distorting the incentives for investment. In principle, the reform program can accommodate universal service objectives in competitive markets by imposing this requirement on new entrants in a nondiscriminatory way or subsidizing network expansion on a competitive basis. In several countries, rollout obligations were part of the license conditions for new entrants into fixed network telephony and transport.

The purpose of a universal access fund is to collect resources for potential subsidies into a central, independent account that is managed on a nondiscriminatory, transparent basis and that is distributed according to clear criteria and procedures. Allocation of the funds is best achieved through minimum-subsidy auctions, in which all potential providers are invited to submit a closed-envelope bid for the minimum amount necessary to connect a locality. The bidder with the least amount of subsidy required will then get the business. This approach has many advantages in terms of flexibility and avoids unwarranted favoritism toward incumbent players. Table 3.5 shows the experiences of several countries with this strategy.

In Peru, the universal access fund was financed by a universal service levy of 1 percent (in Zambia, the CAZ currently levies 5 percent of revenues as license fees from operators). Funds were allocated through a competitive bidding process that encouraged operators to adopt the best technology and other cost-savings practices. The Chilean government followed a similar scheme that allowed it to leverage $2 million of public funds into $40 million in private investment. This resulted in the installation of telephones in 1,000 localities at about 10 percent of the costs of direct public provision. Household ownership of a telephone line increased from 16 percent to 74 percent from 1988 to 2000 and all but 1 percent of the remaining households were provided with public access to telephone.

In Uganda, output-based assistance (OBA) tendering was managed by The Rural Communications Development Fund (RCDF). The fund is financed by a universal service levy of 1 percent of gross operator revenues as well as donor funding (for example, the World Bank contributed $5 million to RCDF). Early applications of OBA focused on improving access to public telephony as well as implementing Internet POP and telecenters. The average subsidy for the public access phones was between $3,300 and $7,500 (about $3.40 per person). Average subsidy per POP has been around $30,000 serving a typical district center population of 25,000. The average cost of the combined Internet POP and telecenter subsidy was about $2.00 per inhabitant.

Table 3.5. Minimum-Subsidy Auctions for Public Rural Telephones, Selected Countries, 2004

	Chile	Uganda	Dominican Republic	Peru	Nepal
Average subsidy per locality	$3,600	$4,342	$6,800	$9,500	$11,200
Localities served	6,059	1,552	500	4,420	1,064
Population served (millions)	2.2	1.9	1.0	1.6	4.0

Source: Based on Navas-Sabater 2005.

The GoZ is already exploring options to expand access to rural communities through private-public partnerships and is currently finalizing a universal access policy and strategy. The key priorities of the proposed universal access strategy include the expansion of the geographic limits of the existing network to all areas with a reasonable demand for services, expansion of the network to remote or high-cost areas, and the provision of access for low-income groups. The primary sources of funds for the rural fund are likely to include a combination of donor funds, the GoZ budget, and contributions from ICT service providers. The CAZ is planning to transfer seed funding of approximately $1 million, which had been set aside for the new agency to cover rural telephony. In addition, the CAZ has committed itself to providing an annual contribution of 5 percent of the current license revenues to the fund. The universal access policy goals defined by CAZ are depicted in table 3.6, and this policy follows practices that have worked well in other countries. As experience elsewhere reveals, however, universal access policies are most successful when implemented in competitive markets that have effective policy and regulatory environments that ensure proper competition, reduce the risk to investment, guard against market abuse by dominant market players, and balance the goals of market efficiency, flexibility, and innovation.

Creating conditions for the deployment of national backbone infrastructure

One of the major causes of the poor quality and high cost of service in Zambia is the lack of a reliable and affordable backbone infrastructure. Currently, all of the existing operators have deployed their own backbone, resulting in duplication of infrastructure and inefficient investment. Although the mobile explosion has had a positive impact on infrastructure, most of the cell sites and switches are interconnected via a wireless-based infrastructure, which is costly, has limited capacity, and is affected by weather conditions (fading and dropped calls).

Backbones facilitate cost-effective interconnections nationally, regionally, and internationally. They allow not only the provision of basic telecommunications services but also for the delivery of advanced value added services such as e-government, e-commerce, and high-speed Internet access. In the case of Zambia, the establishment of a high-capacity infrastructure backbone linked to neighboring countries will create multiple interconnection points to several international and regional backbones and increase the potential for Zambia to be a regional hub for exchanging and transiting regional traffic in Africa.

It is unclear whether Zamtel is in a position to raise the investment cost of the backbone. It has recently commissioned a feasibility study for the backbone infrastructure and invited all operators to pool resources and jointly invest in the backbone infrastructure. The initial reaction of the private operators has not been positive. Typically, backbone networks entail long-term investments with significant

Table 3.6. Summary of Universal Access Targets: Draft Universal Access Policy

Activity/ deliverable	Short-term goals: 18 months (2005–06)	Medium-term goals: (2007–10)	Long-term goals: (2010–12)
Community-based public payphone (voice telephony)	Provide a community payphone in every village or location with 5,000 people at an affordable cost	50 percent of Zambians have access to basic telephone service within 10 km	80 percent of Zambians have access to basic phone service within 10 km
Telecenters offering advanced facilities	Establish six tele-centers as pilot projects in selected districts throughout Zambia	50 percent of districts have minimum of four telecenters	100 percent of districts have a minimum of four telecenters
Online local content	Local content to be locally hosted for above services	50 percent of local content available and hosted in Zambia	80 percent of Zambians have access to online local content
ICT training	An ICT Training Center of Excellence in selected districts as pilot projects	One ICT pioneer institution or ICT training center in 50 percent of districts in Zambia	One ICT Center of Excellence per district
Education and training by mass broadcasting		50 percent of all households are within the range of digital radio and television broadcasting signals	100 percent of households are within the range of digital radio and television broadcasting signals

Source: Authors.

sunk costs and high externalities because they benefit all operators, making them less attractive to private operators. There may also be fears of anticompetitive behavior by Zamtel if it were to operate the backbone and act as a wholesale provider of capacity and a retail provider of services. The fact that Zamtel is still outside the regulatory ambit of CAZ strengthens these fears.

For all these reasons, there could be a good reason for public intervention in mobilizing the necessary financing, ensuring its efficient allocation, and creating a regulatory environment that ensures access to the facilities at appropriate terms. Variants of the mechanisms being considered to further rural connectivity can also promote the development of the backbone infrastructure. The basic approach would fill financing gaps by paying subsidies to the successful bidder. In this case, the output will need to be measured against infrastructure built and the requirement to manage capacity on an open and nondiscriminatory basis. The infrastructure could remain owned by a public entity, a private entity, or a public-private entity. Some countries have entrusted management of the backbone to a third company that provides wholesale services but is, in most cases, not allowed to offer retail services to end users. The main challenge for the regulator is to prevent monopoly control over the backbone infrastructure and to prevent operators with a dominant position from engaging in anticompetitive behavior. Whatever the funding approach or ownership structure, it is important to agree on a management structure for the proposed infrastructure that ensures fair and cost-based access to the backbone infrastructure. The regulation will need to cover access to essential facilities (including colocation and facility sharing), price regulation, and a dispute settlement mechanism. Only then can the backbone deliver its development promise for Zambia and empower Zambians to communicate better with each other, their neighbors, and the rest of the world.

Combining and Sequencing Policies

Policy decisions in sector reform cover not only the range of policy choices to improve sector performance but also combine and sequence different choices. As outlined above, to better leverage the potential of its telecommunications sector, Zambia needs to make at least four broad policy choices, including the following:

- Furthering competition
- Restructuring Zamtel and rebalancing the tariff structure
- Improving the regulatory environment
- Creating policies to ensure universal access

Some elements of the reform agenda could occur almost instantaneously (for example, dismantling Zamtel's de facto monopoly on the international gateway) while other elements may take some time to implement. Improving regulatory capacity and preparing Zamtel for competition, for example, cannot be achieved overnight. The question arises whether the elements that could be implemented rapidly must wait for improvements in other dimensions.

Clearly, no single blueprint exists for the optimal sequencing of reform, but some broad lessons can be learned from the experiences of other countries and from Zambia's own experience thus far.

Cross-country evidence

A salient feature of the international experience is the evidence in favor of introducing competition and regulatory reform before privatization. Fink, Mattoo, and

Figure 3.11. Effects of Sequencing on Mainlines

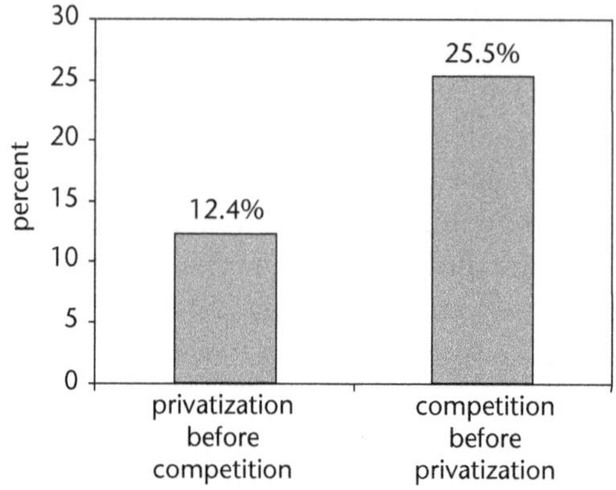

Source: Fink, Mattoo, and Rathindran 2003.

Rathindran (2003) looked at panel evidence from 86 developing countries across Africa, Asia, the Middle East, Latin America, and the Caribbean in the period from 1985 to 1999 to analyze the impact of policy reform in basic telecommunications on sectoral performance. They found that the sequence of reform matters: the generally positive impact of both competition and privatization on mainline penetration is relatively lower if competition is introduced after privatization, rather than at the same time. This result suggests that delays in the introduction of competition—for example, because of market exclusivity guarantees granted to newly privatized entities—may adversely affect performance even after competition is eventually introduced.

This could happen for three reasons. First, because sunk costs have commitment value and can be used strategically, the importance of location-specific sunk costs in basic telecommunications suggests that allowing one provider privileged access may have durable consequences (Bos and Nett 1990). Second, allowing privileged access creates vested interests that may resist further reform or seek to dilute its impact. For example, in South Africa, private shareholders (national and foreign) in the incumbent successfully lobbied to reduce the number of entrants that the government was planning to allow from two to one (Lamont 2001). Third, sequences matter because of the implied changes in the regulatory environment: in one case, the incumbent is a relatively inefficient public operator and the regulator is well informed about the cost structure; in the other case, the incumbent is a relatively efficient private operator and the regulator is less well informed. It could be argued that new entry is easier to accomplish in the former situation.

Wallsten (2002) considers the impact of sequencing privatization and regulation. He finds that countries that established an independent regulator before privatization saw more telecommunications investment, as well as fixed-line and mobile penetration compared with countries that did not. Moreover, investors were willing to pay more for telecommunications operators in countries that established independent regulators before privatization. The increased willingness to pay is consistent with the hypothesis that investors require a risk premium to invest in countries where regulatory rules are unclear.

Sequencing in Zambia: Learning from the past

Zambia followed a two-pronged approach to sector reform, focusing on introducing competition and regulatory reform and delaying decisions to change the ownership structure of the incumbent. The 1994 Telecommunications Act created the CAZ and led to increased private participation and significant liberalization in all segments of the sector with the exception of the fixed line. To a large extent, the introduction of competition resulted in significant benefits and a significant increase in the subscriber base primarily thanks to a boom in the mobile sector.

The following lessons can be learned from Zambia's experience:

- Zambia has introduced competition and, in parallel, undertaken some degree of regulatory strengthening. But both actions have been half-hearted. The incumbent retains monopoly control of the international gateway and the regulator has limited control over the actions of the incumbent. Competition has improved the situation, but the extent of competition, and its benefits, would have been greater if the regulator had been more effective. And the regulator's task would have been easier if it were not confronted with an incumbent that it cannot properly regulate.
- Access to services has increased because of competition, but the institution of an effective universal access policy would have accelerated the growth of the network. And a universal access policy itself would be much more effective in a competitive environment.
- Little progress has been made in aligning Zamtel's operations in each segment with commercial objectives and making the company economically sustainable, despite considerable discussion on the removal of the IGW monopoly.

... to design a proposed course of action for 2006

Given that telecommunications reform has been most successful where competition and regulation were the first building blocks, and given that Zambia has already made some progress on both counts, Zambian telecommunications policy should focus on completing this process by making the regulator independent and extending competition to all segments without exception. Because of the simultaneous presence of operators in several segments, the full benefits of competition will not be seen unless each segment is contestable.

We suggest the following steps:

- Immediately secure the passage of the 2006 Electronic Communications Act (ECA). The ECA draft draws on international best practice, recognizing the realities and opportunities of convergence in the communications, broadcasting, and IT sectors. The draft ECA is a key enabler for the policy and regulatory actions outlined below.
- Immediately ensure the *independence of the regulator* and initiate a *technical support program*, to be implemented over one year. This is key for the success of all other elements of the reform agenda.
- Immediately begin mobilizing resources for a *universal access fund* and identify underserved and inherently unprofitable regions. Tenders should be invited from existing and potential providers, both domestic and foreign. These steps could be implemented over one year.
- Immediately begin the process of *rebalancing of tariffs* and *restructuring Zamtel*, to be implemented over one year. This will help Zamtel to cope with a more competitive market environment. The fact that privatization has been delayed is probably not a serious problem from the sequencing perspective because it gives the government an opportunity to make regulatory improvements and introduce meaningful competition. Change of ownership is an issue that can be addressed in the future, as long as Zamtel begins following commercial objectives immediately.

Given that it will take time to strengthen the regulator and prepare Zamtel for competition, the key sequencing issue is whether there is reason to delay liberalization. Although strengthening the regulator would enhance competition and its benefits, the current weakness of the regulator would not, by itself, be a reason to delay allowing new entry into the market. The real problem is the weakness of Zamtel and the fact that its tariff structure bears little relation to the true costs of specific services. The introduction of full competition without restructuring Zamtel and allowing it to rebalance tariffs would probably spell doom for the incumbent and be politically and socially costly. Without the credible threat of competition, however, such restructuring and rebalancing will have little sense of urgency, as past experience demonstrates. Arguments to indefinitely preserve the IGW monopoly to give the incumbent more time to prepare for competition will only perpetuate the status quo and continue to deprive many Zambians from access to telecommunications.

How can Zambia avert any adverse consequences of immediately unleashing full competition upon the incumbent without being held hostage indefinitely to the weakness of the incumbent or the strength of vested interests? We advocate a *phased approach to liberalization of the international gateway*. Unless some degree of competition is introduced immediately, and there is a credible commitment to introduce full competition at a precise point, the incumbent will not have the incentive to embark on serious reform of its operations and tariff structure. The two phases of transition toward competition should therefore be structured as follows:

- Phase 1, to be implemented immediately, would allow each of the presently licensed operators to operate their own IGW for calls originating or terminating in their network. Because most of the relevant investment for alternative IGW is already made, this would quickly introduce a limited measure of competition in the international segment and alleviate distortions in other segments. Partial liberalization will be on a transition basis for a one-year period to give Zamtel incentives and time to prepare for full competition. It is difficult to say whether the proposed extent and duration of competition is optimal and to predict its precise impact on Zamtel, but it has the virtue of being a well-defined intermediate solution between two extremes, neither of which is presently acceptable. In any case, the more Zamtel benefits from external assistance and effective management during the transition, the less it will suffer during the transition process. Phase 1 would also present an opportunity for the regulator to prepare for unrestricted competition.
- Phase 2, to be implemented after a transition period of one year, would include opening the market to full competition with no restrictions on entry. The total number of players will then be defined by the market. This implies that each customer will be free to choose the provider of international calls, which requires the establishment of cost-based interconnection fees under the supervision of an independent and strengthened CAZ.

The basic trade-off being proposed here is between bringing the benefits of open telecommunications markets to the Zambian people as quickly as possible and avoiding a breakdown of the incumbent. For this proposal to work, two conditions must be met. First, both Zamtel and the regulator will need assistance to develop the capacity to deal with fully competitive markets. Second, both parties need to be confronted with a credible deadline to instill a sense of urgency into their efforts. As with any transitional arrangement, there is a danger that transition could last forever, possibly using the argument that Zamtel's restructuring process is not yet complete. If such renegotiation is anticipated, the whole reform may lose effectiveness. It is therefore essential to use a commitment mechanism to lock in the timing of the two reform phases. The next section will illustrate how Zambia can use international engagement to generate assistance and credibility.

International engagement, external assistance, and WTO commitments

Although telecommunications reform is principally the domain of domestic policy and much could be achieved unilaterally, Zambia may benefit from international engagement. On the one hand, Zambia needs external assistance, both financial and technical, to strengthen its regulatory institutions and to institute effective universal access policies. On the other hand, Zambia could benefit from locking in current and planned reform by making international commitments in regional or multilateral forums. The desirability of such commitments should be assessed and depends on whether the loss in flexibility is outweighed by the gain in credibility.

There is reason to treat assistance and reform as interdependent. The absence of assistance may stymie reform, and the persistence of poor policy may weaken the case for assistance. Zambia needs to assess whether a link could lend credibility to both liberalization and assistance programs. If so, then Zambia could commit internationally to a program of reform over a certain time frame. Liberalization would be one element of this reform, and donors could commit to provide the requisite technical assistance. And this assistance should consist of additional assistance rather than a diversion of existing aid commitments.

Whether or not such a link is made, the arguments in this note suggest four key elements of a comprehensive reform package:

- Zambia's commitment to eliminate all de jure and de facto impediments to competition in all segments of the telecommunications market.
- Zambia's commitment to create an independent regulator that guarantees a level playing field and an entity that oversees the design and implementation of universal access policies.
- Donor commitments to provide technical and financial assistance to improve regulatory institutions, especially the capacity to ensure interconnection and guarantee competitive conditions (estimated requirements: $2.7 million).[5]
- Donor commitments to help institute policies that promote universal access and the development of national telecommunications backbone and to supplement investment in these areas by the private sector and the government (estimated requirements: $15 million).

The government will need to determine the desirability of subscribing to such a package and the appropriate forum for undertaking any commitments. In the past, a large number of developing countries used the telecommunications negotiations under the GATS to anchor their reforms within an international legal framework and guard against policy reversal. WTO commitments constitute legally binding obligations on members, enforceable through the WTO's binding dispute settlement process. The negotiations called for a large number of legally binding commitments to liberalization at precise points that lent credibility to their reform programs and urgency to the efforts of incumbents and regulators to prepare for openness (see table 3.7). It is likely that the regulatory certainty that follows from such commitments reassures potential investors.

If Zambia were to decide to make commitments under the GATS, it could use the flexibility under the agreement to determine the appropriate scope and phasing of its reform program. In addition to market access and national treatment commitments, it could subscribe to the WTO Reference Paper on regulatory principles for telecommunications. Many believe that this paper has played

Table 3.7. Examples of Precommitments to Liberalization in Basic Telecommunications

Latin America
Argentina: No restrictions as of November 8, 2000.
Grenada: Reserved for exclusive supply until 2006, no restrictions thereafter.
Venezuela: No restrictions as of November 27, 2000.
Africa
Côte d'Ivoire: Monopoly until 2005, no restrictions thereafter.
Mauritius: Monopoly until 2004, no restrictions thereafter.
South Africa: Monopoly until December 31, 2003; thereafter duopoly and authorities will consider the feasibility of more licenses.
Asia
India: Review the subject of opening up national long-distance services in 1999 and international services in 2004.
Korea, Rep. of: Will raise in stages foreign equity participation in facilities-based supplier.
Pakistan: Proposes to divest 26 percent to a strategic investor who will have an exclusive license for the operation of basic telephonic services for seven years.
Thailand: Will introduce revised commitments in 2006, conditional on the passage and coming into force of new communication acts.

Source: Members' Schedules of Specific Commitments, http://www.wto.org.

a pivotal role in liberalizing telecommunications and encouraging regulatory reform in developing countries. The paper, which consists of six principles that serve as a "checklist of 'success' of telecommunications reform in many countries" (Henderson, Gentle, and Ball 2005) was conceived as a necessary instrument for the removal of regulatory barriers to market access, and its implementation is aimed at preventing anticompetitive practices by major suppliers (see annex 1). The draft ECA reflects many of the requirements that would be expected to be seen as a WTO-compliant legal framework. The ECA could, therefore, pave the way toward facilitating such commitments.

Zambia has a stake in regional cooperation because of shared infrastructure

Although telecommunications markets are ideally opened on an most-favored nation (MFN) or nonpreferential basis, cooperation on infrastructure services and regulation is both more feasible and more desirable in the regional context with proximate countries at a similar level of development than in the multilateral or Economic Partnership Agreement (EPA) context. The EASSy cable project offers a good example of why attention and negotiating resources should be devoted to regional cooperation in telecommunications. Currently, Zambia relies on expensive satellite communications for connectivity with the rest of the world and suffers from a lack of adequate and cost-effective international bandwidth. To bridge the connectivity gap in the region, a new regional submarine cable system EASSy is being planned. To gain open, fair, and competitive access to the proposed regional infrastructure needed for the development of Zambia's Internet and telecommunications sectors, cooperation at the regional level is required to facilitate cost-based cross-border interconnection and pricing agreements. The EASSy fiber-optic cable project offers Zambia the possibility to gain access to a terrestrial broadband network via its neighbors Malawi and Zimbabwe. Zambia is actively participating in this regional infrastructure initiative, and Zamtel is planning to make an equity investment to the EASSy consortium to build the submarine cable.

Access to the EASSy submarine cable landing points is envisaged through two links: Lusaka-Lilongwe and Lusaka-Harare. For Zambia to gain efficient, fair, and competitive access to the cable through these intermediary countries, an increased degree of regulatory cooperation will be necessary. In particular, Zambia and its neighbors will need to renegotiate and revise existing cross-border interconnection and pricing agreements. A key difficulty for Zambia, however, is that the enforcement of such agreements is beyond the jurisdiction of national regulators. Thus a strong case can be made for the development of regional interconnection guidelines and a regional clearing house for interconnection, and the enforcement of regional competition and dispute settlement frameworks. Existing regional initiatives, for example, those under COMESA, could be leveraged to reach this goal. "Policy Guidelines for Interconnection for COMESA Countries" stress that the principles of domestic interconnection should apply at the regional and international level. If a regional body is empowered to ensure the enforcement of these guidelines, fair and competitively priced access to the EASSy cable for Zambia and other landlocked countries could be safeguarded.

International Assistance

The transition from restricted to full competition needs to be accompanied by a number of complementary actions to produce a socially desirable outcome. Each of these actions would benefit from international assistance. First of all, an important role will be played by the Ministry of Communications and Transport in driving the reform agenda, and it must have the technical capacity to develop implementation strategies. Similarly, additional capacity building of CAZ is needed to ensure effective regulation. Finally, funding will be needed for the national backbone infrastructure and the universal access mechanism, beyond the support needed to draft enabling legislation and create an implementation mechanism. The World Bank–proposed project to provide International Development Association seed funds of $3.5 million in the universal access fund is the first initiative to implement the universal access program on a pilot basis. Scaling up the program for a wider rollout will require additional funds from donors.

To this end, Zambia could harness the current "aid-for-trade" agenda in the context of the WTO's Doha Development Agenda to generate resources for reform in its telecommunications and other services sectors. The Ministry of Commerce, Trade, and Industry can play a significant role at the interface of international trade negotiations and domestic reform. The aim should be to construct a package along the lines suggested above, which will define reforms to be undertaken domestically in a specific time frame, and requests to be made of other countries for assistance (including estimated needs). These two elements can be mutually reinforcing—the promise of reform could make the demands for assistance less resistible, and the promise of assistance could make the demands for reform less resistible.

**Table 3.8. Action Plan for Implementation and Possible
External Support**

Action	Possible external support	Estimated budget[a]
Support the implementation of the Electronic Communications Act		$200,000
Revision of Zamtel license plus issuing new licenses	Legal consultancy to draft Zamtel's license	$100,000
Cost-based interconnection regime	In-house capacity building for developing costing methodology and supporting the regulator. Support drafting RIO.	$300,000
Progressive tariff rebalancing	Advisory support	$200,000
Competitive safeguards	Drafting relevant instruments	$100,000
Commercialization and restructuring of Zamtel	Consultancy on strategies and action plan for commercialization of Zamtel	$500,000
Universal service	Support to draft enabling legislation for the fund and implementation mechanism	$300,000
Universal access	Financial contribution to universal access fund	$5 million
Design of national backbone and proposal for management and operation of backbone	Feasibility study	$400,000
Supporting the funding gap for national backbone	PPP arrangement, including possible use of OBA	$10 million
Targeted capacity building for regulator, policy makers, and competition authority	Training, study tours, workshops	$500,000
Streamlining and reducing taxes	Study and proposal for change	$100,000
Total technical assistance plus investment		$17.7 million

Source: Authors.

Note: OBA = output-based aid; PPP = public private partnership; RIO = reference interconnection offer.

a. These figures are rough estimates of the costs of the project components, based on World Bank experience in contexts similar to Zambia. For more accurate projections of the costs, deeper country-specific analysis would need to be undertaken.

Notes

1. Even if prices in both directions were equal, one would never expect a ratio of 1:1, because of the differences in disposable income between Zambia and other countries.
2. Interviews in Lusaka, March 2006.
3. Annex 2 contains an overview of the kind of ownership restrictions placed on telecommunications operators in other countries.
4. The Statutory Instrument is yet to be converted into subsidiary legislation. The Ministry of Justice has been slow in responding to requests for subsidiary legislations.
5. For a breakdown of these estimates, see table 3.8.

References

Arnold, J., A. Mattoo, and G. Narciso. 2006. "Services Matter for Productivity: Firm-Level Evidence from Sub-Saharan Africa." World Bank Policy Research Paper No. 4048, World Bank, Washington, DC.

Bos, D., and L. Nett. 1990. "Privatization, Price Regulation, and Market Entry: An Asymmetric Multi-stage Duopoly Model." *Journal of Economics (Zeitschriftfiir Nationalokonomie)* 51(3): 221–257.

Fink, Carsten, A. Mattoo, and I.C. Neagu. 2002. "Assessing the Impact of Communication Costs on International Trade." Policy Research Working Paper No. 2929, World Bank, Washington, DC.

Fink, Carsten, Aaditya Mattoo, and Randeep Rathindran. 2003. "An Assessment of Telecommunications Reform in Developing Countries." *Information Economics and Policy* 15(4): 443–466.

Guermazi, B., and I. Neto. 2005. "Mobile License Renewal: What Are the Issues and What Is at Stake?" Global Information and Communication Technologies Department, World Bank, Washington, DC.

Guislain, P., M. Ampah, L. Besançon, C. Niang, and A. Sérot. 2005. "Connecting Sub-Saharan Africa." World Bank, Washington, DC.

Henderson, Angus, Iaian Gentle, and Elise Ball. 2005. "WTO Principles and Telecommunications in Developing Nations: Challenges and Consequences of Accession." *Telecommunications Policy* 29: 205–331.

ITU (International Telecommunication Union). 2005. Trends in Telecommunications Reform. Geneva.

Kenny, C. 2006. "Catalyzing the Development Impact of Information and Communications Infrastructure in Kenya, An Agenda and Role for the World Bank." World Bank, Washington, DC.

Lamont, J. 2001. "South Africa U-turn on Telecoms Competition." *Financial Times*, August 15.

Mulavu, Sikaaba, S. B. Kanyanga, Inonge Imasiku, and Floyd Mwenda. 2005. "Chapter 12: Zambia." In *Towards an African e-Index: Household and Individual ICT Access and Use across 10 African Countries*, ed. Alison Gillwald, 178–89. The LINK Centre, Wits University School of Public and Development Management. http://link.wits.ac.za/papers/e-index-zambia.pdf.

Navas-Sabater, J. 2005. "Universal Access and Output-Based Aid in Telecommunications and ICT." Global Information and Communications Technology Department, World Bank, Washington DC.

Navas-Sabater, J., A. Dymond, and N. Juntunen. 2002. "Telecommunications and Information Services for the Poor: Toward a Strategy for Universal Access." World Bank, Washington, DC.

OECD Communications Outlook. 2005. Organisation for Economic Co-operation and Development, Paris.

Republic of Zambia. 1994. Telecommunications Act. Lusaka.

Rossoto, C.M., B. Wellenius, A. Lewin, and C. Gomez. 2004. "Competition in International Voice Communications." World Bank Working Paper No. 42, World Bank, Washington, DC.

Wallsten, Scott J. 2002. "Does Sequencing Matter? Regulation and Privatization in Telecommunications Reforms." Policy Research Working Paper No. 2817, World Bank, Washington, DC.

WSIS (World Summit on the Information Society). 2006. "Navigating Unchartered Waters: Implementing Regional ICT Strategies," November 16, 2005, Tunis.

Zambia Competition Commission. 2003. Report to the Committee on Communications, Transport, Works and Supply of the National Assembly of Zambia, April.

Annex 1. The Reference Paper on Regulatory Principles

Under Article XVIII of the General Agreement on Trade in Services (GATS) of the WTO, parties are allowed to schedule "additional commitments" in addition to market access and national treatment commitments. These additional commitments are binding on the countries that make them and enforceable through WTO dispute procedures. The drafting of the Reference Paper on regulatory topics was driven by a need to guarantee effective competition in the basic telecommunications sector, especially the need to prevent major suppliers from abusing their dominant market positions. WTO member countries that adopt the Reference Paper commit to the following:

1. *Competitive safeguards*: Members are required to establish competitive safeguards preventing major suppliers from engaging in anticompetitive conduct. The Reference Paper does not establish what these appropriate competitive safeguards are nor does it define anticompetitive practices, because members are required to establish these in their national legislation. However, the Reference Paper does list certain examples of anticompetitive practices, including the following: anticompetitive cross-subsidization; use of information obtained from competitors with anticompetitive results; and withholding technical data.

2. *Interconnection*: Major suppliers (that is, those with the ability to materially affect the terms of price and supply in the market by exploiting their control over "essential facilities" or their position in the market) of members are required to provide interconnection upon request, under nondiscriminatory terms and conditions, and at cost-oriented rates that are transparent and feasible.

3. *Universal service*: Members have the right to define the kind of universal service obligation they wish to maintain, provided that such obligations are not anticompetitive per se, and that they are administered in a transparent, nondiscriminatory, and competitively neutral manner. Universal service obligations may not create unnecessary burdens on service suppliers.

4. *Public availability of licensing criteria*: To the extent that a license is required, members should make publicly available the licensing criteria and the time it will take to decide on a license application and the terms and conditions of individual licenses.

5. *Independent regulators*: Members should ensure that the regulatory authority is separate from, and not accountable to, any supplier of basic telecommunications services, and that their decisions are impartial with respect to market par-

ticipants. This requirement seeks equal, transparent, and objective treatment of all operators in the market.

6. *Allocation and use of scarce resources*: Allocation and use of scarce resources (that is, frequencies, numbers, and rights of way) should be carried out in an objective, timely, transparent, and nondiscriminatory manner, and the allocation of frequency bands should be made publicly available. Details of government-use frequencies do not have to be made publicly available.

Annex 2. Benchmarking License Fee for International Gateway

The experience of countries in Africa shows that, in most cases, the fees for the international gateway are an integral part of the operating license. In cases in which a separate license fees is attached to the international gateway, they are generally in the range of few hundred thousand dollars with a larger percentage paid as an up-front fee and a smaller percentage paid for a period of few years and then completely phased out.

Table A-2.1. African Experience in IGW License Fees

Country	Specific fee for the IGW	Comments
Niger	No fee	International gateway (IGW) is part of the global system for mobile communications (GSM) license. Celtel is already operating its own gateway and Telecel will have the right to do so on January 2005.
Côte d'Ivoire	No fee	Mobile operators have the right to operate an international gateway since February 2004, with no additional fee.
Cameroon	No fee	The right to operate the IGW is part of the license that the two GSM operators paid CFAF 40 billion (Orange) and CFAF 100 billion (paid by the operator who purchased the mobile branch of the incumbent). Note that Orange is only able to handle the traffic and is not allowed to sell international minutes to other operators.
Gabon	No fee	The right to operate the IGW is part of the GSM license that was originally granted for an annual fee of around $100,000.

(Table continues on the following page.)

Table A-2.1. (continued)

Country	Specific fee for the IGW	Comments
Ghana	$2 million for first year, $100,000 annually	Initial IGW as part of license for two fixed operators, new IGW awarded to Scancom. IGW license to operate for period of 10 years, automatic renewal 5 years thereafter.
Uganda	$50,000	A second national license combining the whole range of fixed and mobile services (including international voice services) was granted for an annual fee of around $100,000. Celtel purchased the right to operate an IGW for $50,000 (apparently this is the renegotiated fee for the whole new license).
Malawi	$50,000 for the first year and $35,000 for the second and third years	
Sierra Leone	$100,000 to have access to the IGW plus $50,000 annual fee the following years	One gateway has been issued to Celtel. The gateway will belong to the Sierra Leone Government with the operator having sole responsibility of the building, operating and maintenance of the structure. The government will have the right to determine tariffs based on established international interconnect tariffs. The gateway will be available to all operators in Sierra Leone with uniform tariffs. Celtel will be permitted to recover maintenance cost of space parts and recovery of capital cost over a period of 10 years. At the end of the contract period (10 years), Celtel will negotiate with government for further extension of the contract period.
Botswana	n.a.	Only the incumbent operator is operating the IGW. Liberalization of the gateway is under study.
Kenya	n.a.	The two mobile operators (Safaricom and Kencell) don't have the right to operate their own gateway thus far. The international market is in the process of liberalization, but a monopoly will remain for at least a few months.
Tanzania	n.a.	Only the incumbent is operating the IGW.
Sudan	n.a.	Only the incumbent is operating the IGW.

Source: Authors.

Note: n.a. = not applicable.

Annex 3. Benchmarking—Restrictions on Foreign Investment in Telecommunication

Zambia's restrictions on foreign ownership in the telecommunications sector are neither unique nor surprising in the international context. Because of the strategic nature and importance for economic and social development of the sector, many countries have regarded telecommunications as an integral part of their identity and sovereignty and subjected the sector to foreign ownership restrictions under the telecommunications legislation or a country's foreign investment law. Table A-3.1 describes the kind of restrictions placed on foreign ownership in other countries.

Table A-3.1. Restrictions on Foreign Telecommunication Ownership in Selected Countries

Country	Restrictions
Australia	Once full privatization of the incumbent carrier, Telstra, is implemented, it will be subject to 35 percent limit on total foreign ownership and a 5 percent limit on individual foreign ownership. There is a legislative requirement that Telstra's chair and majority directors have to be Australian citizens and that the head office, base of operations, and place of incorporation remain in Australia. Prior approval is required for foreign involvement in the establishment of new entrants to, or investment in, the telecommunications sector.
Austria	None
Bangladesh	None
Belgium	None
Brazil	According to federal Decree Law No. 2.617 of July 1998, public telecommunications services must be majority owned by Brazilian entities, which means a 49 percent limit on foreign ownership.
Bhutan	None
Canada	Limit of 20 percent of voting shares in facilities-based carrier with 80 percent of board required to be Canadian citizens. Foreigners are permitted to own not more than $46\frac{2}{3}$ percent of the voting shares of a telecommunications common carrier, including direct holdings and indirect holdings through a holding company.
China	49 percent limit, and up to 50 percent for value added services.
Czech Republic	None
Denmark	None

(Table continues on the following page.)

Table A-3.1. (continued)

Country	Restrictions
Finland	None
France	None
Germany	None
Greece	None
Hong Kong (China)	None
Hungary	None
Iceland	None
India	74 percent, with the remaining 26 percent owned by Indian citizens or companies.
Indonesia	35 percent
Ireland	None
Italy	None
Japan	No restrictions on individuals and corporations investing in the incumbent PTO(s) in Japan. However, foreign capital participation, direct and/or indirect, in NTT Corporation, which holds all the shares of NTT East Corp. and NTT West Corp. is restricted less than one-third of ownership.
Jordan	None
Korea, Rep. of	Foreign governments, foreign or domestic corporations with more than 15 percent of its stock held by a foreign government, or foreigners cannot hold more than 49 percent of a share issued by a facilities-based operator in Korea.
Luxembourg	None
Malaysia	30 percent, and permit more than 50 percent but has to be reduced after three years.
Maldives	None
Mexico	Concessions only granted to Mexican nationals. Foreign investment can be no greater than 49 percent except for cellular telephony services where permission is required from the Commission of Foreign Investment for a greater level of foreign participation.
Mongolia	None
Netherlands	None
New Zealand	No more than 49.9 percent of ownership in Telecom New Zealand. No restrictions on other operators.
Norway	None
Pakistan	None
Philippines	40 percent
Poland	None
Portugal	None
Singapore	49 percent on facilities-based operators.

Table A-3.1. (continued)

Country	Restrictions
Slovak Republic	None
South Africa	Sections 35(3) and 35(4) of the Telecommunications Act require the regulator, ICASA, to promote the empowerment and advancement of disadvantaged groups and women by giving them preference in the award of any licenses for up to 30 percent equity ownership or such higher equity ownership percentage as may be prescribed.
Spain	The right to operate networks and provide electronic communications services is reserved to residents of the European Union member states and foreign nationals when provided for by international agreements where Spain is a signatory party. The government may provide exceptions to the rule for all other natural and legal persons.
Sri Lanka	None
Sweden	None
Switzerland	None. Federal government is required to retain majority shareholding in Swisscom.
Taiwan (China)	49 percent
Thailand	49 percent
Turkey	None
United Kingdom	None
United States	Not more than 20 percent directly, or 25 percent indirectly, in a U.S. broadcast, common carrier, or aeronautical radio station license, although the FCC may allow higher level of indirect ownership unless it is not in the public interest.

Source: OECD Communications Outlook 2005, and data compiled by the World Bank.

Note: ICASA = Independent Communications Authority of South Africa; FCC = Federal Communications Commission; PTO = Public Telecommunications Operator; NTT = Nipon Telephone and Telegraph Corporation.

4

FINANCIAL SERVICES: DEALING WITH LIMITED AND UNEQUAL ACCESS

José de Luna Martinez

Overview

In the early1990s, Zambia facilitated the entry of new domestic and foreign banks as well as fully liberalized transactions on the capital account; foreign banks dominated the market. Zambia allows not only foreign investment in banking, but also allows firms and individuals to borrow from and place deposits abroad. At the end of 1995, six international banks accounted for 67 percent of assets, 76 percent of loans, and 64 percent of deposits in the banking system. Large firms raised a significant proportion of their long-term capital needs from abroad, and around one-fifth of the commercial banks balances are placed abroad.

The benefits expected from an open, private, and largely foreign-owned banking system have not so far materialized and access to banking services is low and unequal. Credit to the private sector by banks represented only 8 percent of GDP in 2005, which is lower than the level registered in 1990. Only 5,000 people hold 90 percent of loans. Just 8 percent of Zambia's adult population had a bank account in 2005, one of the lowest ratios in Sub-Saharan Africa. The number of rural branches of banks actually declined in the last decade by 15 percent to 65. Whereas microfinance institutions (MFIs) have grown rapidly in some other Sub-Saharan countries, in Zambia, they serve only 50,000 customers, which is 0.005 percent of the population.

Access to bank credit is not just scarce, it is also extremely expensive. The average annual interest rate on loans was 48 percent in 2005 (the inflation rate was 20 percent). Large firms and goods exporters borrow at rates below the average (the prime rate was 20 percent in 2005). The few small and medium-size enterprises (SMEs) in Zambia that are able to borrow from banks pay the average annual lending rate or higher. MFIs lend at rates of around 50 to 60 percent. Most loans have a short-term maturity (one to three months); few loans have a maturity of one year or more. The few firms with sources of revenue in foreign currency are able to obtain financing from banks in U.S. dollars at significantly lower interest rates.

Bank savings and deposits accounts are not a practical instrument for building savings over time. No interest at all is paid on small savings accounts denominated in kwacha (K) and only large firms receive positive interest rates on their deposits. A K 3.2 million deposit (equivalent to $100) today would lose two-thirds of its real value after six years, if during this period the annual inflation rate remains at 18 percent. In addition to this loss, monthly charges are also deducted by all banks. Five of the 13 banks require customers to have a minimum balance of $156 to $313 or more to open a savings account. In five other banks, the minimum balance to open an account is lower (in the range of $16 to $78). In the context of Zambia, where 58 percent of the population lives on less than $1 a day, these minimum balances prevent most people from having access to basic banking services. Thus, with the exception of high-income households, public servants, and employees of large companies, most Zambians do not have access to products offered by banks.

Macroeconomic and institutional problems are the main reasons why liberalization has not delivered significant benefits, and these reasons are being gradually remedied. The large fiscal deficit (which amounted to 6 percent of GDP in 2003, but has been reduced to 2.3 percent of GDP today) has been financed by borrowing from banks, which has limited the funds available to finance the private sector. The recent reduction in the fiscal deficit and government borrowing has shaken the banks out of their stupor and immediately induced stronger efforts to lend to the private sector. In addition, key institutional weaknesses undermine the effectiveness of the banking sector: 90 percent of land is still collectively owned, making it difficult for individuals to produce collateral; past disbursement by state banks of credit as de facto grants has created a tradition of default; and the judicial system provides few effective procedures to collect delinquent loans. The credit bureau being set up by the Bankers' Association of Zambia is a critical step to improve market information and to strengthen the credit culture. The current plan is to start the credit bureau with negative information on defaulters. That effort should be supported and expanded as soon as technically feasible to include positive information to help clients with a clean credit history enjoy the expanding services and lower costs. Over time, an attempt should be made to extend the credit bureau database to small and medium-size firms that suffer from severe information asymmetries in the Zambian markets.

Limited access is also attributable to financial policy failures, beginning with an inappropriate sequence of reform that has had durable consequences. The financial system was liberalized before establishing a new legal and regulatory framework for the banking system that would encourage prudent risk-taking and market discipline. Ten new bank licenses were issued between 1991 and 1994, increasing the number of commercial banks to 18. Between 1995 and 2001, nine bank failures were estimated to have caused losses to taxpayers and depositors equivalent to 7 percent of GDP. At the end of 2005, nonperforming loans (NPLs) in the banking system still amounted to 8.9 percent of the total loan portfolio. All banks scaled back their lending operations and increased their holding of government securities, which offered high yields at a lower risk for banks. Barclays, the largest bank in Zambia, refrained from any new lending for several years and just began lending again in 2006.

In recent years, significant improvements have been made in the regulatory framework, but some weaknesses remain. Following the first episodes of bank failures in 1995, Zambia established major measures to improve the quality of bank regulation and supervision. In 2002, the Financial Sector Assessment Program (FSAP) carried out by the IMF and the World Bank found that Zambia satisfactorily complies with the Basel Core Principles (BCPs) on Bank Supervision. Of the 30 principles assessed under the BCPs, Zambia was found to be compliant or largely compliant with 19 principles and noncompliant or materially noncompliant with 11 principles. Major weaknesses were found in the areas of independence of the central bank, remedial measures to deal with insolvent banks, management and control of market risks, internal controls, and anti–money laundering initiatives. Following the release of the FSAP report, Zambian authorities drafted a comprehensive Financial Sector Development Plan (FSDP), which contains a series of actions for the period from 2004 to 2010 to strengthen the overall financial system.

Bank regulation in Zambia must be sensitive to the needs of the population if banks are to be encouraged to lend to the poor and to SMEs and, in particular, if MFIs are brought under the umbrella of Bank of Zambia supervision. International regulation, such as anti–money laundering (AML), if applied with no discretion, is not well designed for countries in which only 10 percent of land is registered and much of the population live in temporary dwellings and work informally.[1]

Most SMEs are not registered, do not pay taxes, and do not have audited accounts and, therefore, cannot access financial services offered by banks. In the past, banks have relied on group monitoring and personalized relations to give loans for productive investments carried out by this part of the population and required only a national identity card. Know Your Customer (KYC) rules make such lending illegal, however, if the customer cannot provide documentary proof of residence or proof of employment in the formal sector. Several bank managers told us that these rules were effectively hindering them from making loans they usually would have made to SMEs and individuals. Finally, a proposal to regulate MFIs could have the benefits of protecting depositors, enhancing stability, and mobilizing resources from donors and the formal sector, but it must not inhibit the development of this nascent sector.

The disappearance of past, inefficient instruments of providing the poor with access to financial services left a socially costly vacuum that is only now being addressed. Before liberalization, policy makers played an active role in promoting access to finance through the direct control of financial markets and financial institutions, subsidies, and credit allocation. During the 1990s, policy makers refrained from any such intervention in the financial system with the expectation that foreign and private financial institutions would increasingly serve all segments of the population and private sector. It is now clear that the visible hand of the government is needed to use market-friendly instruments to promote access in the short run, until the fruits of ongoing institutional and fiscal reform are ripe. Government attempts to increase access have more often than not failed to achieve their objectives. Subsidized credit (for example, for housing) typically has ended up benefiting the middle class and those who already have access to credit. Experience from other countries suggests that interventions to widen access are most likely to succeed if they harness market forces by providing incentives to public or commercial banks to innovate and engineer products that enable downscaling to serve the poor to be profitable and sustainable. The experience of South Africa underlines that "moral suasion" on the part of the government can encourage banks to act collectively to profitably meet universal access goals. If the costs of extending services remain prohibitive for commercial banks, a case could be made for government intervention to provide market infrastructure, for example, by renting space in the post offices to banks that wish to expand into rural areas or by subsidizing transaction costs. Any such intervention, however, is unlikely to succeed if it distorts competition in the sector and awards subsidies in a noncompetitive way.

There is little cost and perhaps some benefits from multilateral commitments, and greater benefit but little prospect of deeper regional integration through regulatory harmonization. Given the openness of the Zambian banking sector, and the fact that most of the desired policy interventions do not require impeding market access or discriminating against foreign banks, there is little cost to Zambia to bind existing openness under the GATS. There may be some benefit in so far as such bindings create greater regulatory certainty and thus make the market more contestable and more attractive to new entrants. Creating a more integrated regional market through regulatory harmonization would help Zambia overcome some of the disadvantages of its small market size, but there is little willingness at this point to make the necessary sacrifice in regulatory autonomy.

Through international engagement, Zambia can mobilize financial and technical support to develop more appropriate regulations and for universal access policies. Zambia could request the following:

- Assistance with the continued implementation of the FSDP and long-term institutional and capacity building
- Assistance and continued support for the creation of the credit information bureau
- Assistance with the evaluation and implementation of banking regulation in light of access needs
- Assistance in the assessment of and implementation of proactive universal access policies

Reforms and Access to Banking Services in Zambia

In 1992, Zambia began to deregulate its financial sector and implement a series of economic reforms aimed at establishing the foundations of a market-based economy. In that year, borrowing and lending rates were deregulated and the exchange rate was permitted to be market determined.[2] By March 1993, most foreign exchange controls on current transactions had been removed and in February 1994 the capital account of the foreign payment systems was liberalized. In 1995, the Bank of Zambia (BoZ) allowed commercial banks to hold foreign currency deposits. In 1996, the final phase of liberalization of the foreign exchange market was implemented with Zambia Consolidated Copper Mines (ZCCM) being allowed to retain all its foreign currency earnings and to supply foreign exchange to the market directly.

The liberalization process of the 1990s led to a deep reconfiguration of the Zambian banking system. Before liberalization, the banking system was composed of a group of public and privately owned domestic banks holding approximately 60 percent of the assets of the banking system. A group of foreign banks held the remaining 40 percent of the assets. Between 1992 and 1994, 10 new banks were established by domestic private investors. These new banks, however, along with other domestic banks, failed in the subsequent years for reasons discussed below (see annex 1). As a result, existing foreign banks progressively increased their market share in Zambia.[3] Although in the early 1990s the combined assets of foreign-

Table 4.1. Banking Institutions in Zambia, 2006

Commercial Banks	Total assets		Loans and advances		Deposits		Branches	
	Assets	% of total	Loans and advances	% of total	Deposits	% of total	Branches	% of total
Foreign banks								
Barclays Bank	1,587,948	20	750,489	32	988,120	18	17	11
Standard Chartered	1,214,629	16	344,322	15	967,324	18	15	10
Stanbic Bank	1,122,275	14	414,368	18	735,346	13	9	6
Finance Bank Zambia Ltd	604,535	8	174,556	8	384,176	7	38	24
Citibank Zambia Ltd	560,095	7	80,710	3	338,161	6	2	1
Indo-Zambia Bank	453,116	6	71,532	3	314,287	6	9	6
Bank of China	112,117	1	109	0	93,123	2	1	1
Subtotal	*5,654,715*	*73*	*1,836,086*	*79*	*3,820,537*	*69*	*91*	*58*
Domestic banks								
African Banking Corporation	124,314	2	68,539	3	31,240	1	1	1
Cavmont Merchant Bank	72,510	1	6,381	0	58,836	1	11	7
First Alliance Bank	110,884	1	21,074	1	58,343	1	4	3
Intermarket Banking Corporation	87,108	1	21,292	1	70,170	1	2	1
Investrust Bank	197,333	3	80,109	3	162,912	3	5	3
Zambia National Commercial Bank	1,537,857	20	278,552	12	1,297,752	24	42	27
Subtotal	*2,130,006*	*27*	*475,947*	*21*	*1,679,253*	*31*	*65*	*42*
Total	7,784,721	100	2,312,033	100	5,499,790	100	156	100

Source: Bank of Zambia.

owned banks did not represent more than 40 percent of the banking system assets, at the end of 2005, seven foreign banks—Barclays, Standard Chartered, Stanbic, Finance Bank, Citibank, Bank of China, and Indo-Zambia Bank—held 73 percent of total assets. Moreover, in 2005, foreign banks had 79 percent of the total lending portfolio, had 69 percent of the deposits in the banking system, and operated 91 of the existing 156 bank branches in Zambia.

Among the group of seven foreign banks, three large banks—Barclays, Standard Chartered, and Stanbic Bank—play a dominant role in Zambia's financial system. They hold 50 percent of assets in the banking system, 55 percent of the total loan portfolio, 49 percent of deposits, and 27 percent of all branches.[4]

Nowadays the banking system is not only dominated by foreign-owned banks, but also shows strong signs of soundness and profitability. According to data from the BoZ, at the end of 2005, all of the 13 commercial banks operating in Zambia reported a capital adequacy ratio above the minimum level of 8 percent on risk-weighted assets and a moderate level of NPLs, which was 8.9 percent of the total lending portfolio. In addition, in 2005, banks recorded high profits that allowed them to achieve a 7.4 percent annual return on assets.[5]

Size and Outreach of Zambia's Banking System

Despite the profound reform efforts undertaken by authorities, the growing presence of foreign-owned banks in Zambia, and the soundness and profitability of the banking sector as a whole, the banking system remains small and underdeveloped. At the end of 2005, total assets of the banking system amounted to only $1.7 billion, which represented 35 percent of Zambia's GDP. Other ratios on the size of the financial system indicate that the system has remained small since liberalization. For example, the ratio of total money supply (M2) to GDP reached 22 percent in 2004, which is the same level of 1990, the year when reform measures were implemented, as illustrated in figure 4.1.

Commercial banks in Zambia are small and serve only a small segment of the population and private sector. Five of the 13 banks have less than $5 million in capital each, seven banks have capital in the range of $5 to $30 million, and only one bank (Barclays) has a capital of $52 million.

At the end of 2005, there were 405,888 deposit accounts at all commercial banks in Zambia (including deposit accounts in kwacha and foreign currency). This number is extremely low for a country with a population of 10.5 million people, which includes 6 million people age 18 and above. Figure 4.1 indicates that, on average, only 3.8 percent of the population, or 6.2 percent of the people age 18 and above, have a bank account (putting aside the fact that the figures include accounts by firms and some people may have more than one account). The ratio

Figure 4.1. Size of Zambia's Financial System

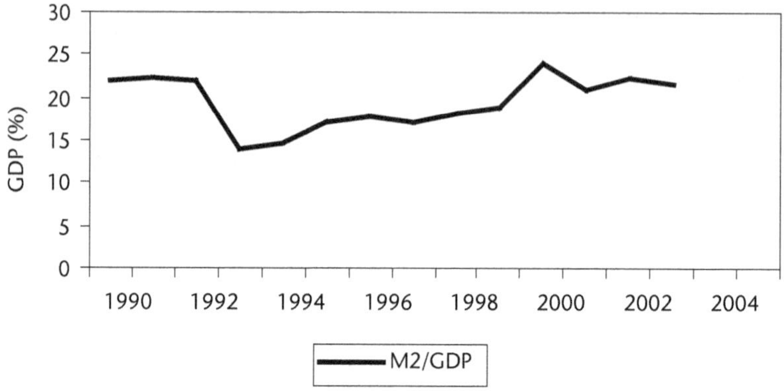

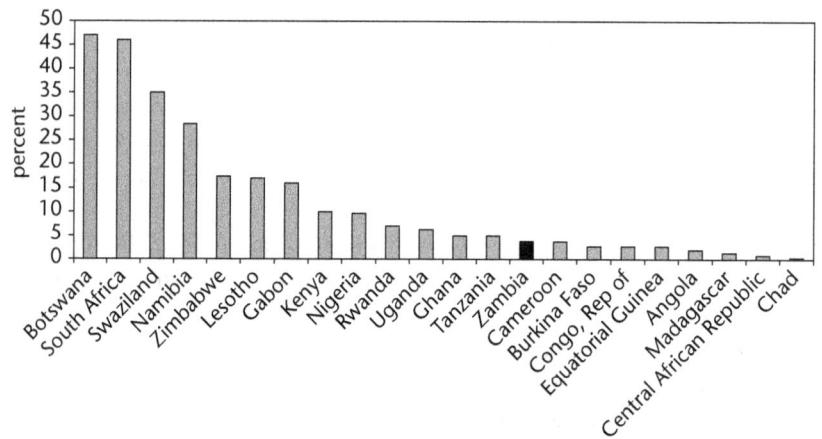

Source: World Bank 2006c.

of bank accounts to population is one of the lowest in Sub-Saharan Africa, as illustrated in figure 4.2.

As shown in figure 4.3, 64 percent of the accounts at banking institutions in Zambia have a balance below K 320,000 ($100), 8 percent of the accounts have a balance between K 320,000 and K 640,000 ($200), and the remaining 28 percent have balances above K 640,000. In terms of value of deposits, 10 percent of account holders (42,000 accounts) have 85 percent of the total deposits in the Zambian banking system.

Figure 4.2. Percentage of Population with a Bank Deposit Account in Africa

Source: Martínez Pería, Soledad, Demirgüç, and Beck (2005) and data from commercial banks in Zambia.

Figure 4.3. Distribution of Bank Deposits in Zambia, March 2006

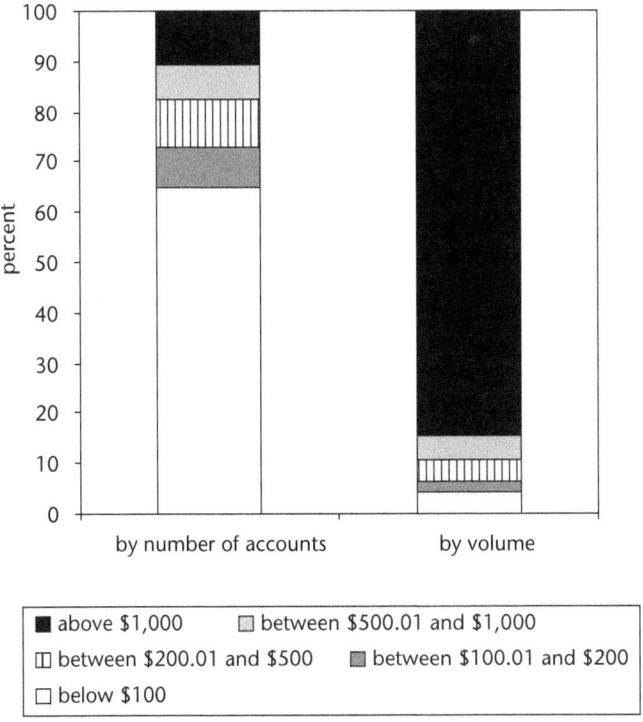

Source: Data from commercial banks in Zambia.

Several studies indicate that the account holders are usually people living in urban areas and with a regular employment in the public sector or a large private firm. A recent survey conducted by the Bank of Zambia concluded that the highest percentage of banked population are salaried employees (48.6 percent), although a high percentage of this salaried population have never had a bank account (41.6 percent) (Bank of Zambia 2006).

One additional characteristic is that the real value of small savings and deposit accounts declines over time, because usually no interest is paid on small savings accounts denominated in kwacha. Only large firms receive positive interest rates on their deposits. In practice, for most households in Zambia, bank savings and deposits are just a way to safeguard coins and notes, not a practical instrument to save money over time. As illustrated in figure 4.4, a K 320,000 deposit (equivalent to $100) today would lose two-thirds of its real value after six years if during this

Figure 4.4. Real Value of a K 320,000 Deposit

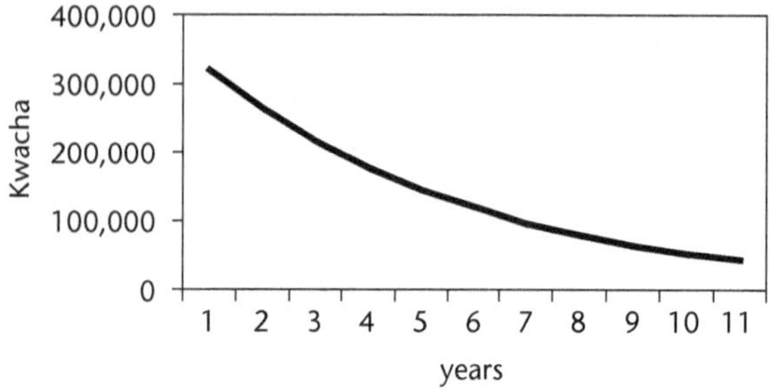

Source: Author's own calculation.

Note: This assumes an annual inflation rate of 18 percent and no interest payments.

period the annual inflation rate remains at its 2004 level (18 percent) and no nominal interest is paid, as is currently the case for small saving deposits in kwacha.

In addition to the lack of interest payments on small saving deposits in kwacha, most commercial banks in Zambia have adopted high balances to open or maintain an account, making it impossible for most people to have a savings or deposit account. As outlined in table 4.2, five banks require customers to have a minimum balance of $16 to $78 to open a savings account. In a group of five other banks, the minimum balance to open an account ranges from $156 to $313. In the context of Zambia, where 71 percent of the population lives on less than $1 a day, the minimum balances currently required by banks are high and prevent most people from having access to basic banking services.

Interviews with bankers revealed that, at this time, most banks in Zambia do not seem to be interested in serving the low-income part of the population. Most banks prefer to target only a small universe of the population, approximately 500,000 people with medium- to high-level incomes, which is defined as the "bankable" group by the bankers themselves. Besides commercial banks, no other types of financial institutions offer savings and deposits in Zambia, which could serve the needs of low-income households that are not served by commercial banks. By law, the approximately 50 MFIs that operated in Zambia in 2005 were not allowed to take deposits from the public.

Interestingly, a recent survey conducted by the Bank of Zambia found that the use of informal financial service providers (not registered or licensed individuals who provide basic financial services to the poor) is relatively high in Zambia. Approximately 8 percent of adult Zambians declared that they save money in the so-called *chilimbas* or savings clubs (Bank of Zambia 2006). Chilimbas can also be used for loans.

**Table 4.2. Minimum Balances to Open and Maintain a Bank
Account, March 2006**

Bank	Account opening balance Kwacha	$	Minimum balance to avoid penalty Kwacha	$
African Banking Corporation Zambia	500,000	$156	500,000	$156
Bank of China	1,000,000	$313	1,000,000	$313
Barclays Bank	N/A	N/A	N/A	N/A
Cavmont Capital	1,000,000	$313	N/A	N/A
Citibank	N/A	N/A	N/A	N/A
Finance Bank	100,000	$31	50,000	$16
First Alliance Bank	250,000	$78	250,000	$78
Indo Zambia Bank	150,000	$47	250,000	$78
Intermarket Banking Corporation	1,000,000	$313	250,000	$78
Investrust	50,000	$16	50,000	$16
Stanbic Bank	50,000	$16	N/A	N/A
Standard Chartered	750,000	$234	750,000	$234
Zambia National Commercial Bank	N/A	N/A	N/A	N/A

Source: Bank of Zambia 2006.

Bank Branches in Rural Areas

The limited access to banking services in Zambia is reflected in the low number of
bank branches serving urban and rural areas. Although in 1990 there were 120
bank branches, in 2005, there were only 152, giving a ratio of one bank branch per
70,000 people in 2005, one of the lowest bank penetration ratios in the world.

As can be seen in figure 4.5, the modest increase in the total number of bank
branches can be mostly attributed to the growth of branches in urban areas. In
1990, 50 percent of all branches were in urban areas and the other 50 percent in
rural areas. This was in line with the government policy at the time. From 1990 to
2004, the number of bank branches increased to 152. However, with the removal
of the requirement to open a rural branch for every urban branch opened, the
proportion of rural branches to urban branches reduced from 50 percent in 1990
to 43 percent in 2004. The change is most notable in the period from 1995 to 2000
when the number of urban branches increased by 16 percent to 79 from 68 compared with a drop of 15 percent to 65 from 77 branches in rural areas.[6]

The concentration of financial institutions in urban areas has been attributed
to the fact that Zambia's rural environment is not particularly conducive to the

Figure 4.5. Number of Bank Branches in Zambia, 1990–2004

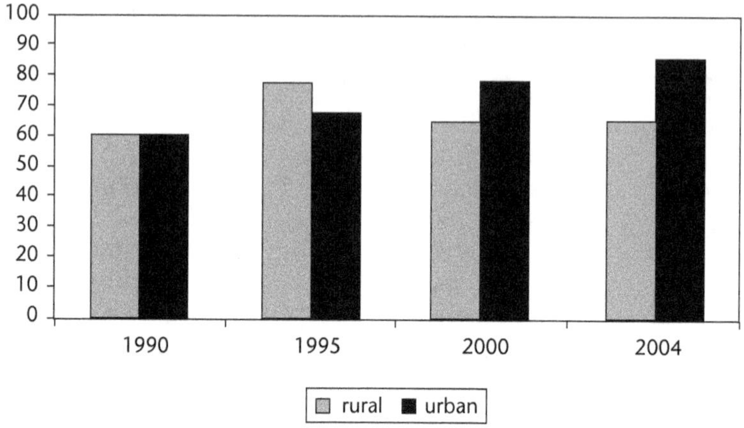

Source: Bank of Zambia.

establishment of viable businesses. One of the main criteria used by banks to determine whether to establish a branch in a particular locality is the economic activity and level of business. The main form of economic activity in rural areas is peasant farming. Where there is commercial farming on a significant scale, the banks may be inclined to serve potential clients from existing branches in the nearest urban center, visiting the client only when required.

The costs of operating in rural Zambia are relatively high. Like most other developing countries, Zambia suffers from a lack of basic infrastructure in the rural communities. Electricity supply in outlying areas is unreliable and, in some areas, nonexistent. Telecommunications are poorly developed, making it difficult to communicate with head office and other branches. This adversely affects the smooth and efficient operation of a payment system. Much of the country is covered by gravel roads; where roads are paved, away from the main line of rail, they are in bad need of repair. These factors contribute to significantly raising the costs of operating in these areas. In most cases, they are prohibitive for investment into the provision of financial services.

Credit to Households and Private Sector in Zambia

Access to credit remains extremely limited in Zambia. Between 1990 and 2004, bank credit to the private sector, measured as a percentage of GDP, dropped slightly from 8.8 percent to 8.1 percent (see figure 4.6). At the same time, banks increased their holding of government securities.

Figure 4.6. Zambia: Domestic Credit to the Private Sector by Banks

Source: World Bank 2006c.

The number of firms and households borrowing from banks in Zambia also remains extremely low. In 2005, authorities estimated that the total number of outstanding loan accounts amounted to only 46,908, which includes 39,074 of accounts for individual people; the balance are accounts for firms, government entities, and so on. In other words, in Zambia only 0.37 percent of the population has a credit (or loan) account with a commercial bank.

As illustrated in figure 4.7, approximately 50 percent of all loan accounts are represented by credits and advances below $100.[7] Only 5,687 borrowers (4,028 individuals and 1,659 firms) had loans that represented 91 percent of the total loan portfolio of commercial banks in Zambia, reflecting the high concentration of wealth in the country.

In terms of volume, at the end of 2005, 73 percent of the total loan portfolio of banks was composed of loans granted to private firms. The remaining 27 percent was composed of loans granted to individuals and households. In the case of loans to private firms, 69 percent of credit is concentrated in the following sectors: agriculture, forestry and fishing, wholesale and retail trade, and manufacturing.

In Zambia, bank credit to private firms is not only scarce but also extremely expensive. The average annual interest rate on loans was 48 percent in 2005 (compared with a 20 percent inflation rate). Interviews with selected banks revealed that only large firms borrow at rates below the average (prime rate was 20 percent in 2005). The few SMEs in Zambia that are able to borrow from banks pay the average annual lending rate. Given the exorbitant level of existing lending rates, most loans have a short-term maturity (one to three months); only a few loans have a maturity of one year or more. Those few firms with sources of revenue in foreign currency are able to obtain financing from banks in U.S. dollars at lower interest rates.

Figure 4.7. Distribution of Bank Loans and Advances, March 2006

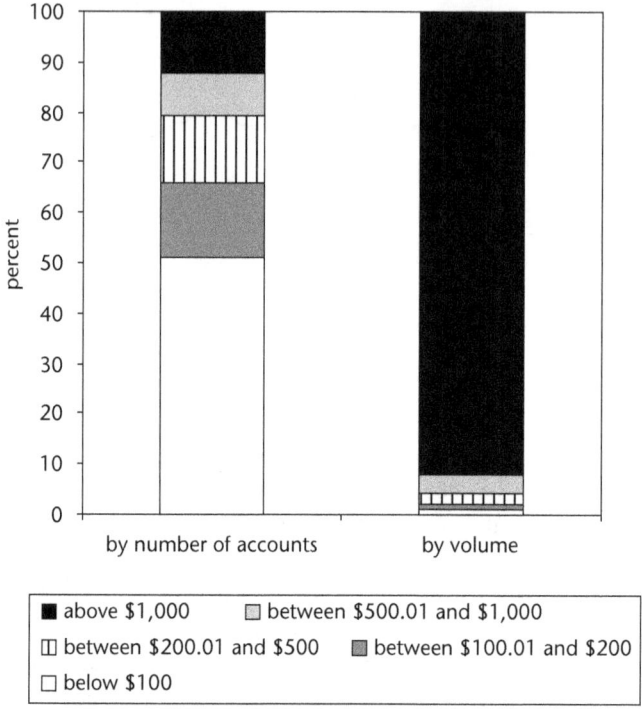

Source: Data from commercial banks in Zambia.

When owners of small enterprises in Zambia were asked how they would deal with a crisis in their businesses, 27 percent responded that they would borrow from family, friends, or neighbors; 22 percent would use savings; and 14 percent would accept a donation. Only 2.5 percent said they would borrow from a bank, 4 percent from an MFI, and 7 percent from an informal moneylender (Bank of Zambia 2006).

With the exception of high-income households, public servants, and employees of large companies, most Zambians do not have access to financing products offered by banks. Low salaries, lack of jobs in the formal economy, and high interest rates have precluded Zambian workers from having access to any type of consumer credit offered by the banking system.

In Zambia, most of the consumer lending consists of salary loans. These personal loans are granted to employees of public institutions and large private firms. The monthly payment is directly deducted from the worker's salary by the employer and remitted to the banking institution. Other types of consumer credit,

Figure 4.8. Distribution of Bank Credit to Private Firms in Zambia, 2005

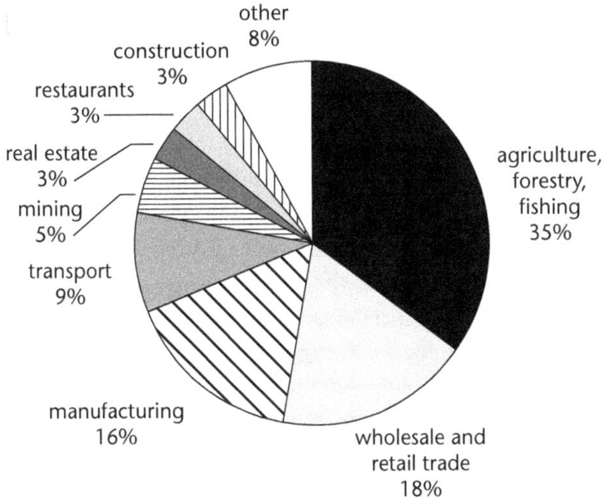

Source: Bank of Zambia.

such as credit cards and loans to acquire vehicles, do not exist in Zambia. Mortgages are offered by a few banks, but the aggregate volume of mortgages is still extremely low.

The abovementioned developments have resulted in a financial system that serves only a few people and firms in Zambia. Historically, the banking sector has been unwilling to lend to the medium, small, and micro sectors of the economy because of the high levels of risk associated with this sector. The harsh economic conditions that prevailed in the country in terms of high interest levels and volatile exchange rates meant borrowers found it difficult to repay their loans, which led to poor repayment rates. The situation was exacerbated by the inefficient legal system, which made it difficult to seek redress through the courts, and by the small-value transactions that made it uneconomical to do so.

Role of MFIs in Zambia

Unlike other countries in Sub-Saharan Africa where MFIs have grown by providing financial services to low-income households, in Zambia, MFIs remain extremely limited. According to data from the Association of Micro-finance Institutions of Zambia, MFIs only serve 50,000 customers, representing 0.005 percent of Zambia's population. The small number of MFIs in Zambia is unusual even in the context of other low-income countries where MFIs have achieved a larger outreach. MFIs are small, and combined, they do not represent more than 2 percent of the assets of banking institutions.

As noted, MFIs are not authorized to take deposits from the public. As a result, their main sources of funds come from the commercial banks and the donor community. Because of their low volume of operations and high operating costs, loans granted by MFIs have higher interest rates than those offered by commercial banks. Most households borrow only short-term loans (one month) from MFIs to meet family needs or, in the case of firms, to address short-term liquidity needs.

During the past years, MFIs have suffered multiple problems. MFIs have failed to become self-sustainable and many do not meet basic reporting and financial disclosure requirements. Moreover, the public has been defrauded by unscrupulous persons posing as MFI officers (see Chiumya 2006). To address these problems, authorities have designed a new regulatory framework for this type of financial institutions that would create two categories of MFIs—one based on size and one based on capital. According to the new Banking and Financial Services (Microfinance) Regulations of 2006, the minimum capital for deposit-taking MFIs is K 250 million ($78,125) and for nondeposit MFIs is K 25 million ($7,812). The scope of permissible activities for MFIs would vary for each group of MFIs. Larger and more capitalized institutions would be allowed to take deposits from the public and lend, whereas smaller institutions would be allowed to lend, but they would not be allowed to take deposits from the public. Eventu-

Figure 4.9. Assets of MFIs (as percent of assets of all financial institutions)

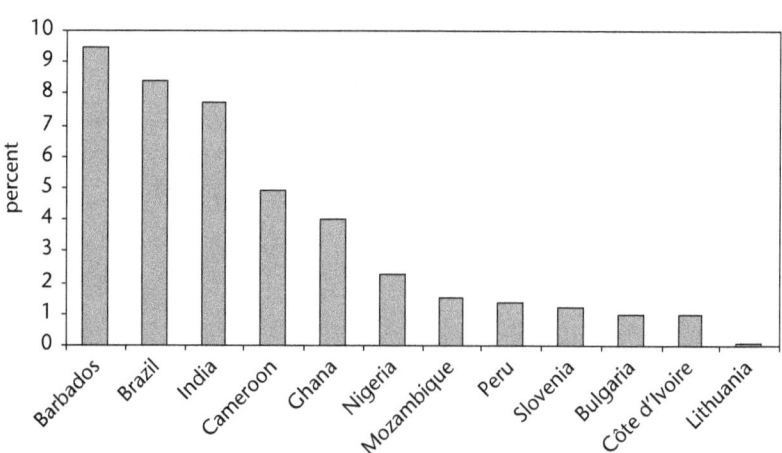

Source: World Bank database on FSAPs (2000–05).

ally, authorities expect the new regulatory regime will trigger a consolidation process among MFIs that will result in fewer but stronger MFIs in Zambia.

At this time, the major challenge for authorities is to establish a regulatory framework that promotes the protection of people's money, transparency, and sound governance of MFIs, and ensures the growth and long-term self-sustainability of the microfinance sector. Rules on secured and unsecured lending are critical, including a broad definition of the types of "assets" that can be used by borrowers to use as collateral for their loans. These regulations should be aligned with the economic condition of MFI clients in Zambia. Zambian authorities may wish to consider the experiences of successful cases of microfinance, such as in Jamaica, where MFIs serve 50 percent of the population on a sustainable basis.

Why has liberalization not delivered benefits?

Various mutually reinforcing factors may explain the lack of growth and limited outreach of the Zambian banking system since liberalization, including the following:

- Inadequate sequencing of liberalization reforms
- Insufficient economic growth, widespread poverty, and few jobs in the formal economy
- Crowding out of bank funds to finance the public sector
- Deficiencies in the basic infrastructure for financial sector development

Sequencing of Liberalization Reforms

Following the prevailing development approach advocated by the international community in the early 1990s, Zambia—like many other developing countries—transformed its closed and repressed financial system into an open and deregulated one. The problem is that this transformation was done without first building an effective legal, regulatory, and supervisory framework, which—combined with proper market incentives and monitoring—would encourage prudent risk-taking in banking institutions and ensure market discipline.

Following the liberalization measures of the early 1990s, it became more attractive for private investors to establish new financial institutions and make high profits from lending and trading operations in foreign exchange and treasury bills. Additionally, minimum capital requirements for establishing banks become progressively low because of the depreciation of the kwacha. Ten bank licenses were issued between 1991 and 1994, with the number of commercial banks in operation increasing from 10 in 1990 to 18 in 1994, as illustrated in figure 4.11.

Figure 4.10. Sequencing of Financial Sector Reform in Zambia

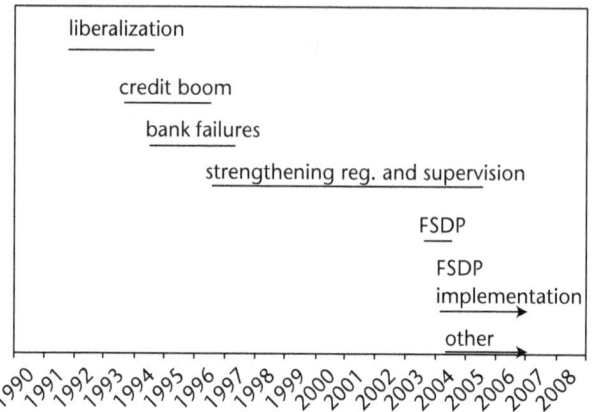

Source: Author's creation.

In the absence of an effective set of minimum prudential rules (in terms of proper loan classification and provisioning, internal controls, corporate governance, credit risk management, and so on) and the lack of risk-management capacity within commercial banks, the liberalization process of 1992–93 led to the rapid growth of financial institutions; a credit boom—bank credit to the private sector increased from 4.7 percent to 8.4 percent of GDP between 1993 and 1995; and, subsequently, a series of bank failures in 1995 and 1996.

Figure 4.11. Zambia: Growth in the Number of Banks, 1990–2004

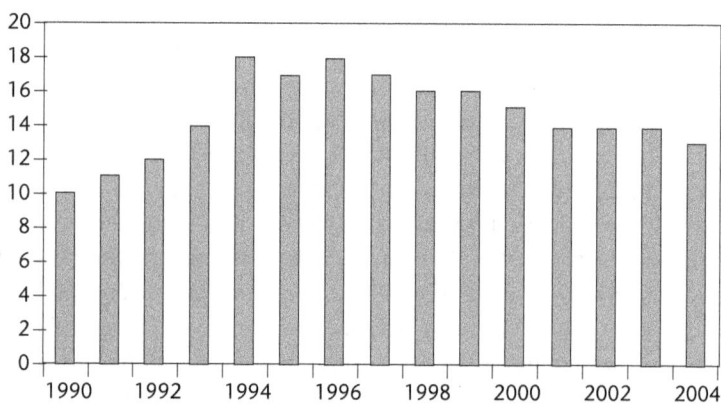

Source: Bank of Zambia.

Risky lending to attract new customers, lower revenue from foreign exchange operations, lower treasury bill yields, periodic shortages of liquidity, and limitations to raise capital eroded the solvency of many banks, causing nine bank failures between 1995 and 2001 that brought enormous losses to taxpayers and depositors (approximately 7 percent of GDP).

Bank failures had negative effects on the entire banking system, leaving a large stock of NPLs. At the end of 2005, NPLs in the banking system still amounted to 8.9 percent of total loan portfolio. Moreover, several banks scaled back their lending operations and increased their holding of government securities, which offered high yields at a lower risk for banks. Barclays, the largest bank in Zambia, refrained from any new lending for several years. It was only in 2006 that it started to lend again.

As the Zambian crisis has shown, a different sequencing of reforms may have avoided some of the problems faced by the banking system in the 1990s. In particular, more efforts could have been put toward strengthening the quality of regulation and supervision before liberalization is conducted (Maimbo 2002).

Following the first episodes of bank failures in 1995, Zambia established major measures to improve the quality of bank regulation and supervision. Between 1995 and 2000, bank regulation and supervision was significantly strengthened. In 2002, the IMF and World Bank completed an extensive review of the financial system, conducted under the aegis of the FSAP. In this review, it was found that Zambia satisfactorily complies with the BCPs on Bank Supervision, which constitute the most important international standard in bank regulation and supervision. Of the 30 principles assessed under the BCPs, Zambia was found to be compliant or largely compliant with 19 principles and noncompliant or materially noncompliant with 11 principles.

Major weaknesses were identified in the areas of independence of the central bank, remedial measures to deal with insolvent banks, management and control of market risks, internal controls, and anti–money laundering measures. The BoZ has been working to address the deficiencies found in the FSAP assessment and much progress has been accomplished, bringing regulation and supervision of banks closer to international standards.

Many deficiencies in the legal and regulatory framework still hold back financial sector development. Fortunately, authorities are showing enormous commitment to address these deficiencies. Following the release of the FSAP report, authorities drafted an FSDP, which contains a series of actions for the period from 2004 to 2010 to strengthen the overall financial system.

Poor Economic Performance and Macroeconomic Environment

Zambia, which until two decades ago was one of the most prosperous countries in Sub-Saharan Africa, now ranks as one of the least developed countries in the world.

The poor performance of Zambia's economy over the past 30 years as evidenced by the declining per capita GDP, which is now only a fraction of the level it was at independence, has significantly affected the level of poverty in the country. In 2004, 73 percent of the population was officially classified as poor (that is, below the national poverty line). Poor people do not have bank accounts either because no bank branches are located in their communities or because the minimum balances to open and maintain a bank account are extremely high, given their income level.

The situation has been exacerbated by the lack of jobs in the formal economy. Formal sector employment, which has not exceeded 20 percent of the labor force for a number of years, declined to 10 percent from 12 percent between 1996 and 2004. Following international standards on anti–money laundering and combat for terrorism financing, banks in Zambia have adopted guidelines that prevent them from providing services to customers that cannot be identified or cannot demonstrate their source of income. Although Zambians have national identification documents, many people can not prove their source of income.

A similar situation affects private sector firms in Zambia, in particular SMEs. There are no official statistics on the number of SMEs in Zambia, but it is believed that many of them are not registered, do not pay taxes, and do not have audited accounts. As a result, they can not access financial services—either savings, deposits, cash management, lending, guarantees, etc.—offered by banks.

An additional challenge faced by Zambia is related to the HIV/AIDS problem. Principally, HIV/AIDS threatens the country's capacity-building efforts because it strikes the educated and skilled as well as the uneducated. Consequently, it reverses and impedes the country's capacity by affecting human productivity and life expectancy. The long periods of illness of the skilled personnel in employment has translated into severe loss in economic productivity, which leads to considerable loss to the employer in terms of staff hours. Today, life expectancy in Zambia is only 36 years, largely because of the HIV/AIDS problem.

During the past years, banks in Zambia have operated in an environment characterized not only by low economic growth and falling per capita incomes, but also by high inflation, a large fiscal deficit, exchange rate volatility, and an external debt burden.

Between 1997 and 2001, inflation in Zambia averaged 24.3 percent, which was largely caused by the fiscal deficit, the high growth of money supply and depreciating kwacha, and occasional shocks such as the effects of drought. A significant fall in inflation requires, among other things, a reduction in the government's budget deficit, which will reduce its need to borrow from domestic markets to finance the deficit.

For many years, persistent fiscal indiscipline led the government to increase its reliance on domestic borrowing for funds. As a consequence, loans currently rep-

**Table 4.3. Zambia: Macroeconomic Indicators,
1997–2005**

Indicators	1997–2001	2002	2003	2004	2005
Real GDP growth	2.4%	3.3%	5.1%	5.4%	5.1%
Real per capita GDP growth	0.2%	0.9%	2.7%	2.9%	2.6%
Real per capita GDP*	$313	$325	$334	$343	$352
Consumer prices**	24.7%	22.2%	21.4%	18.0%	18.3%
Overall fiscal balance, including grants (in percent of GDP)	–4.4%	–5.1%	–6.0%	–3.0%	–2.3%
Trade balance (in percent of GDP)	–5.0%	–6.9%	–7.2%	1.5%	0.8%
External debt to official creditors (in percent of GDP)	181.6%	135.4%	107.9%	77.8%	54.3%
Nominal effective exchange rates (Index: 2000=100)	127.0	85.4	70.8	69.0	78.6

Source: World Bank 2006c.

*In U.S. dollars, at 2000 prices, using 2000 exchange rates.

**Annual average percent change.

resent about one-third of total assets only, while total deposits are equivalent to about 70 percent of assets. High treasury bill rates with their zero-risk weighting for capital requirements and use in the MLAR have induced banks to hold large amounts of government securities. This concentration is especially high for small banks, with security holdings equivalent to one and a half to two times that of outstanding loans. Foreign exchange liquidity is also relatively high, as banks lend only about 20 percent of foreign exchange deposits, compared with kwacha loans equivalent to 70 percent of deposits.

Deposits raised by banks in Zambia are not just used to purchase government securities. They are also placed in foreign institutions abroad, as illustrated in figure 4.12. In 2002, 26 percent of total bank assets were placed in instruments in other financial institutions outside Zambia.[8] However, the trend toward using local deposits to purchase government securities or invest overseas has reversed in recent years in favor of more domestic loans, as shown in the asset structure of banks in Zambia. Between 2002 and 2005, the share of loans in the total assets of banks increased from 19 percent to 30 percent.

The macroeconomic environment in Zambia has improved since 2004 when average annual inflation eased to 18 percent, the first time in decades that annual

**Figure 4.12.   Zambia: Balance Sheet Structure of Banks,
2002–05**

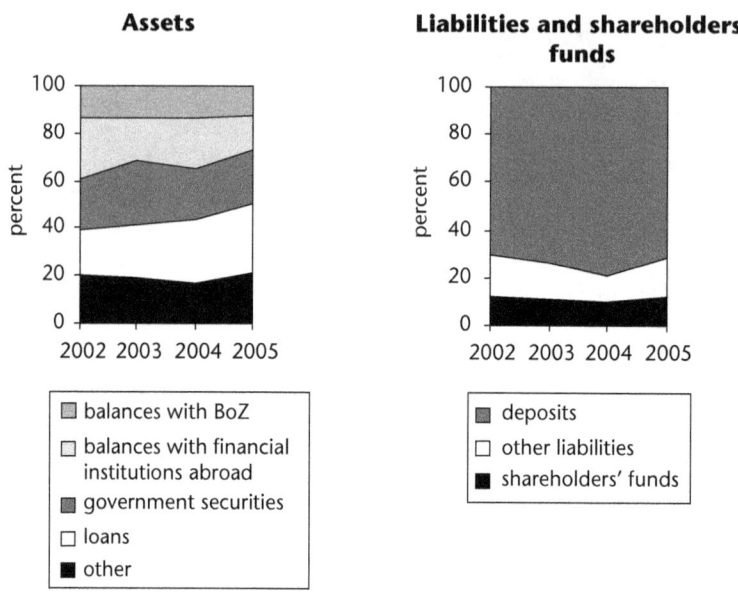

Source: Data from Bank of Zambia.

price growth has been below 20 percent. The fall in interest rates in the last couple of years, stabilization of the exchange rate, and reduction in domestic borrowing by the government has meant that banks are increasingly being forced to rely on their traditional source of revenue, namely, the provision of credit. This has resulted in various initiatives, including the introduction of unsecured lending to salaried employees.

Since November 2003, interest rates on government securities have declined sharply. This is attributed to the following factors: the reduction in the statutory reserve ratio from 17.5 percent to 14 percent in October 2003, the reduction in government borrowing, and the stability of the kwacha against the U.S. dollar because of the improvement in the external environment. With declining real interest rates on government securities, commercial banks are expected to lower their own lending rates and increase credit to the private sector.

Weak Payment System Infrastructure

Financial sector development presupposes, among other requirements, a well-functioning, efficient, and reliable clearing and payments system. The payment system provides an essential conduit for the circular flow of money and execution of monetary policy. In addition, properly designed payments systems can contribute to financial system stability and promote access to banking and financial services. Over the years, several weaknesses in Zambia's National Payments System have contributed to undermining the development of the Zambian financial markets.

In the case of the check-clearing system, for instance, the use of checks has declined for a number of reasons, including high frequency of checks issued against insufficient funds, delays in clearing funds on checks, and poor and slow processing and operational systems in banks. The implication was that bank customers who were paid by check were at the mercy of their bankers. This situation created huge amounts of float as a result of funds being tied up in the clearing process.

The BoZ has made significant progress in modernizing the payments system in Zambia by reforming the legal framework for payment systems, establishing electronic check clearing, improving the security of check paper, and introducing machine-readable checks, as well as direct debit and credit clearing (DDACC) to pay bills and salaries, and a large value clearing system (that is, real-time gross settlement system). The number of days for clearing a cross-country check has been reduced from 21 to 10 days, while interprovincial and local clearing days were reduced to 6 and 4 days, respectively.

Currently, the few banks with automated teller machines (ATMs) and point-of-sale (POS) terminals operate on an individual basis. ATM and cash point cards are used by 7.5 percent of the adult population, while other transaction mediums such as credit cards, debit cards, and DDAC (direct debit and credit) are used by less then 1 percent of the adult population (Finmark Trust 2006). Measures need to be developed and implemented that will ensure that these facilities are shared by payment system participants, including non-bank participants.

Deficiencies in the Legal, Regulatory, and Judiciary Framework

At this time, three issues require attention to promote financial sector development: the ineffective judicial system, the lack of credit information available, and the weak insolvency regime.

Zambia has a relatively well-developed legal and judicial system compared with other African countries, but there is scope for improvement in several areas. The legal process has resulted in delays in the timely disposal of cases involving the collection of bad loans. Collection efforts have been weak for defaulters in public financial institutions, as well as in failed banks. Failure to take strong measures against questionable banking practices that led to bank failures also contributed to serious moral hazard.

Although the operation of the courts continues to attract criticism, the increased emphasis on mediation and arbitration as alternative dispute resolution mechanisms is welcome. This process has done much to refute complaints over delays in the handling of commercial disputes. Nevertheless, the financial community continues to attribute difficulties in collecting loans to legal procedures and the ease with which borrowers can block creditor efforts to collect delinquent loans.

Authorities have identified the following shortcomings of the legal and judicial system. The hope is that these shortcomings will be addressed through the FSDP and with the support of the donor community:

- Delays in delivering judgments
- Lack of reported judgments
- Bureaucratic procedures leading to delays in the enactment of new laws
- Fragmented laws relating to the financial sector
- Lack of guidelines and directives under principal acts
- Lack of adequate legal framework for regulating foreign currency transactions
- Lack of financial sector consumer protection laws
- Inadequate skills for enforcement of the law relating to financial crimes
- Underreporting of financial crimes to the relevant law enforcement agencies

The credit bureau being set up by the Bankers' Association is a critical step to improve market information and to strengthen the credit culture. The current plan is to start the credit bureau with negative information on defaulters. That effort should be supported and expanded as soon as technically feasible to include positive information. This will help clients with a clean credit history enjoy expanding services and lower costs. Over time, the credit bureau database should be extended to small and medium-size firms, for which little information is available and that need to use their good credit record to supplement their limited collateral.

In the past, the collection efforts against defaulting borrowers in some public financial institutions, as well as failed banks, have been ineffective. In Zambia, it is widely believed that the treatment of the management of failed banks during the late 1990s was lenient. No legal action was taken in some cases in which banking laws were violated, and some managers were allowed to take jobs elsewhere in the financial system. Failure to take strong measures against the questionable banking practices that led to bank failures and ineffective collection efforts has contributed to the widespread belief that misconduct in the financial sector will not be prosecuted.

The BoZ needs to develop more effective arrangements to deal with bank failures. It should establish accountability for the management of bad loans. A cumbersome process of liquidating insolvent banks has resulted in loan recovery difficulties, partly because borrowers' capacity to continue borrowing from the banking system does not seem to be affected by nonpayment to banks in liquidation.

Need to Adapt Prudential Requirements to Zambia's Needs

One of the growing challenges for Zambia is that the adoption and enforcement of a number of international standards of prudential regulation are in tension with the goal of increasing access for low-income households. Three particular regulations appear to be negatively affecting access to finance: the zero-risk weighting on government securities, enforcement of KYC rules, and reform of collateralized lending.

As discussed above, banks in Zambia prefer to buy government debt securities because of the zero-risk weighting of government securities (recommended by the Basel Capital Accord), and thus the need to provide regulatory capital for banks is lower. This situation is not only faced by banks in Zambia, but also throughout Sub-Saharan Africa. Banking sector claims on governments in the region, as a percent of total claims, have increased from 19 percent in the period from 1990 to 1994 to 26 percent in the period from 2000 to 2004 (IMF 2006).

Another regulatory constraint in increasing access to finance is related to the KYC rules issued by Zambia as part of its efforts to join international efforts to prevent money laundering and terrorism financing. KYC rules require banks to strictly verify the identity of their customers and their sources of income. In a country with 90 percent of the workforce in the informal economy, however, the requirement of income verification has become a major obstacle preventing the wider provision of banking services. Although it is important for banks to know their customers and verify that they have the capability to repay their loans, more flexibility is needed in Zambia in terms of documents and practices used by banks to assess the creditworthiness of their prospective clients.

Several banks in Zambia have adopted guidelines that prevent them from recognizing movable assets as collateral. As a result, electrodomestic appliances and other types of movable assets—which constitute the main or only assets owned by the poor—cannot be pledged as collateral to obtain a loan. Moreover, unsecured lending is penalized through high provisioning requirements. As a result, the poor people cannot access lending products from commercial banks.

Although it is important to prevent money-laundering activities, maintain the integrity of a banking system, and ensure that banks manage credit risks appropriately, the above regulatory requirements need to be revised to ensure that they do not prevent banks from serving low-income households in Zambia.

Box 4.1. Testimony of the Difficulties Faced by a Banker in Serving Low-Income Households in Zambia Because of the Know Your Customer (KYC) rules

"... KYC does not favor nor meet the needs of our poorer people to have access to finance. We are required to demand the following:

A utility bill, for example for water, electricity or telephone. Many Zambians live in areas where these facilities are either non-existent or the bills are in the name of someone else, such as a landlord. In order to avoid paying tax on the rental income, most landlords will not allow their bills to be used. The other reason for their reluctance is plain suspicion that they may be held liable for the borrowing, jealousy or the mobility of these tenants who change accommodation often as rates can be raised at any time.

In the rural areas and in the villages, all these documents do not exist but the chief or traditional ruler can verify your address. Which financial institution will accept this proof? KYC does not give them the leeway to vary these rules as the Central Bank also enforces these rules and banks are rated on their compliance.

They also need passport size photos and copies of identity cards. The latter is available as it is a national requirement to have a registration card but photos in certain locations are difficult to obtain.

Banks also ask for a minimum balance in their deposit accounts. These minimum balances prevent people from using banks.

For small businesses, they must produce the documents asked for under the Companies Act or Societies Act or Co-operative Act. There are Certificates of Incorporation, certificates of registration as well as tax clearance certificates, trading licenses and so on. These can all be obtained with patience and some literacy levels to deal with the bureaucracy. There are different offices and ministries involved as well as fees at every point.

In the case of a pilot group of 10 from the market here, we got them to provide their IDs and passport size photos and we then used our version of the group lending model by having them give a small deposit towards the loan individually, opening one account in their group name, and then giving them a lump sum each. The deposit was used to open the account as our minimum deposit was met and also acted as a commitment. They have since paid back two installments and they are on time and doing well. They have increased their stocks and got the council to give them a better location. We will increase the loan amounts once full repayment is made."

Source: Testimony of a commercial banker in Zambia. Reproduced with permission.

Fragmented Regional Markets

Significant benefits likely will result from regional integration of financial services markets. A central consideration is the inclusion of significant scale economies in banking, securities markets, and payment systems. For instance, modern banks, insurance companies, pension funds, payments systems, and securities markets all use computer-based technology that is scale dependent for efficient operation. Even in their smallest configurations, these technologies often exceed the needs of institutions in small financial systems. As a consequence, larger financial markets tend to have an increased number of participants and consequently are more competitive. This leads to lower financial product pricing, increased access to finance, and increased levels of innovation than in smaller financial systems. An additional benefit is that, in larger markets, the regulatory infrastructure tends to be of higher quality and lower cost than in smaller markets (World Bank 2006a).

There is a spectrum of possible levels of financial integration. Some envisage an extreme situation in which all economies in Southern Africa have unified their financial systems, which operate with a single currency, single monetary authority, and a single regulator and supervisor. Others have a less ambitious view of regional financial sector integration, in which all financial sector institutions can operate across borders without facing any hurdle while maintaining domestic currencies and regulatory institutions.

The Common Market for Eastern and Southern Africa (COMESA) has not made substantial progress in terms of financial integration. The treaty calls for the integration of financial structures and, since 1999, member states have been working to harmonize their regulatory frameworks. The COMESA Bankers' Association has also been set up to exchange information and strengthen correspondent relationships among banks. Jansen and Vennes (2006), however, conclude that regional integration has not proceeded smoothly despite regulatory cooperation at the highest levels. In addition, they found that countries that were part of COMESA and the Southern African Development Community (SADC) were experiencing political problems and issues stemming from incompatible and overlapping legal obligations. Hence, little progress has been made on these ambitious regional integration agendas.

Macroeconomic divergence is not by itself a reason to hold back from increased integration. Global financial markets provide a good example of how markets based in vastly different economies, in terms of macroeconomic balances, can be closely linked and even interdependent. Indeed, differences in economic prospects, different transactional cost structures, and varying risk premiums usually influence the flow of capital and portfolio choices; and these differences can actually encourage financial transactions.

Economic and political concerns, however, are raised by integration in Southern Africa. On the issue of harmonizing financial infrastructure, for example, less developed countries in the region do not need to invest in a sophisticated payment system architecture that will not be used in the foreseeable future. These countries should not give a high priority to developing regulatory frameworks and standards for certain financial instruments (such as synthetic products) and institutions (such as option exchanges). On the political side, policy makers have expressed their concern that "integration" in Southern Africa actually means "convergence" to South African structures and processes, which could facilitate further domination by South African institutions.

In the interim, it is desirable to work toward creating better-integrated financial markets that are similar, in terms of functioning, to global financial markets. Hence, the focus should be on creating an environment in which market participants have the same information set, identical benchmarks, and similar pricing mechanisms for different risks so that financial sector participants can work across countries in the region without hurdles or prohibitive transaction costs. This would require that Southern African markets have a certain commonality, compatibility, and interoperability with respect to the following: a physical infrastructure that provides timely and reliable trading and fund flow mechanisms; timely access to reliable data that conform to the same standards; and a well-understood and well-established dispute resolution mechanism with accompanying enforcement capabilities.

Proactive policies to promote access to financial services

Promoting access to finance has proven to be a complex issue in Zambia, as well as in most developing countries. Since independence, Zambia has actively pursued policies to promote financial sector development. During that time, it swung from the extensive use of government controls on the financial system in the 1970s and 1980s to the establishment of a market-friendly environment and deregulated financial system in the 1990s, in both cases with disappointing results.

A larger and more inclusive banking system is needed to alleviate poverty and establish the foundations of sustainable economic growth and development of Zambia. Sound and efficient banking institutions mobilize savings and channel them to productive uses, allowing firms to reach their growth potential and improving productivity. Moreover, inclusive financial institutions open up opportunities for energetic and able entrepreneurs. They enable people to smooth consumption and help households and firms manage their risks.

The financial services needed by poor households and small enterprises in Zambia include not only credit, but also the simple and essential tools of a safe and low-cost way to save, efficient payment and remittance services, and affordable insurance against numerous hazards.

No "magic bullets" will rapidly resolve the limited supply of financial services in Zambia. Efforts are needed on various fronts to remove the obstacles and bottlenecks that drag on the growth of the banking system, including the establishment of a credit bureau, modernization of the payment system, strengthening of the legal and judiciary framework, promotion of market discipline, establishment of efficient mechanisms for resolution of bank failures, and the strengthening of bank supervision.

In addition to the above financial sector reforms, efforts are needed to preserve macroeconomic stability, reduce the fiscal deficit, improve the business environment, create new jobs in the formal economy, increase the average income of households, and reduce the number of firms operating in the informal economy. Thus, a combination of financial sector reforms, macroeconomic stability, and a better business environment is needed for a deeper and more efficient banking system that promotes economic growth and prosperity in Zambia.

In the short-term, however, a relevant question for Zambia and the donor community is whether government intervention to foster financial development and broaden access is necessary and, if so, what form should that intervention take.

At an international level, there seems to be an increasing consensus (see De la Torre, Gozzi, and Schmukler 2006) that a market-friendly role indeed exists for the visible hand of the government to promote access in the short run, while ongoing institutional reforms are under way. The important qualifier is that the government needs to be highly selective in its interventions, always trying to ensure that they work with the market, never against it.

Instruments that distort the functioning of markets often fail to improve access to services or do so at a high cost in terms of efficiency

This has been the case with credit guarantee systems in Zambia and elsewhere in the region. Credit guarantee systems are mechanisms in which a third party, the *guarantor*, pledges to guarantee loans to a particular group of borrowers. Credit guarantee systems reduce the lender's expected credit losses—even if the probability of default remains unchanged—acting as a form of insurance against default. Around the world, public credit guarantee systems are widespread. The largest and more established guarantee schemes are followed primarily in developed countries, including Canada, Japan, the United States, and several European countries. The general experience with credit guarantee systems, especially in developing countries, has been poor to mixed: most systems have depleted their reserves because of high credit losses and bad investment decisions and, in many cases, they have been designed to channel funds to certain sectors without due regard to loss rates.

Box 4.2. Credit Guarantee Scheme Operations in Zambia (1987–93)

The Zambian Credit Guarantee Scheme (CGS) was set up in 1987 and was operated by the Bank of Zambia (BoZ). The objective of the CGS was to provide protection to financial institutions against losses incurred for credit exposures to small enterprises. The fund was financed from the net profits of the BoZ with a view toward it becoming self-supporting in the "shortest" time practicable. Honoring of any guaranteed exposure to a financial institution was to be made upon the BoZ being satisfied that, at the time such loan was made or funds advanced, financial institutions acted in good faith and in accordance with good banking practice.

The CGS, although well intended, faced problems on two fronts. First there was general apprehension with having the BoZ back the CGS. Ideally, such activities would be more appropriately placed under a development banking institution. Second, an element of moral hazard was evident over time as borrower repayment rates deteriorated. This was partly on account of the knowledge that such exposures were guaranteed by the central bank. To this extent, therefore, the self-sustainability of the fund in the longer term became questionable. Because of these reasons, particularly the first, the credit guarantee scheme was abolished in 1993.

Source: Interviews with Bank of Zambia officials.

Critics of public credit guarantee systems argue that these schemes cannot decrease asymmetric information problems in credit markets and are even likely to increase them. Public guarantee systems may increase moral hazard for borrowers and lenders: borrowers who know that their loans are guaranteed by the government may not feel obligated to repay them, and lenders may have fewer incentives for screening and monitoring borrowers, because guarantees cover their credit losses. An open question, therefore, is whether credit guarantee systems can be designed in a market-friendly way, reducing their unintended consequences while at the same time promoting private financial market activity.

If programs are well designed to reach their target, and if the institutional capacity exists to implement the project and avoid political capture, then they can have an equalizing effect. This was demonstrated with the Enterprise Development Program (EDP) and the activities of the marketing board in Zambia.

Despite the widespread acknowledgment of its failure as a sustainable line of credit to increase access, the Zambia EDP may be an example of how financial intermediary lending can have a positive impact by providing scarce medium-term lending for investment and export production to SMEs (OED 2004, p. iii).

Under this project, the funds were channeled through the BoZ, but measures were established to strengthen the BoZ's capacity to monitor on-lending and successfully resist political pressures to capture the funds. In addition, the facility allowed local banks to freely determine on-lending rates, thereby allowing competition between banks that were receiving funds from the project (World Bank 2003).

New instruments attempt to reconcile equity with efficiency

Soft and hard commands on providers can work, but they must be designed realistically and flexibly to allow the private sector to choose the most efficient and sustainable means of extending access. In South Africa, in response to pressure from the government or "moral suasion" (for example, the government suggested that it would introduce new regulation if no action was taken by banks to improve access amongst poorer groups), representatives of the financial services industry signed the Financial Sector Charter in 2003. In doing so, the industry attempted to increase the number of poorer people (Living Standard Measure 1-5) with a bank account from 32 percent to 80 percent by 2008. To achieve this goal the key players in the sector have collaborated to design the Mzansi account, which offers fewer services, but has lower transaction charges, such as cash deposits and ATM withdrawals. The product has been highly successful with 180,000 new customers in the first six weeks. Thus, government pressure has pushed banks to innovate and to engineer a product that allows downscaling to be sustainable and even profitable. This example underlines the notion that allowing banks to decide on the extent, process, and technology of their expansion not only avoids conflict with the regulator, but also results in the kind of innovation and sectorwide coordination necessary to achieve the set objective.

Access to financial services might be better attained by exploiting the synergies between services sectors to increase the likelihood of achieving access goals

Banks have found it challenging to move profitably to downscale markets because of the nature of demand in poorer and rural areas, which is small but transaction intensive. As a result, many countries have moved toward "correspondent banking" as a way to broaden the range of delivery points and allow for small-scale banking. Banks outsource services typically undertaken at branches—like receiving loan applications, making deposit withdrawals, and paying invoices—to nonfinancial institutions with a significant network of outlets, such as convenience stores or lottery houses. In Zambia, banks could achieve this through the use of the postal network. This has been highly successful in Brazil, for example, where it was estimated that the cost of providing banking services through the existing post office was 0.5 percent of the cost to build a new branch (De la Torre, Gozzi, and Schmukler 2006). Building effective and strong partnerships between state-owned postal operators and financial institutions has proven to be a complex and cumbersome process, however, as the divorce of Zampost and the National Savings and Credit Bank underlines. A recent report on lessons for expanding access to financial services through the postal networks highlights two particular weaknesses that undermine the potential for public-private partnerships. First, private banks are loath to work with an institution that is not run on a commercial basis, is dependent on a nontransparent provision of subsidies between the separate services being offered by the post office, and that has little tradition of accountability (World Bank 2006b). The second problem is the lack of investment in Information and Communications Technology (ICT) in many postal networks in Africa, which provides another argument for bundling access to postal and banking services with access to telecommunications networks.

If services are effectively bundled, they will benefit from the positive spillovers of joint consumption. This approach underlines the recent "Zyonse" product, which was developed by the National Resources Institute for smallholder farmers in Zambia. The packaged financial product consists of insurance, primarily covering weather insurance; production credit and the ability to collateralize produce to improve crop marketing; and easy access to commodity finance. The product is to be offered by financing banks, with the insurance cover provided by credible insurance companies. Farmers ultimately pay the insurance premium, but it may be initially financed by the banks. The loan covenants require farmers to deposit and market their produce using the warehouse receipt system (Onumah 2005).

In general, bundling of services will create a significant regulatory challenge to ensure competitive and cost-based access to shared networks—the problem that motivated some of the separations. If banks are to use the postal network, they must continue to remain institutionally separate from the postal service, coming under supervision of the central bank. Regulating access to networks has proved to be a challenge even within a single sector. In South Africa, incumbent banks have been accused of erecting barriers in the payments system against smaller banks that want to introduce new technologies (World Bank 2006b). In Zambia, Zamtel does not provide cost-based access to its fixed-line network, thus limiting competition in the Internet sector. The problems will be greater if multiple services are to be provided from the same network, but the potential benefits in terms of access provide good reasons to look for solutions.

Although the specific form of intervention is an issue that needs to be analyzed and discussed in a separate document, interventions should be relatively small and temporary, and should be terminated when the underlying causes of the problem of access have been removed. Mechanisms must be in place to prevent political capture that may undermine the temporary nature of the interventions or their compatibility with the long-run objective of institutional reform and financial market development. Promarket activism should favor a policy strategy that explicitly creates room for a process of discovery and learning by doing as the interventions are implemented, and may be useful in giving the authorities a first-hand understanding of what legislation or enforcement mechanisms are missing for certain innovations to take off. The ultimate goal is to broaden access in ways that create financial markets where they are missing and that enhance the functioning of existing markets.

Notes

1. Some 90 percent of the workforce is estimated to work in the informal economy.

2. Since independence, the foreign exchange market has undergone various changes. From 1964 through the early 1980s, the foreign exchange market was characterized by administrative controls, with the kwacha firstly being pegged to the U.S. dollar then later to the Special Drawing Rights. In the 1980s through the 1990s, the exchange rate was determined by a quasi-market system and later by a Foreign Exchange Committee. The market was finally liberalized in 1992.

3. Foreign banks have operated in Zambia uninterruptedly since the early 1900s. Even during the phase of nationalization of strategic sectors in the 1970s, foreign banks remained untouched.

4. Of the remaining seven banks, the Zambia National Commercial Bank, a state-owned bank, is the second-largest institution operating in Zambia, holding 20 percent of the banking system assets. Five other banks owned by local investors—African Banking Corporation, Cavmont Merchant Bank, First Alliance Bank, Intermarket Banking Corporation, and Investrust Bank—together hold 8 percent of the banking system assets. Finally, one bank, the Indo Zambia Bank is a joint venture between the Governments of Zambia and India and holds the remaining 6 percent of the banking system assets.

5. In addition to commercial banks, the financial sector includes non-bank financial institutions (composed of the three building societies, some microfinance institutions, the National Savings and Credit Bank [NSCB], the Development Bank of Zambia, and 37 change bureaus and leasing companies), insurance companies, pension funds, and the capital markets.

6. A better indicator of how well rural population is served by bank branches is the number of people living close to a branch. Unfortunately, that information was not available at the time of this study. In addition, the indicator of the number of branches does not consider whether former branches in rural areas were closed because of the decline of the population caused by migration to urban areas.

7. The large number of loans below US$100 can be attributed to the large number of nonperforming loans that are still in the books of banks and that have become small over time.

8. Many reasons explain why banks in Zambia, as well as in other countries in Africa, have large amounts of deposits abroad. First, they need to maintain these deposits abroad to finance imports because these are usually collateralized for letters of credits outside. Second, corresponding banks usually demand these balances to continue with corresponding relations. Much more research is needed to determine the causes for the placement of deposits abroad.

References

Chiumya, Chiara. 2006. "The Regulation of Microfinance in Zambia." Essays on Regulation and Supervision. CGAP, Washington, DC.

CGAP (Consultative Group to Assist the Poor). 2006. *Access for All*. Washington, DC: CGAP.

De la Torre, Augusto, Juan Carlos Gozzi, and Sergio L. Schmukler. 2006, April. "Innovative Experiences in Access to Finance: Friendly Roles for the Visible Hand?" World Bank, Washington, DC.

Detragiache, Enrica, Thierry Tressel, and Poonam Gupta. 2006. "Foreign Banks in Poor Countries: Theory and Evidence." International Monetary Fund Working Paper 06/18. IMF, Washington, DC.

FinMark Trust. 2006. "FinScope Zambia: Measuring Financial Access in Zambia." Report prepared for the Bank of Zambia, Lusaka, Zambia.

IMF (International Monetary Fund). 2006. *Regional Economic Outlook. Sub-Saharan Africa.* Washington, DC: IMF.

Jansen, Marion, and Yannick Vennes. 2006. "Liberalizing Financial Services Trade in Africa: Going Regional and Multilateral." WTO Staff Working Paper No. ERSD-2006-03, World Bank, Washington, DC.

Maimbo, S. 2002. "Explaining Regulatory Failure in Zambia." *Journal of International Development* 14: 229–48.

Martínez Pería, María Soledad, A. Demirgüç, and T. Beck. 2005. "Access to and Use of Banking Services Across Countries." World Bank Policy Research Paper, World Bank, Washington, DC.

Ministry of Finance and National Planning of the Republic of Zambia. 2004. "Financial Sector Development Plan, 2004–2009." Lusaka, Zambia.

Onumah, Gideon. 2005. "Feasibility of Introducing an All-Inclusive Financial Product in Zambia to Improve Access to Rural Finance." National Resources Institute, London.

OED (Operations Evaluation Department). 2004, May 6. "Review of Bank Lending for Lines of Credit." World Bank, Washington, DC.

World Bank. 2003. "Implementation Completion Report on a Credit for an Enterprise Development Project." World Bank, Washington, DC.

———. 2004. "South Africa: Technology and Access to Financial Services." World Bank, Washington, DC.

———. 2006a. "Regional Financial Sector Integration in Southern Africa: Issues and Opportunities." World Bank, Washington, DC.

———. 2006b. "The Role of Postal Networks in Expanding Access to Financial Services." World Bank, Washington, DC.

———. 2006c. *World Development Indicators.* Washington, DC: World Bank.

Annex 1. Statistical Data

Table A-1.1. Banks Licensed in Zambia, 1906–94

Name of bank	Year of incorporation
Standard Chartered Bank	1906
Barclays Bank	1918
Stanbic Bank	1956
Zambia National Commercial Bank	1970
Citibank	1979
Meridien Bank BIAO*	1984
Indo-Zambia Bank	1984
African Commercial Bank*	1984
Finance Bank	1984
Manifold Investment Bank*	1987
Zambia Export and Import Bank*	1987
Cooperative Bank*	1989
Commerce Bank*	1989
Union Bank Zambia*	1991
Cavmont Merchant Bank	1992
First Alliance Bank	1992
New Capital Bank	1992
First Merchant Bank Zambia*	1992
Mercantile Bank*	1993
Meridien BIAO Bank*	1993
Ital Bank*	1993
Continental Bank*	1993
Safe Deposit Bank*	1993
Prudence Bank*	1994
Credit Africa Bank*	1994

Source: Bank of Zambia.

Note: * = failed banks.

Table A-1.2. Banks in Liquidation

Name of bank	Liquidation date
Meridien BIAO Bank	September 1995
African Commercial Bank	February 1996
Zambia Export and Import Bank	May 1997
Prudence Bank	February 1998
Credit Africa Bank	March 1998
Manifold Investment Bank	March 1998
First Merchant Bank Zambia	March 1999
Commerce Bank	January 2001
Union Bank Zambia	March 2001

Source: Bank of Zambia.

5

AIR TRANSPORT: REVITALIZING YAMOUSSOUKRO

Charles Schlumberger

Overview

The aviation market of Zambia is small and has witnessed uneven growth. The passenger movements at the four international airports (Lusaka, Ndola, Livingstone, and Mfuwe) in 2005 amounted to 675,000, of which 80 percent were international arrivals. Overall, the traffic at Zambian airports has grown by 3.1 percent per year on average, which is in line with the general growth of air traffic in Africa. Although international traffic has grown by 7.1 percent per year on average between 1995 and 2004, domestic traffic has decreased at an average rate of 5.3 percent per year. This decline is attributed to the liquidation of the nationalized Zambia Airways in 1994, which operated subsidized domestic flights. The air cargo market plays an important role for the country's exports of perishable products, such as cut flowers and vegetables, which are mostly destined for Europe (the United Kingdom and the Netherlands). In 2005, there were five weekly cargo freighters operating to Lusaka with a total dedicated capacity of 175 to 250 tons (about 40 tons per aircraft). But, in early 2006, the number of flights had declined to two per week with a total capacity of about 80 to 100 tons, and a significant proportion of vegetable exports was being sent by road to Johannesburg and then by air to Europe. The reason for the reduction in flights is reported to be the high cost of fuel in Lusaka, as well as the diseconomies arising from the small volume of exports that do not fill an aircraft.

For a small market like Zambia, which has a stake in tourism and horticulture, openness is vital and was even accomplished in principle through regional agreements, but these agreements have not been fully implemented. Somewhat unusually, Zambia liquidated its loss-making national airline in the mid-1990s and liberalized entry into its market. Furthermore, the implementation of Fifth Freedom liberalization in the African Union was agreed on in the Yamoussoukro Decision (YD), which became fully binding in 2002. Even three years after becoming fully binding, however, the agreement has had little impact on Zambia and its neighbors. Given the failure of the YD, the Common Market for Eastern and Southern Africa (COMESA) has agreed to liberalize air transport services among its member states with regulations and a mechanism similar to the YD. But here, too, implementation has been partial and subject to delays.

As a consequence, Zambia's international air transport remains based on relatively restrictive bilateral air service agreements (BASA). The Government of Zambia (GoZ) has signed 72 BASAs over the past years of which only eight are currently in use. The most important bilateral relationship is with South Africa, with whom traffic between five city pairs was agreed. The capacity of these traffic rights was only partially used until recently, when traffic rights were assigned to a low-cost carrier, which operates under a Zambian operator's certificate. Both Zambia and South Africa have denied Fifth Freedom rights to other countries: the Republic of Egypt (Cairo-Lusaka-Johannesburg) was refused by South Africa in 2001, Libya (Tripoli-Lusaka-Johannesburg) was refused by Zambia in 2001, Ethiopia (Addis Ababa-Lusaka-Johannesburg) was refused by Zambia in 2005, and Nigeria (Lagos-Lusaka-Johannesburg) was refused by Zambia during BASA negotiations. A request by Kenya to fly Nairobi-Lusaka-Harare was refused by Zambia in 2005.

High operating costs seem to be deterring airlines from flying via Zambia. High jet fuel prices drive these high operation costs. Jet fuel, which is refined in Zambia by a 50 percent government and 50 percent privately held refinery, is reported by the Zambian Export Growers Association (ZEGA) to be more than 50 percent more expensive than fuel in neighboring countries. According to British Airways, they pay more than 40 percent more to refuel in Lusaka than in Johannesburg or Nairobi. The International Air Transport Association (IATA) has recently examined the high fuel cost in Zambia and called for a reduction. The price is thought to be controlled by a Zambian refinery, which is not operating efficiently, and so far there has been no reduction. In addition, jet fuel is taxed with 17 percent value added tax (VAT) and an import duty of 5 percent.

Weaknesses are evident in the regulatory framework and oversight mechanism. According to the latest International Civil Aviation Organization (ICAO) Universal Safety Oversight Audit (USOAP) the regulatory framework and oversight mechanism remain unsatisfactory. The shortfalls noted include a lack of technical guidance material and the poor structure of the Department of Civil Aviation. ICAO particularly noted weak implementation of surveillance obligations and the failure to resolve safety issues.

Although a full assessment has not been carried out, signs of weakness are evident in the domestic airport infrastructure. For example, Zambia does not possess a civilian radar system and is limited to using procedural air traffic control. The overflight income from air traffic control services is quite low and safety might not be ensured with increased traffic.

The feasibility and desirability of forming a new national carrier, the subject of a study commissioned by the Government of Zambia, must be carefully assessed. The interim report (SH&E, Ernst & Young 2005) examines the possibility of starting a new national "Flag Carrier," which would operate one narrowbody and one wide-body aircraft on the two main routes to Johannesburg and London. Although the intention is primarily to attract private investors, a proposal suggests that the government retain a share of ownership. The conclusion of the study is that, in most scenarios, the airline would not be profitable. Some local industry representatives maintain that the study was based on inappropriate assumptions. Regardless of the merits of such a venture, the primary goals at this stage should be to create an open, competitive, and well-regulated market for domestic and international transport.

It may be desirable to carry out an assessment of the domestic airport infrastructure network. New technologies such as Automatic Dependent Surveillance-Broadcast (ADS-B) could be evaluated as an alternative to investing in costly radar systems.[1] The establishment of a Global Navigation Satellite System (GNSS) to be used during approaches to secondary airports would greatly increase safety. The World Bank is currently financing such approaches in several countries. The typical cost is about $1 million for six to eight approaches.

Priorities for Reform

Air transport service liberalization

Given the importance of tourism and horticulture for the Zambian economy, a high priority must be the creation of a liberalized and competitive market for air transport services. Comprehensive liberalization requires action at the unilateral, regional, and multilateral levels. The government should push its own reforms to the logical limit and eliminate the few restrictions it still maintains, such as those that arise from the denial of Fifth Freedom rights to third countries.

Zambia is limited in what it can achieve on its own, however, because introducing competition on any international route requires the agreement of the other country involved. Zambia should, therefore, support the full implementation of YD and, perhaps more realistically in the short run, the relevant legal notice under COMESA. Liberalization also should be pushed within the Southern African Development Community (SADC) and, as far as possible, negotiations are needed for BASAs, which establish conditions similar to YD, impose no capacity constraints, and allow up to Fifth Freedom rights. A liberalized air transport market at the regional level is in Zambia's best interests for at least two reasons: the development of tourism requires efficient and economical regional connections so that tour operators can bundle Zambia's safari parks with neighboring countries' beaches and other attractions; and a liberalized regional market can reduce the costs of intercontinental transport by facilitating the emergence of a more efficient hub-and-spoke model from which Zambia is likely to benefit, regardless of whether it is the hub or at the end of a spoke.

A liberalized regional market is not, however, sufficient to ensure competitive and efficient intercontinental connections. In the absence of frequent direct flights, Zambia will continue to be affected by the degree of liberalization on routes between other countries, such as South Africa and the United Kingdom. No instrument is immediately available to Zambia to deal with restrictions between third countries—air traffic rights have been excluded from the scope of even the GATS. Zambia and other least developed countries should, nevertheless, use various international forums to press for the elimination of protectionist arrangements in air transport that inhibit their exports.

Reform of the fuel market

The government should address inefficiencies in the oil refinery and the lack of competition in the fuel market to lower the price of fuel, which is today the highest in the region. The government should conduct a review of the existing pricing rationale and consider reducing the high import tariff and taxes on fuel.

Reforms to address the shortcomings in the regulatory framework and oversight mechanism

The authorities must focus on the creation of an autonomous Civil Aviation Authority, with administrative and financial independence, development of regulation and technical guidance material, and capacity building for continued surveillance obligations. These shortcomings need to be remedied to ensure the development of a safe, secure, efficient, and reliable air transport sector, as well as to support international liberalization (all liberalization frameworks have provisions to refuse the granting of traffic rights for safety reasons, which can include weaknesses in the regulatory framework and oversight mechanism). The World Bank assists countries with these efforts. Projects providing technical assistance for regulatory reform in the air transport sector typically cost between $1 and $3 million.

The size and structure of the Zambian air transport market

The aviation market of Zambia is one of the smallest aviation markets of the Southern African continent. The passenger movements at the four international airports in 2005 amounted to 675,000, of which 80 percent were international arrivals.[2] Growth over the past five years has been relatively flat, after a surge in 1999, followed by initially decreasing and then slowly recovering traffic. Overall, the traffic at Zambian airports has grown by 3.1 percent per year on average, which is in line with the general growth of air traffic in Africa (SH&E, Ernst & Young 2005, p. 33). Although international traffic has grown by 7.1 percent per year on average between 1995 and 2004, domestic traffic has decreased at an average 5.3 percent per year. This is mainly attributed to the disappearance of Zambia Airways in 1994.

Of the country's four main international airports, Lusaka (LUN) accounts for about 60 percent of all passenger movements, followed by Livingstone (LVI) with 23 percent, Ndola (LNA) with 11 percent, and Mfuwe (MFU) with 3 percent. About 82 percent of traffic is international. Next to the international airports, there are five provincial airports and more than 130 airstrips. Traffic data of these airports are not known in detail. With the exception of a few domestic scheduled flights, however, airport traffic consists mainly of on-demand or general aviation flights.

The main international routes with 92 weekly international flights of about 8,500 seats are as follows: (1) Livingstone–Johannesburg (2,193 seats per week each way);

Figure 5.1. Passenger Movements at Lusaka Airport

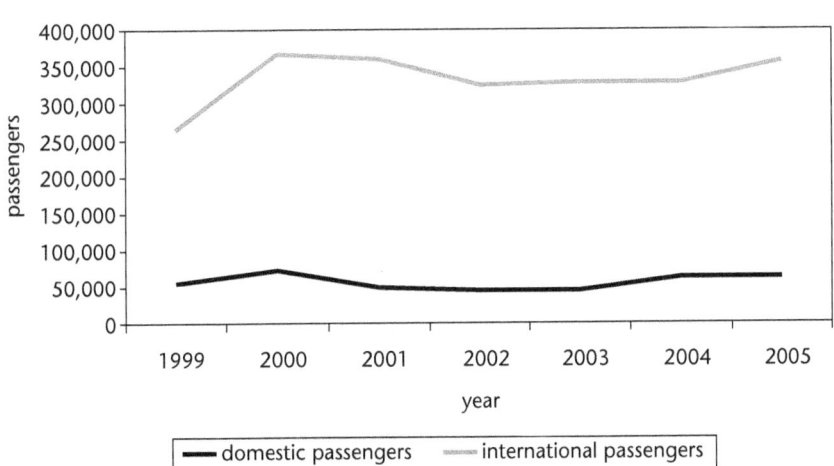

Source: SH&E, Ernst & Young 2005.

(2) Lusaka–Johannesburg (1,948 seats); (3) Lusaka–Nairobi (1,336 seats); (4) Lusaka–London (648 seats); (5) Ndola–Johannesburg (966 seats); and (6) Lusaka–Harare (588 seats). In addition, a few weekly flights travel to Ethiopia, Malawi, and the Democratic Republic of Congo (SH&E, Ernst & Young 2005, p. 53).

The market can be divided into three different categories: domestic and regional traffic, African continental traffic, and intercontinental traffic.

The Domestic and Regional Markets

The domestic and regional air traffic markets[3] are currently served by two Zambian carriers with scheduled air service, Zambian Airways, which operates five BE1900 aircraft, and Proflight Commuter Services, which operates one Jetstream 32.[4] Both carriers are fully owned by Zambian nationals. In addition, carriers have bilateral agreements with neighboring countries, including Angola (130 seats per week each way), Kenya (1,336 seats), Malawi (206 seats), Harare (588 seats), and the Democratic Republic of Congo (108 seats) (SH&E, Ernst & Young 2005, p. 53). The few air taxi operators do not represent a major factor for the domestic or regional market.

The domestic network to the four main airports include Lusaka–Ndola (576 seats per week each way), Lusaka–Mfuwe (402 seats), and Lusaka–Livingstone (330 seats).

The current size of the domestic market is estimated at 50,000 to 70,000 passengers per year.[5] The market has two segments. The primary segment is the tourist traveler who visits a few attractions in Livingstone and Mfuwe. This travel is highly seasonal (May to October), but it has recently experienced a significant growth. The second segment is the business-related traveler whose visits relate to the increased mining activities in the Copperbelt region. The business destinations of Ndola and Solwezi are not cyclical, although they are less profitable than the tourism sector. Local operators estimate that both segments are equally important on a yearly basis.

Given the increase of both segments in 2005, the potential for growth of the domestic market is quite significant. Because the road network to the main cities of the country is relatively good, the main growth primarily will come from tourists and business travelers.

The current size of the regional market is estimated to be between 180,000 and 200,000 passengers per year, of which at least half travel between Zambia and Kenya (Johannesburg [JNB] and Addis Ababa [ADD] excluded). This segment includes mainly tourists connecting over Nairobi (NBO), regional business travelers, and regional tourist travelers.

The growth potential of the regional segment is significant. The increased number of travelers using the NBO hub and the increase in regional travelers present an opportunity for Lusaka to become a regional hub. On one hand, the road network is often not a good alternative for travel. On the other hand, the southern countries of the COMESA region now have the opportunity to initiate liberalization procedures within the newly established COMESA framework. In addition, Lusaka represents a natural regional hub because of its geographic location halfway between Johannesburg and Nairobi.

African Continental Traffic

The major destination outside of the COMESA neighboring countries is South Africa. Total current traffic is estimated at about 250,000 to 300,000 passengers per year.[6] This market segment has significant growth potential. The BASA between South Africa and Zambia allows 3,000 weekly seats for each country between JNB–LUN, that is, 310,000 seats per year, of which 130,000 are being used.

Recently, Zambian Airways has introduced low-cost flights between JNB–LUN by wet-leasing an aircraft from the South African low-cost carrier Kulua.com.[7] The operation has been considered a great success with rapid take-up by travelers shifting from bus to air service. The cost for a one-way ticket is $100, which is close to the bus fare and much lower than current economy-class tickets. As a result, bus operators have lowered their prices, although the traditional carrier South African Airways (SAA) has maintained its fares. It is alleged that the market potential of this route is limited by anticompetitive behavior on the part of SAA. They are reported to have retaliated against competition on several occasions by lowering their fare to the point where competitors had to abandon certain routes. Statistical evidence of this behavior was not available for this report.

Two weekly flights currently operate between LUN and ADD. Even with quite high load factors, however, this market represents only about 25,000 passengers per year.

The growth of African continental traffic depends mainly on the possibility of carriers flying through Lusaka using Fifth Freedom rights, particularly into Johannesburg. Several requests have been made, but they have all been declined by the South African authorities or by the Zambian authorities: Egypt (Cairo-Lusaka-Johannesburg) was refused by South Africa in 2001, Libya (Tripoli-Lusaka-Johannesburg) was refused by Zambia in 2001, Ethiopia (Addis Ababa-Lusaka-Johannesburg) was refused by Zambia in 2005, and Nigeria (Lagos-Lusaka-Johannesburg) was refused by Zambia during BASA negotiations.

With progress made toward liberalization of air transport services within COMESA, new traffic might originate in the northern hemisphere to fly into or through Lusaka. A request from Kenya to fly Nairobi-Lusaka-Harare was refused by Zambia in 2005. Some Fifth Freedom rights have been granted for cargo flights and some additional flights are under consideration. Emirates Cargo was granted Fifth Freedom rights to serve LUN out of NBO.

Intercontinental Traffic

Intercontinental traffic is currently limited to three flights per week between London and Lusaka operated by British Airways (BA) with 40,000 to 50,000 passengers per year. Despite the fact that BA has a 70-year history in operating to Lusaka, the direct flight to Lusaka is not considered a highly profitable operation. The main reason is that there is a very thin market for business or first-class travelers to Zambia. Given the competitive rates between Europe and South Africa, BA's economy-class fares for LHR–LUN vary between $600 and $1,000. Given the high fuel prices in LUN, and the fact that return catering needs to be transported from London, and that additional security expenses are necessary in LUN, the profitability of this flight remains marginal. BA could consider operating just a feeder operation from JNB to LUN, as was done in the recent past when it subcontracted the JNB–LVI segment to Comair.[8]

LVI has been considered as a second direct intercontinental destination. Because tourist infrastructure remains limited, tourists mostly travel to LVI as an add-on to their visits to other neighboring countries, and the tourist season remains seasonable, little potential exists for direct intercontinental traffic for this destination.

The air cargo market, which plays an important role for the country's exports consisting of perishable products, such as cut flowers and vegetables mostly destined for Europe (the United Kingdom and the Netherlands), has experienced a similar trend to other segments. International cargo (domestic cargo is insignificant), which is mainly operated in and out of Lusaka by regular cargo flights, surged and dropped in 2001 and recovered by 2005. It is reported, however, that high fuel prices and alternative road transport have recently reduced cargo flights and lower figures may be expected in 2006.

In 2005, five weekly cargo freighters operated to Lusaka with a total dedicated capacity of 175 to 250 tons (about 40 tons per aircraft). But, in early 2006, the number of flights had declined to two per week with a total capacity of about 80 to 100 tons, and a significant proportion of vegetable exports were being sent by road to Johannesburg and then by air to Europe. The largest obstacle for air cargo is reported to be the high cost of fuel in Lusaka and the diseconomies arising from

Figure 5.2. International Freight, 1999–2005

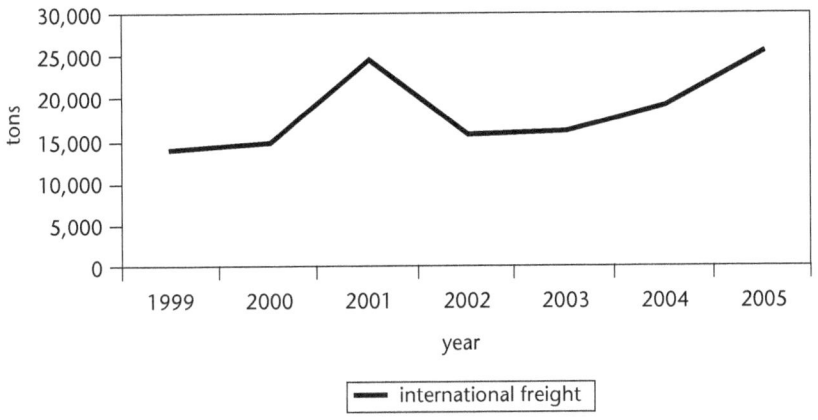

Source: SH&E, Ernst & Young 2005.

the small volume of exports that do not fill an aircraft. Overall, the air cargo export market is estimated at 150 tons per week (4,000 flowers and 4,000 vegetables on a yearly basis).[9]

Air transport policy and liberalization

Air Transport Policy

Zambia's Air Transport Policy is defined in its National Air Transport Policy paper, which was published in May 2002 by the Ministry of Communications and Transport. Recognizing the importance of air transport for the development of the economy, the paper argues that the air transport industry is small due to poor infrastructure, small passenger loads, and the lack of properly managed tourist destinations.

The implementation of the air transport strategy has made modest progress. Policies to create a competitive and liberalized environment (including the assignment of international traffic routes) and to ensure effective regulation (based on international standards, ICAO), are discussed below.

The Re-creation of a National Airline

The objective of encouraging private investment in the air transport industry as well as providing incentives for start-up operations of Zambian air services has

> ### Box 5.1. Key Objectives in the National Air Transport Policy, 2002
>
> Following are the key objectives outlined in Zambia's National Air Transport Policy:
> - The creation of a competitive and liberalized environment
> - Ensuring effective regulation, based on international standards (ICAO)
> - Ensuring safe, efficient, and cost-effective services
> - Promoting air transport through trade and development
> - Attracting private investment in airports and airlines
> - Protecting the domestic market, while supporting Zambian carrier in obtaining equal international traffic rights
> - Promoting international joint ventures with Zambian carriers
>
> Based on these objectives, the Government of Zambia shall pursue a strategy that includes the following:
> - Institutional reforms to provide an adequate regulatory framework
> - Encouraging private investment in the air transport industry
> - Assigning and negotiating multiple domestic and international destinations for Zambian registered carriers
> - Providing incentives for start-up operations of Zambian air services
>
> *Source:* Republic of Zambia 2002.

not been addressed. However, the GoZ did launch a study for the formation of a national airline in Zambia. The interim report examines the possibility of starting a new national "Flag Carrier," which would operate one narrow-body and one wide-body aircraft on the routes to Johannesburg and London (SH&E, Ernst & Young 2005). Although the idea is to attract primarily private investors, the GoZ would retain 10 percent control to ensure national ownership. The conclusion of the study is that most scenarios would not render the venture profitable. Some local industry representatives maintain that the study was based on false assumptions. The final version should reflect a better picture.[10]

The creation of a new national carrier, as examined in the study, must be evaluated with skepticism. Even if the GoZ holds only a minority stake, this skepticism is important because of Zambia's negative experiences with a national flag carrier, which are similar to other countries' experiences. Finally, it is highly doubtful that the GoZ would find private investors, given the projected high risk and low return of the new carrier. Instead, the GoZ should focus on its objective of creating a competitive and liberalized environment, supporting Zambian carriers by obtaining equal international traffic rights and promoting international joint ventures with Zambian carriers.

Jet Fuel Pricing

The high operating cost in Zambia is primarily a problem of high jet fuel prices. According to ZEGA, jet fuel is 55 percent more expensive in LUN than in JNB. BA's fuel costs are more than 40 percent more in LUN than in JNB or NBO.[11] Jet fuel is refined in Zambia by a 50 percent government and 50 percent privately held refinery. In June 2005, the IATA examined the high fuel cost in Zambia and requested a reduction of 20 percent as an initial step toward achieving a more reasonable and sustainable price structure.[12] The pricing seems to be strongly influenced by the Zambian refinery and so far no reduction has been achieved. In addition, jet fuel is taxed with 17 percent VAT and an import duty of 5 percent, despite the fact that usually fuel is entirely tax free.

Other than high fuel prices, the operating costs in Zambia remain rather reasonable. The current appreciation of the local currency against the U.S. dollar must be considered a temporary effect.

Air Transport Liberalization

In terms of the creation of a competitive and liberalized environment, the domestic air transport sector can be considered liberalized. All domestic operators confirmed that obtaining the necessary operators' certificate is relatively easy. Given the very small domestic market, however, competition regulation and regulatory supervision are necessary to ensure that the market remains fair.

International air service continues to be based on BASAs. The GoZ has signed 72 BASAs.[13] Of these, however, only the following eight are currently in use: United Kingdom, South Africa, Angola, Kenya, Malawi, Zimbabwe, Ethiopia, and the Democratic Republic of Congo. The most important bilateral relationship is with South Africa, for which traffic between five city pairs was agreed: Johannesburg to Lusaka (3,000 seats per week each side), to Ndola (2,700 seats), to Livingstone (2,200 seats), to Mfuwe (400 seats), and from Pilanesberg to Livingstone (400 seats). The capacity of these traffic rights was only partially used until recently, when traffic rights were assigned to a low-cost carrier on the JNB–LUN segment, which operates under a Zambian operator's certificate. Further liberalization has been constrained because of resistance from bilateral counterparts. This is especially an issue when requesting Fifth Freedom rights for traffic stopping in LUN.[14] As noted earlier, South Africa has systematically rejected all requests for Fifth Freedom rights. According the Department of Civil Aviation, however, South Africa has even rejected a request for a designated cargo carrier to fly directly via a third country to JNB to receive freight for the JNB–LUN leg. Such a request (if no freight was unloaded in JNB) would not even constitute a case of

Fifth Freedom and should be granted. Zambia also has rejected requests for Fifth Freedom rights from Libya, Ethiopia, Nigeria, and Kenya. It is not in Zambia's best interests to deny these rights because doing so raises the cost of air travel, with secondary effects on the dependent sectors, such as tourism and horticulture.

Liberalization of international air transport in Africa is a declared objective of the African Union. The implementation of up to Fifth Freedom liberalization was agreed in principle in the YD, which became fully binding on August 12, 2002. If the conditions established in the YD are met, it will become enforceable continentwide because it has been endorsed by the African Union Heads of State under the African Union Treaty framework of 2000. The legal basis for ratification of the YD is the Treaty of Abuja, which has been adopted by most of the 52 African states. In the four years since it became fully binding, however, few cases of new air traffic rights granted through the application of the YD mechanism have been observed. Evidence of the nonapplication of the YD ranges from the lack of implementation of the conditions set (for example, the failure to establish competition rules, a dispute settlement mechanism, and a monitoring body) to simply ignoring the YD by continuing to use traditional, restrictive BASAs.

As a result of this lack of progress, several regional organizations have begun to implement the YD among their regional member states. COMESA has agreed to liberalize air transport services among its member states in the spirit, and with similar regulations and mechanisms, of the YD.

In COMESA Legal Notice No. 2, the Council of Ministers adopted a two-phase timetable for the implementation of a liberalized air transport industry in COMESA. Phase I became effective in October 1999, allowing free movement of intra-COMESA air transport and nonscheduled passenger traffic up to twice a day between city pairs. Beyond that, flights are subject to bilateral agreements, allowing multiple designations of airlines and eliminating capacity restrictions. This phase has been partially implemented. Cases have been observed, however, of limiting tourist charters. Phase II deals with the establishment of an Air Transport Regulatory Board, which would implement liberalization policies, handle dispute resolutions, and harmonize policies in COMESA. The necessary regulation has been prepared and is currently under consideration by the secretariat of COMESA. Phase II should eventually abolish all restrictions and establish free movement for all intra-COMESA air services. This freedom should include cabotage and Fifth Freedom rights and, thus, would actually implement the YD and other regulations.

The implementation of the COMESA liberalization of air transport services among its member states has experienced some delay given that the introduction of phase II was planned for October 2000.[15] COMESA has been active in supporting requests for granting liberalized air service agreements within the framework of Legal Notice No. 2, and it likely that this liberalization effort will succeed. This should be achieved through direct and active involvement in COMESA implementation activities. In addition, the GoZ should begin to negotiate traffic rights within existing or new BASAs, which are compatible with Legal Notice No. 2 for Zambian carriers.

A liberalized air transport market at the regional level is in Zambia's interests for at least two reasons: (1) the development of tourism requires efficient and economical regional connections so that tour operators can bundle Zambia's safari parks with neighboring countries' beaches and other attractions; and (2) a liberalized regional market can help reduce the costs of intercontinental transport by facilitating the emergence of a more efficient hub-and-spoke model from which Zambia is likely to benefit, regardless of whether it is the hub or at the end of a spoke.

A liberalized regional market is not, however, sufficient to ensure competitive and efficient intercontinental connections. In the absence of frequent direct flights, Zambia will continue to be affected by the degree of liberalization on routes between other countries, such as South Africa and the United Kingdom. No instrument is immediately available to Zambia to deal with restrictions between third countries—air traffic rights have been excluded from the scope of even the GATS. Zambia and other least developed countries should, nevertheless, use various international forums to press for the elimination of protectionist arrangements in air transport that inhibit their exports.

Regulatory and Oversight Mechanism Environment

In terms of ensuring effective regulation, based on international standards (the ICAO), Zambia has made progress. According to the last ICAO USOAP, however, the regulatory framework and oversight mechanism remain unsatisfactory (see annex 2). The shortfalls include a lack of technical guidance material and the current structure of the Department of Civil Aviation. Zambia was found especially weak on continued surveillance obligations and the resolution of safety issues.

To support the implementation of Zambia's National Air Transport Policy, and to ensure the development of a safe, secure, efficient, and reliable air transport sector, the GoZ must address shortfalls of the regulatory framework and oversight mechanism. Because all of the liberalization frameworks include provisions to refuse the granting of traffic rights for safety reasons, which can include shortcomings of a regulatory framework and oversight mechanism, these shortcomings could block international liberalization. They also may badly damage the country's reputation when the ICAO audit reports are made public in March 2008.[16]

The World Bank is currently supporting several states in Africa in reaching acceptable international standards for effective regulation and safety oversight. In the case of Zambia, the focus must be creation of an autonomous Civil Aviation Authority, the development of regulation and technical guidance material, and capacity building for continued surveillance obligations. Projects providing technical assistance for regulatory reform in the air transport sector typically cost between $1 and $3 million (see the example project in box 5.2).

Box 5.2. Technical Assistance for Regulatory Oversight: The Case of Mozambique

The Government of Mozambique obtained funding from the World Bank for technical assistance for the Mozambique Civil Aviation Institute (IACM) to enhance its safety oversight capacity. The project objective is to improve the safety, regularity, and efficiency of air transport operations in Mozambique to better meet the country's air transportation needs, to encourage the growth of trade and tourism, and to attract business and investment to the country. The project will last for 18 months and started in December 2005.

The project has various components. The government will hire consultants to assess and suggest amendments to the primary aviation legislation and regulations. The objective is to develop a regulatory framework containing complete and detailed regulations to enable the effective implementation of the provisions of ICAO Standards and Recommended Practices (SARPs), as set out in the Chicago Convention Annexes 1, 6, and 8.

In addition, to enhance the safety oversight capacity of IACM the following tasks will be undertaken:

- **Civil Aviation Authority System:** A system will be put in place that makes all accident and incident reports available to air operators for inclusion in their accident prevention programs.
- **Personnel Licensing:** A framework will be developed to ensure that all licenses issued by Mozambique conform to the correct specifications.
- **Aircraft Operation Certification and Supervision:** Air navigation regulations will be developed to enable the implementation of Annex 6 SARPs.
- **Airworthiness of Aircraft**: Airworthiness regulations will be developed for the certification of aircraft registered in Mozambique.

The capacity-building program includes the preparation of handbooks and materials for inspectors of the IACM. It also provides training, for example, in accident investigation. Finally, some special equipment, such as laptop computers or portable global positioning system (GPS) receivers, will be financed.

Source: World Bank project documents.

Infrastructure

Airport Infrastructure

Zambia has four international airports, five provincial airports and more than 130 airstrips. The four main and international airports are managed by the National Airports Corporation Limited (NACL). Provincial airports are under the responsibility of the Department of Civil Aviation.

The NACL has prepared a detailed five-year plan, which aims to maintain and modernize is airport infrastructure. Although it is able to finance the necessary maintenance, it cannot invest in major improvements, such as the necessary extension of the runway in Livingstone. The long-term focus of NACL is the full commercialization of its operations, which would also allow public-private partnerships.

The general condition at the main airport in Lusaka can be considered satisfactory. The runway is more than 3,900 meters long, which accommodates all types of aircraft. In addition, the airport has several types of published precision and non-precision approaches, including GNSS-based Radar Navigation Area Navigation (RNAV) approaches.[17] The security situation remains unsatisfactory, however, as access to the restricted area is possible because of damaged perimeter fencing.[18]

The mission to Lusaka was not able to gather information on the condition of the other airports managed by the NACL. They are perceived to be relatively satisfactory by operators. The only necessary major improvement is the extension of the runway at Livingstone, which would permit larger aircraft to operate.

The mission was not able to obtain information on the condition of airports under the responsibility of the Department of Civil Aviation. However, five of these airports have published instrument approaches.[19]

Overall, given the thin aviation market, the existing airport infrastructure of the country can be considered satisfactory. In view of future development, however, the mission recommends that the government assess the domestic airport infrastructure network.

Airport Traffic Control Infrastructure

The airport traffic control (ATC) infrastructure of Zambia is maintained and operated by the NACL. The country does possess a civilian radar system and is limited to procedural air traffic control.

The overflight income from ATC services are quite low, particularly given the fact that major overflight routes pass through Zambia.[20] Furthermore, it might be difficult to negotiate higher fees because of the lack of adequate surveillance infrastructure. With increased traffic, the country will need to invest in new surveillance technology. It is recommended that the government evaluate new technologies, such as ADS-B.[21]

In addition, several operators would welcome the establishment of GNSS approaches to secondary airports. Such approaches would greatly increase safety and, because they are independent of ground installations, would have a permanent character. The World Bank is financing the installation of such approaches in several countries. The typical cost is about $1 million for six to eight approaches (see the example project in box 5.3).

Box 5.3. ATC infrastructure financing: The case of Tanzania

The World Bank is currently preparing an ATC infrastructure project for Tanzania. The objective is to finance a modern Automatic Dependent Surveillance–Broadcast (ADS-B) system. ADS-B is a new technology that allows pilots in the cockpit and air traffic controllers on the ground to "see" aircraft traffic with greater precision than previously has been possible. ADS-B–equipped aircraft broadcast their precise GPS-based position via a digital datalink along with other data, including airspeed, altitude, and whether the aircraft is turning, climbing, or descending.

Box Figure 1.

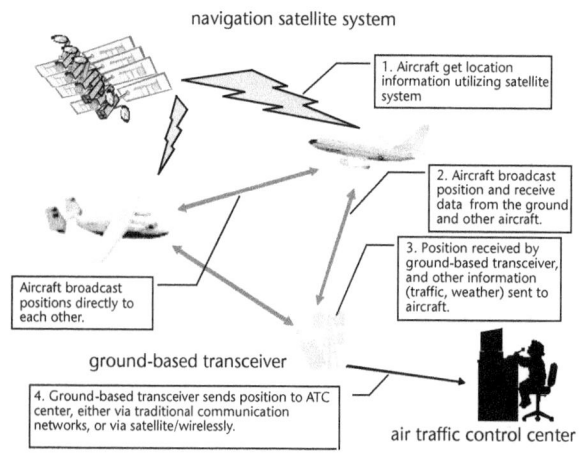

Having good surveillance capabilities on the ground is of obvious help in avoiding obstructions and other traffic. However, the capability of seeing, on one display in the cockpit, all surrounding terrain, the weather conditions en-route, and all other traffic, significantly lowers the risks that are leading to accidents with lighter aircraft. In the United States, the FAA launched a test program in the state of Alaska where operators using the ADS-B system reduced their fatal accident rate by over 50%.

Source: World Bank project documents.

Box 5.3. (continued)

ADS-B presents the best fit choice for bringing airspace control to countries lacking such infrastructure. The technology is optimal because of its low cost of introduction, its much lower maintenance cost, its accuracy compared with traditional radar, and its independence from most other infrastructure networks. Complete coverage of a country such as Tanzania (945,087 km²) would require the installation of about 10 ground-based transceivers and could be achieved for less than $2 million. By contrast, a single radar installation today costs about $6 million. Aircraft would have to be equipped with the transceivers and GPS equipment. Assuming no GPS devices have been previously installed, the basic cost per unit would be $20,000. In Tanzania, with 210 aircraft registered, this would add $4.2 million to the introduction. Even if half of the aircraft were registered for commercial use, and it would be deemed necessary to add the cost of multifunction displays, the cost would still only increase by about $2.1 million, bringing the total installation, including training and interfacing with the current radar system, to about $10 million.

Other Air Transport Infrastructure

Other air transport infrastructure will have to be evaluated in an assessment of the domestic airport infrastructure network. The Zambian Air Services Training Institute (ZASTI) must be considered as part of the country's air transport infrastructure, which must be conserved. ZASTI, which is designed to host up to 120 resident students, was created in the late 1960s. In the 1980s, it had been modernized through support from the United Nations Development Programme (UNDP). Although it still offers training in three areas: flight school (pilot training), engineering school (mechanics), and ground handling school (including ATC, fire and rescue, metrological services, communication, and security), the institute lacks students and funding.[22]

Given that the ZASTI is relatively well maintained and has qualified staff, the GoZ should consider privatizing institute. This is especially important because one of the major development constraints identified by operators was the lack of qualified technical personnel. In addition, Zambia benefits from relatively low labor cost and good weather conditions, which would benefit basic pilot training. The institute might have the potential to become a regional training center, if it was well managed and commercialized.

The World Bank could evaluate and support the privatization. Depending on necessary restructuring, such a project component typically would cost between $100,000 and $500,000.

Notes

1. ADS-B is a function on an aircraft or surface vehicle that broadcasts position, altitude, vector, and other information for use by other aircraft, vehicles, and ground facilities.

2. These airports include Lusaka (capital), Ndola, Livingstone, and Mfuwe.

3. Given the fact that South Africa is not part of COMESA, this technical note considers destinations in South Africa as continental traffic. Also, destinations that are further than two hours' flight time are not considered regional.

4. Zambian Airways recently merged with Airwaves.

5. Zambian Airways (60,000 passengers per year) and Proflight (10,000 passengers per year) in 2006. These figures were given by the airlines during interviews in March 2006.

6. Adjusted data for 2005, based on SH&E, Ernst & Young 2005, p. 53.

7. A leasing arrangement whereby a company agrees to provide an aircraft and at least one pilot to another company. A dry lease refers to leasing only the aircraft.

8. Interview with British Airways managing director in Lusaka on March 29, 2006.

9. Figures on freight obtained from Zambian Export Growers Association.

10. Apparently, the final version remains pending because the GoZ did not transfer the required payment.

11. Interview with British Airways managing director in Lusaka on March 29, 2006.

12. IATA investigated aviation fuel prices in Zambia and compared them with other airports in the region. This limited study demonstrated that the Zambian prices are between 12 and 40 percent higher than other airports in the region.

13. Annex 1 provides a list of the first 54 BASAs. Many more have been signed, often followed by modifications through memorandums of understanding (MOU).

14. In the BASA with South Africa, Fifth Freedom rights may be exercised by a designated carrier of either party provided that no air service is performed by a designated carrier of the other party between that third country and South Africa or Zambia. In addition, it was agreed that the designated carriers of South Africa may exercise Fifth Freedom traffic rights on the Ndola-Nairobi and Ndola-Entebbe sectors.

15. COMESA Legal Notice No. 2 (1999), Article 2 (b).

16. On the recent conference of the director general of civil aviation, the ICAO decided to release all future safety audits of contracting states starting at the latest March 2008.

17. GNSS = Global Navigation Satellite Systems; GPS = Global Positioning System.

18. According to a security assessment of British Airways (BA), the main problem of LUN is access to the restricted area of the airport. As a result, BA must finance private security personnel to guard the aircraft when on the ground. This is unsatisfactory, because it represents a security risk, as well as increased cost for the operator.

19. Most approaches are nondirectional beacon (NBD) approaches, which are not very reliable. A recent Japanese grant helped upgrade approaches to modern VHF Omnidirectional Radio Range (VOR) approaches. Operators, however, would like to see the development of several GNSS approaches, which are independent of ground installations.

20. Apparently, ATC overflight income is only about $2 million per year.

21. Please see box 5.3 for a description of this technology.

22. The flight school has seven aircraft (five single-engine C150 and two multiengine PA30), but only one aircraft is operable. The Instrument Flight Rules (IFR) trainer is operational, but the school currently lacks students.

References

ICAO (International Civil Aviation Organization). 2004. "Universal Safety Oversight Audit Report" (February). ICAO, Montreal.

Republic of Zambia. 2002, May. "National Air Transport Policy." Ministry of Communications and Transport, Lusaka, Zambia.

SH&E (Simat Helliesen & Eichner) and Ernst & Young. 2005. "Formation of a National Airline in Zambia, Interim Report" (November). Lusaka, Zambia.

World Bank. 2005. "East Africa Air Transport Survey." World Bank, Washington, DC.

Annex 1. Bilateral Air Services Agreements with Zambia

According to the Ministry of Transport, Zambia has 72 signed bilateral air services agreements. However, the mission received the attached list of the following 53 countries:

Angola	Maldives
Botswana	Mauritius
Burundi	Namibia
Cameroon	Netherlands
Cape Verde	Nigeria
China	Portugal
Congo, Dem. Rep. of	Romania
Côte d'Ivoire	Rwanda
Congo, Rep. of	Saudi Arabia
Cyprus	Senegal
Belgium	Seychelles
Bulgaria	Singapore
Egypt, Arab Rep. of	South Africa
Ethiopia	Sri Lanka
France	Sudan
Gabon	Swaziland
Gambia, The	Tanzania
Germany	Thailand
Ghana	Togo
India	Uganda
Italy	United Arab Emirates
Japan	United Kingdom
Kenya	United States
Korea, Rep. of	USSR (former)
Lesotho	Yugoslavia (former)
Liberia	Zimbabwe
Malawi	

Annex 2. ICAO: Critical Elements of a Safety Oversight System, February 2004

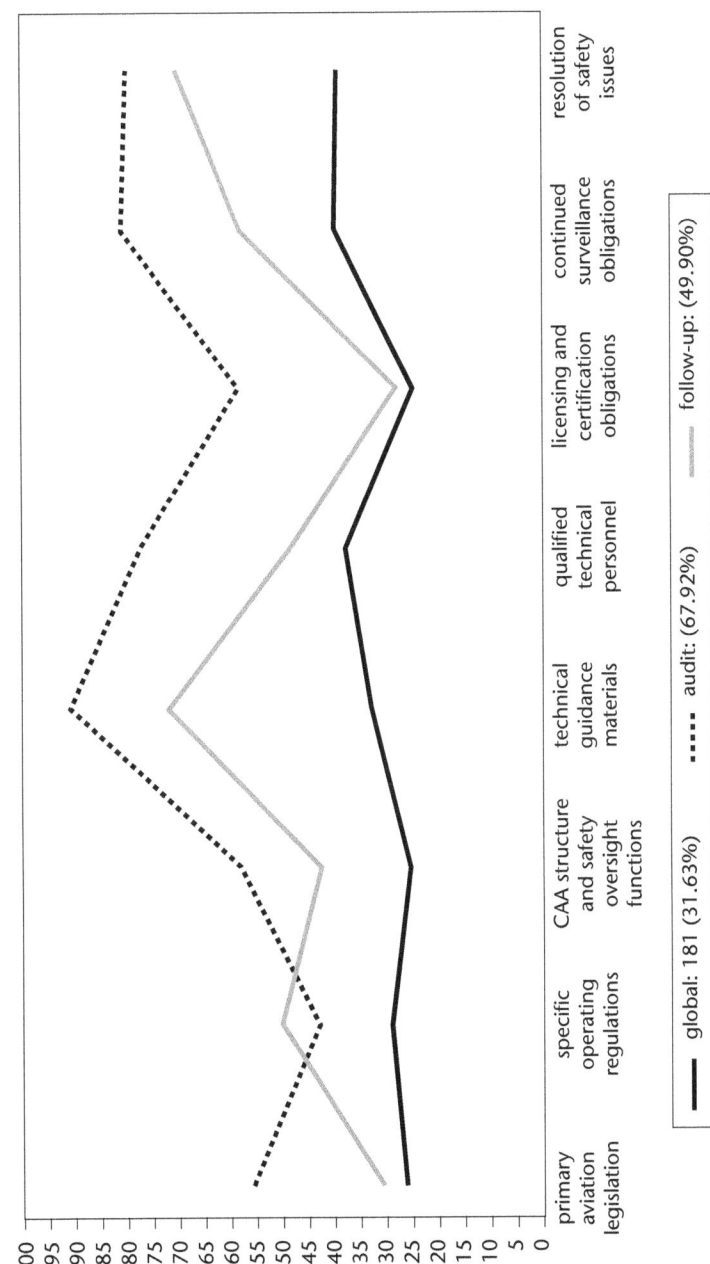

Source: ICAO 2004.

6

TOURISM:
UNFULFILLED PROMISE

Olivier Cattaneo

Overview

By virtue of its endowments (including its wildlife and the Victoria Falls), the peacefulness of the country and the friendliness of its people, Zambia undoubtedly has significant potential in tourism. A recent study funded by UNDP/GEF suggested that better management of Zambia's wildlife resources could generate economic activity of up to $1 billion a year. Although Zambia faces significant competition from other countries in the region with similar endowments, and within the country, the tourism sector must compete for resources with other vital sectors of the economy, Zambia's advantage in tourism and the advantages of tourism for the economy cannot be doubted.

The advantages remain largely unexploited and are producing only limited developmental benefits. Zambia attracts only 600,000 tourists a year—compared with more than 2 million tourists for Zimbabwe at the peak of its popularity. Compared with its neighbors, Zambia has the second lowest (after Zimbabwe) rate of contribution of tourism to GDP (4 percent compared with about 10 percent for Botswana, Tanzania, Namibia, and South Africa) and employment (3.7 percent compared with more than 11 to 12 percent for Namibia and Botswana). In 2005, real growth of the travel and tourism sector was 10 times faster in Botswana and Tanzania than in Zambia, and the significant appreciation of real exchange rate alone cannot explain these differences. Furthermore, the benefits have been unequally spread. Tourism has been increasingly concentrated in the Livingstone area, despite the high tourism potential of other poorer provinces: 82 percent of the tourists visit the Victoria Falls and the Mosi-oa-Tunya area, and 93 percent of employment in nature-based tourism activities is concentrated in Livingstone and the rapids. Preliminary cross-country estimates suggest that Zambia is receiving significantly fewer tourists than would be warranted by its fundamental endowments, and if it were to improve its business climate and infrastructure, the country could receive a much larger share of tourism flows (51 percent more tourists, that is, 295,000 per year).

The highest priority for policy action is the elimination of impediments and distortions created by regulatory policy. Investment in tourism has been stifled by high costs, in terms of both time and money, and the lack of predictability of licensing and administrative requirements to open and operate a tourism business. Up to 74 licenses are required (no exhaustive list exists), which can take between six months and one year to obtain and which cost as much as K 10 million for even a five-room guest house.[1] A simplification and improvement of the quality of regulations is necessary. For example, as a result of the poor quality of the classification system, two-thirds of hospitality establishments remain unclassified and many inhabit the informal economy.

The government must review all administrative and licensing requirements with a view to removing measures that do not serve any valid policy objective and to ensuring that any measure serving a valid policy objective does so efficiently, transparently, and predictably. Ultimately, the cost of compliance with licensing requirements should be reduced by at least 50 percent. It is notable that reducing the cost of opening a business by 75 percent in Uganda resulted in an increase of 40 percent of public revenue because more businesses joined the formal sector. Reducing the time needed to fulfill the legal requirements to open a business in Vietnam from between six months and one year to a maximum of two months, and reducing the cost by 50 to 75 percent, led to a tripling in three years of business registrations. Several countries suffering from overregulation have managed, like Mexico, through a "guillotine" reform, to reduce the number of licenses required to do business by 50 percent.

At the same time, there is a need to rationalize the domestic tax system and prevent wasteful tax competition with other countries in the region. The corporate tax, at 35 percent, is higher than the level of 15 percent in competing countries, such as Botswana, and 30 percent in South Africa, Tanzania, and Zimbabwe. Similarly, the value added tax (VAT) at 17.5 percent is higher than in competing countries, which is as low as 10 percent in Botswana, as are customs and excise duties on tourism inputs (petrol is three time more expensive in Zambia than in South Africa and wine is four times more expensive). Tourism is in general excluded from tax incentives provided to nontraditional goods exporters, such as the reduced corporate tax (15 percent). However, certain tourism service providers (for example, Sun International, a foreign firm with large investments in Livingstone) have succeeded in negotiating a lower corporate tax, and tourism in the Livingstone region is exempted from VAT. The result is de facto discrimination against domestic service providers and an accentuation of existing regional inequalities in the development of tourism. There should be greater uniformity of treatment within Zambia. If incentives are provided to export, they should apply for both goods and services exports, to all regions and to all service providers, irrespective of nationality. Zambia should also seek to coordinate tax policy with other countries in the region to prevent wasteful tax competition.

Zambia should develop efficient institutions and policies to manage tourism resources. Today, six public and more than a dozen private bodies are involved in the sector's management with only limited efforts at coordination. Surveys of tourism businesses suggest that as many as 90 percent regard these bodies as either unprofessional and obstructive or inefficient and unpredictable. In particular, the management of wildlife in national parks and game management areas is unsatisfactory and poses a serious risk of depletion to tourism resources with low returns to the Zambian government and communities. Unquestionably, the market alone will not address key conservation and wildlife management issues. Intervention is necessary. But, as in other areas, public monopolies are not necessarily the best instrument. Zambia needs to develop arrangements that allocate responsibility to the most efficient provider, public or private, national or foreign, rather than following the present, heavy reliance on public institutions, such as Zambia Wildlife Authority (ZAWA) or bilateral negotiations with selected providers. For example, we can think of arrangements analogous to those being considered in other sectors: resources could be mobilized from a tourist tax and donors and allocated through competitive tenders awarded on the basis not only of promises of revenue but also conservation, local employment, and infrastructure development. The UNDP/GEF–funded study recommends that $50 million be invested in the improved management of national parks and game management areas.

The largely untapped potential of tourism in Zambia

Zambia Has a Comparative Advantage in Tourism Trade

Although nature-based tourism is an extremely competitive sector in Southern Africa, Zambia has a unique combination of assets that could make it a major tourist destination. Regarding its natural endowments, Zambia has strong potential for tourism development: wildlife (such as the big five animals of Africa—lion, leopard, buffalo, elephant, and rhino—and more than 700 species of birds), landscapes (waterfalls, lakes, hot springs, caves, and so on), and nearly 2,000 archeological and historical sites. Among these attractions, some qualify as brand names, such as the Victoria Falls, which was included in the United Nations Educational, Scientific and Cultural Organization (UNESCO) list of World Cultural Heritage.

Zambia faces strong competition in the region. Most of Zambia's neighbors have comparable endowments and compete in the same segment of the tourism market: nature and wildlife. In terms of species diversity, including threatened species, Zambia remains on track with the region's average, although it is better endowed than Botswana and Zimbabwe, its two main competitors (see table 6.1). In terms of cultural sites, one of Zambia's sites is included in the UNESCO list of World Cultural Heritage (Mosi-oa-Tunya/Victoria Falls), which it shares with Zimbabwe. Only two of its competitors do not have any listed world heritage site (Tanzania and Namibia), while others have up to seven sites listed (see table 6.2).

Despite this competition, Zambia does have a unique advantage in tourism, which stems from its powerful combination of attributes. First of all, its pristine wildlife and natural remoteness can be marketed as the "real African experience," and its brand-name products and cultural endowments set it apart from its African competitors (see annex 1). Secondly, the country is peaceful and its people are friendly. Zambia is free of many of the political and other constraints that are faced by its competitors (see table 6.3). Thus, despite strong competition, this combination of assets positions Zambia to play a greater role in the regional tourism market.

Zambia could get a higher economic return from specializing in tourism than in other sectors

Although Zambia has important endowments for tourism, it does not necessarily have a comparative advantage in the sector. Several studies have tried to measure

Table 6.1. Species Diversity in Southern Africa

	Area (000s km²)	Mammals	Birds	Fish	Flowering plants	Red List
Botswana	582	154	569	81	2,000	60
Malawi	118	190	650	1,000	6,000	125
Namibia	824	154	640	97	3,159	182
South Africa	1,219	247	774	220	20,300	634
Tanzania	945	310	1,016	250	11,000	716
Zambia	753	229	732	156	4,600	120
Zimbabwe	390	196	634	132	6,000	108

Source: SADC 2005; World Conservation Union 2004.

Note: The Red List is a list of endangered species compiled by the World Conservation Union.

Table 6.2. UNESCO World Heritage Sites in Southern Africa, 2006

	Cultural	Mixed	Natural
Botswana	• Tsodillo (2001)	None	None
Malawi	None	None	• Lake Malawi National Park (1984)
Namibia	None	None	None
South Africa	• Fossil Hominid Sites of Sterfontein, Swartkrans, Kromdraai, and Environs (1999) • Mapungubwe Cultural Landscape (2003) • Robben Island (1999)	• Kahlamba/ Drakensberg Park (2000)	• Cape Floral Region Protected Areas (2004) • Greater St Lucia Wetland Park (1999) • Vredefort Dome (2005)
Tanzania	None	None	None
Zambia	None	None	• Mosi-oa-Tunya/Victoria Falls (1989)
Zimbabwe	• Great Zimbabwe National Monument (1986) • Khami Ruins National Monument (1986) • Matobo Hills (2003)	None	• Mana Pools National Park, Sapi and Chedwore Safari Areas (1984) • Mosi-oa-Tunya/Victoria Falls (1989)

Source: UNESCO 2006.

the trade and development potential of tourism compared with other sectors. Tourism trade has a "multiplier" effect, because it generates direct and indirect economic and development benefits, including direct and indirect jobs. The Tourism Satellite Account tries to capture this effect, including the trade of traditional tourism service providers (airlines, hotels, car hire companies, and so on) and upstream industries and services, such as fuel and catering companies, laundry services, and accounting firms (see annex 3). For Zambia, it is estimated that the travel and tourism economy contributes in total to nearly 4 percent of GDP and creates more than 55,000 jobs, which is 3.7 percent of total employment (World Travel and Tourism Council 2005b).

A recent study funded by UNDP/GEF suggested that good management of Zambia's wildlife resources could generate economic activity of approximately $1 billion a year. On the basis of this study, the government and other donors have committed to invest $150 million in the wildlife sector over the next 10 years (100

Table 6.3. Weaknesses of Zambia Competitors

Tanzania	• Current East African problems—fear of terrorism • More commercialized—boutique African experience • Cannot tap into the South Africa market easily or add on to South Africa tours
Zimbabwe	• Current sociopolitical situation—especially discourages Europe and South Africa markets • Victoria Falls is overcommercialized
South Africa	• Not seen as a safari destination—does not offer the "real" Africa, boutique Africa game viewing, and less spectacular parks • Poor crime, violence, and safety perceptions
Botswana	• Okavango swamps not as well known as Victoria Falls • Weak/limited national destination marketing • Too highly priced for South Africa market • Only in a few markets • Overpopulated elephants—culling will be detrimental in markets
Kenya	• Current East African problems—fear of terrorism • More commercialized—lower-market African experience • Cannot tap into the South Africa market easily or add on to South Africa tours • Destination a little tired—nothing new

Source: Grant Thornton Kessel Feinstein 2003.

million for infrastructure improvements and 50 million for the public management of national parks and game management areas).[2] Although this study and others of the same type should be interpreted with great care, in particular because of the high value of the multiplier used to capture the overall economic impact of tourism, it highlights the important trade and development potential of nature-based tourism in Zambia.[3] It also stresses the high return on investments that can be realized in the nature-based tourism sector compared with other sectors.

Conversely, several critics point to "leakages" from the tourism sector, which represent tourism receipts that do not benefit the receiving country, for example, because inputs of goods and services are sourced abroad and profits are repatriated out of the country. The example of the distribution sector in Zambia (Shoprite, see chapter 1 of this study) shows that leakages do not affect only the tourism sector, and sourcing of goods and services abroad can vary over time without being to the detriment of the local economy. The World Bank Country Economic Memorandum made a "conservative" estimate that 30 percent of receipts were being leaked—that is, as much as 70 percent of gross foreign exchange earnings remained within Zambia (World Bank, 2004c, p. 180).

The Tourism Potential of Zambia Remains Largely Untapped

On the demand side: Zambia's success appears limited and still fragile

For the last five years, demand for Zambian tourism has been continuously grow-ing. International tourist arrivals surged from about 400,000 in 1999 to more than 600,000 last year. Projections based on these data suggest that Zambia could attract more than 2 million tourists by 2015, generating significant trade and eco-nomic activity (Ministry of Tourism, Environment and Natural Resources 2006).[4]

In part, the increase in demand has resulted from major investments by multi-nationals and the development by private actors of a diversified range of tourism products and marketing strategies. For example, Sun International partially attributed the increased occupancy of its Livingstone hotels to the contribution of its in-house tour operator, which included Zambia in its package tours.[5] The improvement of services, in particular in the Livingstone area, has attracted new categories of tourists. The share of overseas tourists (Europeans) has significantly increased to become more important than the share of business visitors from neighboring countries: today, 65 percent of the visitors are on "holiday," compared with only 25 percent in 2001, and these tourists are mostly Europeans (41 percent compared with 23 percent in 2000) or South Africans (28 percent compared with 15 percent in 2000) (Zambia National Tourist Board 2002, 2005). In parallel, the amount spent per visit has grown, to the benefit of the local economy: on average, tourists spent $167 per day in 2005, compared with $53 in 1998—of which 39 per-cent is for accommodation, 16 percent is for drinks and food, 6 percent is for leisure activities, 32 percent is for shopping, and 6 percent is for local travel (Zam-bia National Tourist Board 2002, 2005; World Bank 2006).

Despite this stimulus from investment, however, the growth in demand of the past decade remains fragile and Zambia has not yet developed a sustained global brand. First, Zambia represents only 4.3 percent of the safari market share (World Tourism Organization 2006). Second, the performance remains vulnerable to macroeconomic conditions. Looking, for example, at the real growth of tourism and travel (T&T) demand and visitor exports in 2005, Zam-bia is the second-worst performer in the region (after Zimbabwe). While real growth of the sector stagnated at 1.3 percent in 2005, demand grew 10 times faster in Botswana and Tanzania (12.8 percent and 11.5 percent, respectively). In previous years, tourism growth in Zambia was comparable, if not superior, to its neighbors. Reasons for the poor performance in 2005 given by the tourism sec-tor industries include the appreciation of the kwacha by more than 30 percent over the course of a few months, which, combined with a high rate of inflation (16 percent), negatively affected the competitiveness of Zambian tourism serv-ices providers. Third, the growth in demand since 1999 in large part can be

Figure 6.1. Tourism Bed Nights, 1999–2003

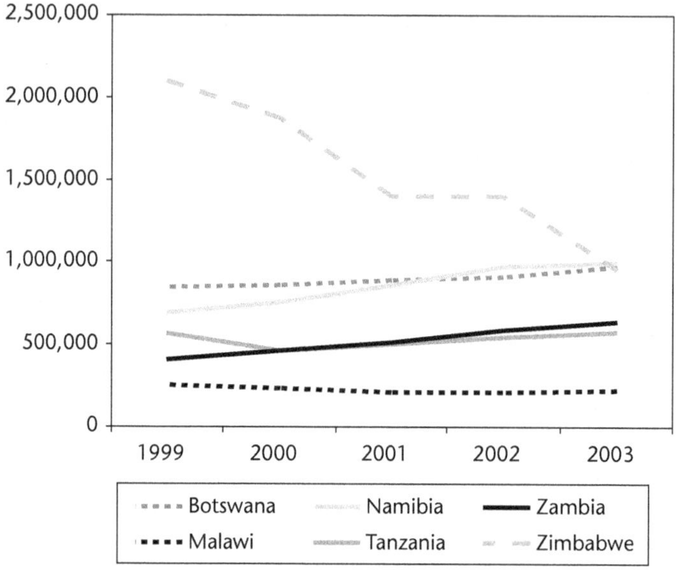

Source: Regional Tourism Organization for Southern Africa 2005.

attributed to the political distress of its immediate competitor, Zimbabwe. In 1999, Zimbabwe received more than 2.1 million tourists; since then, however, this number has dropped by half, and T&T returns of the country have dropped by two-thirds (World Travel and Tourism Council 2005b; Zimbabwe Tourism Authority 2006). Zambia, along with Botswana, has been the main beneficiary of the Zimbabwean crisis and has received a fare share of the diverted tourism traffic and returns.

On the supply side: Zambia has inadequately and unevenly used its resources
The tourist footprint reveals striking and growing inequalities in the distribution of tourism activities and income in Zambia. The Livingstone area, extended to Mosi-oa-Tunya, has benefited the most from tourism growth. The South Luangwa and Lower Zambezi parks are the most developed, but they have grown at a slower pace. The western provinces have benefited from South African tourism, but they remain isolated. The northern territories, despite their high potential, remain off the tourists' path. Large parks like Kafue and North Luangwa have been largely unexploited.

These inequalities are not justified by the distribution of Zambia's tourism attractions (wildlife, waterfalls, archeological sites, etc.), which is more even across the

Table 6.4. Zambian National Parks Tourist Entry

	2000	2003	Average annual growth rate
Kafue	2,200	2,619	6.00%
Lower Zambezi	3,503	3,631	1.20%
Mosi-oa-Tunya	14,998	19,712	9.50%
Victoria Falls	31,248	95,076	44.90%
South Luangwa	16,837	18,712	3.60%
Total	68,786	139,750	26.70%

Source: Guillon 2005 (based on ZAWA 2001 and 2004).

territory. Thus, the concentration of tourism flows is not dictated by the scarcity of tourist attractions, but rather by the inadequacy of infrastructure and access to basic services in remote areas. The northern territory best illustrates this gap between high tourist potential (with the highest concentration of archeological and historical sites and waterfalls in the country) and low tourism outreach and receipts. This reflects a general trend in the country that wealth and living conditions vary greatly across regions. A tourism policy should be tied to a broader strategy for increasing economic opportunities beyond urban centers and the existing railway line.

Figure 6.2. National Park Tourist Entry Trends by Destination, 2000 and 2003

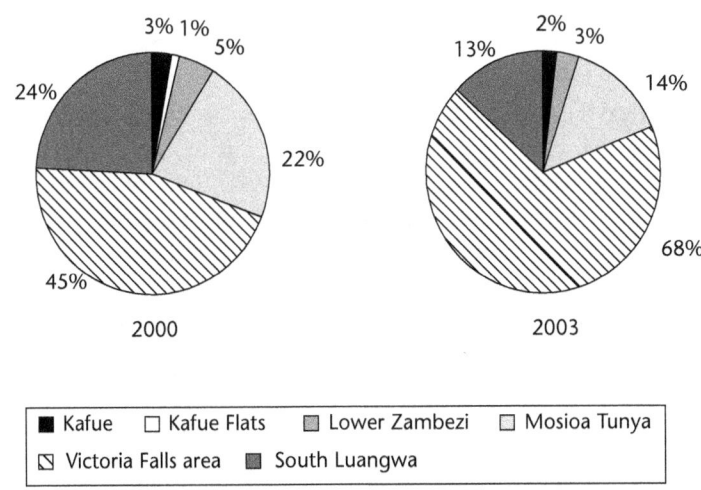

Source: Based on Pope 2005 and ZAWA 2005.

Geographic inequalities pose a double threat for the harmonious and sustainable development of tourism in Zambia: the massive growth of tourist arrivals and their concentration in Livingstone could undermine the image of Zambia as the "real, unspoilt Africa"; and the concentration of tourism in limited sites encourages tourists to shorten their stay in Zambia (for example, one night in Livingstone) and hook up to other destinations in neighboring countries that are more easily, and cheaply, accessible by air.

On the first point, Zambia should preserve its "uniqueness" and continue to play the card of the "real African experience." The paradox today is that, despite a low national tourist density, the optimum vehicle density value of 0.1 vehicles per kilometer for high-quality, low-density tourism is already exceeded in the most popular areas because of the limited road network (in particular, in the wet season) (Pope 2005). The second point represents a serious challenge for Zambia's tourism strategy: 60 percent of the tourists spent less than four days in Zambia, most commonly to visit the Victoria Falls and a nearby national park (World Bank Survey 2006). This results in a high concentration of tourism trade receipts.

Only a better and geographically more extensive utilization of Zambia's tourism potential will make development sustainable. Tourist accommodation units remain sparse across the country and often of poor quality—with the exception of luxurious premises for high-end tourists, most often lodges. In nature-based tourism, the Livingstone area represents 39 percent of all beds and 45 percent of all bed nights, reflecting higher levels of occupancy (Pope 2006). While nonspecific tourism activities are often offered in house and are included in packages (game drives and walks), more specific activities (bungee jumping and helicopter flights) are usually "extras" provided by specialist firms. Here, again, because of the lack of a critical tourist mass in areas other than Livingstone, these tourism activities and service providers are concentrated in the Livingstone area (see annex 2 and table 6.5). The development of such activities elsewhere has the potential to extend the length of the tourists' stay, as well as benefit remote areas of the country. Operators identify the major constraints to working in the more remote areas as the lack of access to infrastructure (transport, of course, but also electricity, water, and sanitation) and basic services (the most qualified workers refuse to work in tourist resorts in remote areas, and local populations do not have basic education and skills).

The demand for longer stays and more diversified activities across Zambia will most likely be supply driven, as has been the case in Livingstone following the massive investment of Sun International. A number of foreign investors have expressed interest in the sector (for example, Legacy Group, Kingdom Group, Sun International, Wilderness Safari, Conservation Corporation, Protea, Accor, and

Table 6.5. Employment Distribution in Nature-Based Tourism Activity Providers, by Region

Region	Permanent employees
Kariba Lakeside	16
Livingstone and the rapids	535
Lower Zambezi	0
Lunga, Kafue, Kafue Flats	0
Lusaka	24
Northern	0
South Luangwa	0
Western and North-Western	0
Totals	575

Source: Pope 2006.

others) and could contribute to the harmonious development of tourism across the country, particularly given that the Livingstone area is close to saturation.

Macroeconomic evidence suggests that Zambia is not fully exploiting its tourism potential

It is estimated that the T&T economy currently contributes nearly 4 percent of GDP and more than 55,000 jobs, that is 3.7 percent of total employment. These positive results should, however, be placed in the context of the performance of its neighbors. Here, again, it appears that Zambia poorly exploits the potential of tourism: compared with its regional competitors, Zambia has the second-lowest contribution of tourism to GDP and employment after Zimbabwe (see annex 4). In other terms, the government's strategy to use tourism as a tool for diversification of the economy has not yet been successful, and the economic potential of tourism remains largely untapped in the country. In Botswana, Tanzania, Namibia, and South Africa, the T&T economy already accounts for about 10 percent of GDP, which is the objective set by the Zambian government, but it is far from being reached. On the employment front, the percentage of jobs in the tourism sector in Zambia is half of the average percentage for the whole Sub-Saharan Africa and up to three to four times lower than in some of its immediate competitors in the south.

A quick econometric exercise confirms this conclusion: Zambia is receiving significantly less tourists than what its first-nature attractions would warrant. If it were to improve its performance in infrastructure and its business climate, the country could receive a much larger share of tourism flows—51 percent more tourists, that is, 295,000 per year (see box 6.1).

Box 6.1. Evaluating Zambia's Performance and Potential in Tourism Services

Zambia has many obvious natural advantages that make it a potentially attractive destination for tourists. But how successful is the country in harnessing these advantages and converting them into a source of income? How does Zambia fare in international comparison when it comes to attracting foreign tourists?

To investigate this question we look at the determinants of tourism flows in a data set comprising all countries for which we have information available. We run a set of simple regressions in which we estimate the number of international tourism arrivals (in natural logarithms) as a function of a set of country characteristics,[a] and then enter an indicator variable for Zambia to evaluate how much the country deviates from the general pattern, given its own characteristics.

When choosing the kind of variables that we consider relevant for the development of a successful tourism business, we make a distinction between two broad classes of explanatory variables. As a first step, we only consider variables of "first nature," by which we mean characteristics that are unalterable, that is, cannot be affected by policy. These include two proxy measures of the natural attractions of a country, such as biodiversity and preservation of wildlife (measured by the number of threatened birds species present in the country), and the share of a country's surface that is under natural protection (such as a national park). We further include a proxy measure for the cultural and natural attractions of a country, for which we chose the number of UNESCO-recognized cultural and natural heritage sites in a country.[b] Finally, we also add as a measure of political stability an index of tensions caused by "racial, nationality, or language divisions" (developed by the International Country Risk Guide, where lower values are associated to a higher degree of tension).

The results of this analysis based only on first-nature characteristics are illustrated in columns I and II of box table 1. The explanatory variables are significant in almost all cases and have the expected signs: The more natural endowments a country has (as measured by national parks and wildlife preservation), the more tourists it tends to attract. Similarly, the more cultural heritage sites and the less political tensions it has, the higher its attractiveness to foreign tourists.

Interestingly, *Zambia turns out to be a negative outlier with respect to the pattern detected in the cross-country sample.* In other words, *Zambia is receiving a significantly smaller number of tourists than what its first-nature attractions would warrant.* This suggests that if one were to judge tourism potential solely on the basis of a country's endowments, with respect to natural and cultural attractions, Zambia has much untapped potential in harnessing tourism.

But tourists do not come for beauty alone. An attractive tourist destination must also deliver the amenities that tourists need, and these fall into two broad categories. First, the state of basic infrastructure matters, and the most obvious proxy measure for this is the extension of paved roads. Second, incoming tourists need to be accommodated and serviced by local tourism establishments, such as tour operators, hotels, and restaurants. It is not easy to find a direct measure for the existence of this kind of infrastructure, and even if such a measure existed it would be subject to a reverse causation from the number of tourist arrivals itself.

Box Table 1. Zambia's Performance in the Tourism Sector

International tourist arrivals (in logs)		I	II	III	IV	V	VI
	Zambia	−1.48***	−0.89**	−0.30	0.11	−0.20	−0.21
		(0.45)	(0.34)	(0.34)	(0.46)	(0.30)	(0.31)
First-nature characteristics	Wildlife proxy	0.02***	0.00	0.01***	0.01**	0.01**	0.01**
		(0.01)	(0.00)	(0.00)	(0.00)	(0.00)	(0.00)
	National parks	0.05***	0.03*	0.03**	0.02	0.02*	0.02*
		(0.02)	(0.01)	(0.01)	(0.01)	(0.01)	(0.01)
	Cultural attractions (UNESCO)		0.15***	0.12***	0.11***	0.11***	0.11***
			(0.02)	(0.02)	(0.02)	(0.02)	(0.02)
	Ethnic tensions Index		0.38***	0.26***	0.13	0.16*	0.14
			(0.08)	(0.08)	(0.10)	(0.09)	(0.09)
Second-nature characteristics	Road infrastructure (% of roads paved)			0.02***	0.02***	0.02***	0.02***
				(0.00)	(0.00)	(0.00)	(0.00)
	Cost of starting a business				−0.00***	−0.00***	−0.00***
					(0.00)	(0.00)	(0.00)
	Cost of obtaining a license					−0.00***	−0.00*
						(0.00)	(0.00)
	Cost of enforcing a contract						−0.01*
							(0.00)
	Credit information Index					0.13*	
						(0.07)	
	R^2	0.09	0.54	0.63	0.66	0.64	0.65
	N	133	116	108	102	101	101

Note: *, **, *** indicate statistical significance at the 10, 5, and 1 percent level

(Box continues on the following page.)

Box 6.1. (continued)

Therefore, it seems more adequate to use as explanatory variables the conditions under which such businesses can be established, which are part of the business climate. If it is difficult to start and operate a business in a given country, then tourists are less likely to find a comprehensive range of services at their disposal. In line with this reasoning, we include several measures from the World Bank's *Doing Business* database, which are available for a large number of countries. These measures include the cost of starting a business (as percentage of per capita income); the cost of obtaining a license and all necessary permits to build a warehouse (as percentage of per capita income); and the cost of enforcing a debt contract in the local judicial system, as percentage of the debt value. We control also for the credit information index, as a measure for the development of local credit markets.

We find the measures for both infrastructure and the business climate to be highly significant predictors of tourism flows as we enter them in different specifications in columns III to VI of box table 1. Tourists are attracted to countries where they face fewer infrastructure problems and to such countries where the business climate facilitates the emergence of the kind of secondary businesses on whose services international tourists rely.

When including these second-nature characteristics into our analysis, we find that Zambia is no longer an outlier to the general pattern. In other words, although on the basis of first-nature attractiveness Zambia should be receiving a larger share of tourism flows than it actually does, the country's tourism performance is more adequately explained when one considers Zambia's performance with respect to infrastructure and business climate. The country's below-average performance on these variables explains why Zambia is not able to reap more benefits from tourism than it currently does.

Unlike the first-nature characteristics, the second-nature issues are not something that a country is stuck with forever. Infrastructure can be made a policy priority, and all of the constraints to a favorable business climate can be addressed by adequate policy. Some of them, like a tedious licensing process to establish a new business, can even be remedied by a stroke of pen.

The analysis presented here suggests that Zambia could be receiving a much larger share of tourism flows if it were to improve its performance in infrastructure and business climate. Our regression analysis suggests that the country could attract 51 percent more tourists if it were performing on par with South Africa with respect to these variables. This would amount to almost 295,000 additional tourists per year. Given its natural endowments, Zambia has the potential for doing much better with respect to tourism, but the development of the sector is hampered by shortcomings in the area of regulation and infrastructure.

Source: World Bank staff 2006.

a. The values are averages from 1999–2003.

b. For Zambia, for example, these include the Victoria Falls as a natural heritage site.

Harnessing tourism trade: Directions for government policy

Zambia Needs to Eliminate Administrative Constraints on Investment and Business Operation

The burden of licensing and other administrative requirements: Reducing cost and increasing predictability

Businesses operating in the tourism sector cite licensing and other administrative procedures as the main obstacle to doing business. Up to 74 licenses are required to operate a hotel that offers different types of tourism activities, such as gaming or hunting. The number of licenses required per se is not a problem. However, the following obstacles do exist:

(1) The cost associated with compliance is too high. It is estimated that the annual cost of compliance for a basic five-room guest house is about K 10 million (see table 6.6). The Hotel and Catering Association of Zambia has suggested that it is possible to reduce this cost by 50 percent, given that the cost of licenses is often disproportionate to the service provided by the corresponding administrative bodies.

(2) According to businesses, licensing agencies lack professionalism and efficiency, and can be obstructive—with significant variation in the satisfaction level from agency to agency (see table 6.9). The overall system lacks transparency. No tourism industry regulator was able to communicate an exhaustive list of the licenses required to operate a business, despite repeated meetings. In practice, it appears that the number of licenses obtained by each business varies dramatically both within and across regions. Similar variations exist in compliance costs (see figure 6.3). In part, this is explained by the varying number and cost of local requirements (see table 6.7). It also results, however, from a high level of unpredictability, which can become a major source of informal trade and unfair competition for properly established businesses.

(3) Unpredictability was a major concern expressed regarding land policy, where leases could only be obtained for shorter periods than desired by businesses, and where legal commitments could be disregarded by the public authorities.

(4) A long time is required to obtain all the licenses. In particular, opening a business can take six months to a year. As shown in figure 6.3, the indirect cost of obtaining licenses in terms of lost days of work is often higher than the direct cost in terms of fees. The system for approval and renewal of liquor licenses was designed to process 200 applications a year, despite the fact that there are an estimated 4,000 sellers of alcohol in the city of Lusaka alone.

Table 6.6. Annual Procedure Costs for a Five-Room Guest House

Renewable annual costs	
Health	K 500,000
Fire	K 400,000
A second license under fire to keep gas	K 300,000
Ministry of Tourism	K 950,000
Liquor	K 200,000
Press Advertisement for Liquor	K 94,000
Restaurant	K 500,000
Annual Trading Business Permit	K 100,000
ZNTB Authorization Licenses	K 2,205,000
LCC Annual Rates (GH/Class B)	K 4,000,000
HCAZ Membership	K 250,000
Total	*K 9,499,000*
Other costs and administrative requirements	
Medical Examination Certificate for Food Handlers	
City Engineers Report	
Chief Fire Officers Report	
Medical Officer of Health's Report	
Tax Clearance	
Waste Management Contract	

Source: Estimates based on interviews with the Hotel and Catering Association of Zambia.

Note: GH = guest house; HCAZ = Hotel and Catering Association of Zambia; LCC = Lusaka City Council; ZNTB = Zambia National Tourist Board.

(5) It also appears that the more remote and isolated the business, the lower the level of compliance and of satisfaction with regulatory agencies (see figure 6.3).

Closely related is the virtual lack of operation of the accommodation grading system. Hotel standards are monitored by the Hotels Board of Zambia, and the National Tender Board is responsible for monitoring the quality of restaurants; however, few inspections have been conducted in the past few years because of the lack of resources and transport (World Bank 2004c). As a result, Zambia's hotel accommodations and restaurants do not meet the required standards, and two-thirds of the hospitality establishments remain unclassified. Illegal guesthouses, motels, and lodges have mushroomed over years. This illustrates how burdensome and complex administrative measures do not serve the valid policy objectives at their origin: instead of ensuring quality of service, the system of administrative control relegates Zambian hospitality establishments to gray areas or informality. Without a strict application of quality control, the reputation of Zambia as a tourist destination is threatened by malpractice.

Figure 6.3. Cost of Regulatory Compliance, 2005 (U.S. dollars)

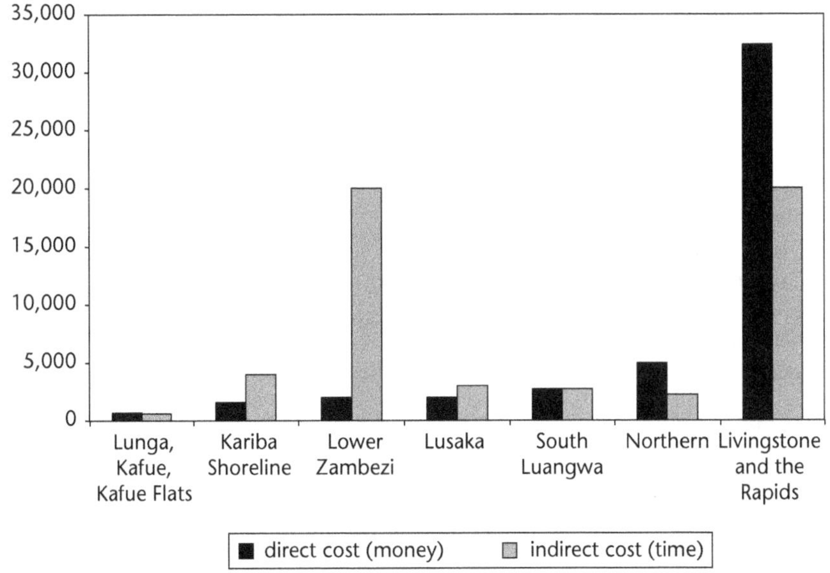

Source: Pope 2006.

Note: Direct cost is the maximum amount declared by a nature-based tourism business to comply with licensing requirements; indirect cost is the maximum amount declared in working days equivalent to get all required licenses. These costs account for acquiring up to 5–8 licenses in Kariba Shoreline; up to 2–4 licenses in South Luangwa, Northern, and Lower Zambezi; up to more than 12 licenses in Livingstone and the Rapids; and up to 8–12 licenses in Lunga, Kafue, and Kafue Flats. On average, the cost declared by surveyed businesses is much lower, and the number of licenses held by each of them varies significantly, revealing the unpredictability and inequality of the system. Although the indirect cost can be overvalued, the direct cost is probably a conservative estimate of the full-compliance cost.

Informality has a cost for businesses in terms of their ability to access credit, and the security and predictability of business. It appears, however, that this cost remains, in the eyes of many small Zambian businesses, lower than the cost of entering the formal sector because of the money and time necessary to obtain the required licenses. The government should find the least burdensome administrative measures that allow it to achieve legitimate policy objectives related to security (fire reports) or public health (liquor and medical licenses).

There was reportedly an initiative to create a "one-stop shop," which could facilitate doing business. Progress on this front has been slow, however, because of the vested interests of certain agencies in the collection of licensing fees. One-stop shops have not always been successful and have sometimes become one-more-stop shops—experience shows that the shop must have enough authority to either issue licenses or accelerate the process of gaining specific approvals. In Tanzania, the Investment Center houses nine senior officials from diverse ministries and

Table 6.7. Livingstone City Council Charges on Tourism

Type of charge levied	Cost
Commercial properties (tourism and others)	3 percent of the evaluation roll
Hotels	From K 10.2 million (ungraded) to K 154 million (five-star)
Lodges	From K 3 million (grade E) to K 5 million (grade A)
Development charges in the tourism sector	K 600,000
Subdivision of plots in the tourism sector	K 1.5 million
Scrutiny fees for tourism per square meter	K 500,000
Petroleum storage license for commercial use	K 700,000
Flat rate tourist levy in addition to the national hotel levy	(cost not specified)
Liquor license	K 100,000 (penalty of K 500,000 for trading without a license)
Various small fees payable to the Registrar of Companies	For example, annual return fee of K 400,000 or application to register a business of K 15,000

Source: Pycroft 2004, based on Kazilimani, *Zambia's Non-Tax Revenues and Earmarked Taxes*, 2004.

normally manages applications to open business within a few days. This rapid turnaround is due in part to a "no-objection" provision written into the invest-ment code—unless a ministry objects within 14 days, the center is entitled to approve the application (World Bank 2004b). The Zambia Investment Center has already proven its ability to play this role, for example, by collecting all licenses required to open a business.

To address these issues, a first step would be to undertake a review of adminis-trative barriers and assess their efficiency against their cost in terms of the devel-opment of the sector: (1) measures that do not serve any valid policy objective could be removed; (2) measures that serve a valid policy objective but at excessive cost, in terms of time or money, could be replaced by more efficient instruments. It should be noted that this simplification process and the reduction of some licensing fees would not necessarily result in a reduction in public income—on the contrary, it would create an incentive for many businesses to join the formal sector. For example, a reduction by 75 percent of the cost of opening a business in Uganda resulted in a 40 percent increase in public revenue (see box 6.2). Zambia could undertake a "guillotine" regulatory reform, not necessarily limited to the tourism sector, but similar to that implemented by many developed and develop-ing countries, including Kenya. The reform in Mexico eliminated about half the regulations and simplified almost all those that remained (see box 6.3). This process is not merely about deregulation, but rather quality assurance.

Box 6.2. Fighting Informality by Easing Business Registration: The Examples of Vietnam and Uganda

The high cost of business registration discourages new firms from entering the formal economy. Vietnam and Uganda illustrate successful strategies for reducing these costs.

Vietnam

Before a new Enterprise Law was enacted in January 2000, business registration and licensing requirements were extremely burdensome in Vietnam. Entrepreneurs were required to submit detailed business plans, curricula vitae, character references, medical certificates, and other documents along with their applications for registration. On average, registering a business took about three months, and required visits to 10 different agencies and submissions of about 20 different documents with official seals. Additional licenses were often required before firms could start operating. Some of these licenses did not appear to serve vital public interests (such as those to operate photocopying machines). It took 6 to 12 months to fulfill the legal requirements to establish a business at a cost of $700 to $1,400. The new law reduced the costs of establishing a new business. The time to establish a new business came down to about two months—with business registration taking only 15 days—and total start-up costs were reduced to about $350. Vietnamese entrepreneurs responded. Fewer than 6,000 new businesses had registered in 1999, but the number shot up to more than 14,000 in 2000 and to more than 21,000 in both 2001 and 2002.

Uganda

A recent pilot program in Entebbe reduced the time and monetary costs to register a business. By streamlining licensing processes and reducing the number of previously required approvals and assessments, the time to register a business was reduced from two days to about 30 minutes. This reduced the cost of registering a business by 75 percent. Although business registration is only one of several steps to start a new business in Uganda (businesses have to register for tax purposes and many need additional licenses), the cost can be significant because registration needs to be repeated annually for most businesses. The pilot program increased business registrations, with an estimated four times as many businesses registering in Entebbe the year after the pilot. Despite the lower fees, the higher number of registrations meant that revenue collections increased by 40 percent. With administrative savings of 25 percent in staff time and 10 percent in financial resources, the program also benefited the municipal authority.

Source: World Bank 2004b, based on background papers by Raymond Mallon (Vietnam) and Cerstin Sander (Uganda) 2004.

Box 6.3. The Regulatory Guillotine: A Model for Zambia?

The regulatory guillotine reform has been used by several countries that suffered, like the Zambian tourism sector, from the excess and poor quality of regulations imposed on business opening and operation. Pioneered by Sweden in 1984, the experience has spread over to Organisation for Economic Co-operation and Development (OECD) countries, transition economies, and, more recently, developing countries.

As defined by the Jacobs (Jacobs and Associates) and Astrakhan (World Bank) study, the guillotine process can be broken down into the following steps:

1. The government establishes the scope of the guillotine, that is, defines precisely the kinds of regulatory instruments to be included.
2. The government adopts a legal instrument that sets out the guillotine process, schedule, and institutions.
3. The legal instrument contains a set of explicit and simple criteria that define which regulations pass and which regulations fail. Three common criteria are as follows:
   - Is the regulation legal (has it been published and is it authorized by parliamentary law)?
   - Is the regulation necessary for the future policy priorities of the country?
   - Is the regulation business friendly?
4. The regulations are passed through three filters or review processes. In each filter, unnecessary, outdated, and illegal rules are identified, and excluded from the list:
   - In the first review, all government agencies establish lists of their regulations within the scope of the guillotine by a certain date, and justify those regulations that they want to keep.
   - In the second review, the lists are reviewed by a central review unit that carries out the same review of regulations that passed the first review.
   - In the third review, the lists are reviewed by stakeholders and recommendations are given to the central review unit.
5. Once the final review is completed, a centralized list is created by adding all the ministries' lists together. When the deadline is reached, any regulation not on the list is automatically cancelled without further legal action or further legal action is scheduled to eliminate any rules not on the list (the guillotine drops).

6. The list defines the contents of a comprehensive electronic registry of all regulations in force, and it is recognized in law as the legal database of regulations for purposes of compliance.
7. In future, all new regulations and changes are entered in the registry within one day of adoption and/or publication. The registry should have legal security—no regulation not in the registry can be enforced against a business.

The scope of the study can vary: Zambia could decide, for instance, to apply the method to the tourism sector only, and ask the network of regulators in the sector to establish a registry of applicable rules. The first benefit would be to provide the government (for the first time) with a comprehensive list of existing rules. Like in the Swedish model, all regulations that are not registered would automatically be cancelled without further legal action. Then the regulators would have to comment on each rule and justify why it is not outdated or unnecessary. In the Swedish education sector, for example, 90 percent of the regulations were eliminated. In Mexico (1998), nearly 3,000 formalities were reviewed, with on average 45.8 percent of rules suppressed and 97 percent simplified by the end of the process (which took five years). The macroeconomic effects of the reform can be significant: for an economy-wide deregulation, South Korea gained over five years about 8.5 points of GDP and reduced unemployment by 1 point.

Closer to Zambia, Kenya engaged in 2005 in a guillotine reform, which engaged 178 ministries and public bodies. At the beginning, it was estimated that Kenya had about 600 regulations pertaining to doing business. After a first census, it appeared that their number reached more than 1,300. This suggested that the ministries and regulatory bodies, including at local levels, had a direct financial interest in creating new licenses and business fees because these revenues supported increased staff and increased opportunities for corruption. In the first phase (12 weeks), the government established the listing of all regulations and reviewed selected licenses considered to be the highest priority; in a second phase (eight months), the government plans to review the reminder of the 1,200 licenses. Out of the 86 licenses reviewed in the first phase, the government already suppressed 35 licenses and simplified 4 others. The second phase will be critical for the success of the reform, and a larger strategy will be needed to avoid reregulation.

Source: Jacobs and Astrakhan 2006.

The tax system and investment incentives: Restoring equality

The Zambian tax system consists of three different layers: (1) the general level, with taxes levied either on value added or turnover, which applies to all businesses in the tourism sector; (2) the level of subsector and geographic exemptions or incentives, which aims to facilitate diversification of the economy and to promote certain subsectors of tourism or areas of growth and trade; and (3) the level of individually negotiated exemptions and incentives, which primarily aims to attract FDI to Zambia. Although this three-layered system sounds reasonable, services sectors (including tourism) have been largely ignored, leaving the tourism operators with a tax level much higher than their competitors in the region. In combination with poor access to finance for small and medium-size enterprises (SMEs), this system also creates an incentive for many businesses to stay in the informal sector, and increases the gap between local and foreign entrepreneurs, who are able to benefit from tailor-made tax holidays and other incentives. The disparity of treatment between Zambians and foreigners has helped to fuel the debate on empowerment. In sum, tax incentives are a source of arbitrary inequalities, as pointed out by the Foreign Investment Advisory Service of the World Bank in its December 2004 report: "Although the tax/incentive scheme in Zambia is broadly pro-growth, tax policies and rates are not being evenly and consistently applied in the tourism sector" (World Bank 2004d, p. 20). Most recent initiatives, like the proposed Zambia Development Agency Act, have unfortunately not remedied this situation.

Box 6.4. Level 1: General Level of Taxes for Tourism Activities

Corporate Tax = 35%
VAT = 17.5%
Service Charge = 10%
No preferential treatment on customs and excise duties

General nonsector-specific exemptions:
• Income from small enterprises registered under the Small Enterprises Development Act of 1996 is exempt from tax (1) for the first three years of operation in an urban area, and (2) for the first five years of operation in a rural area.

Tourism sector–specific exemptions or incentives:
• Wear-and-tear allowances.

To look at the first level, the corporate tax rate is 35 percent. This is high relative to competitors in the region: in Botswana, the rate is 15 percent; in South Africa, Tanzania, and Zimbabwe, it is 30 percent. For businesses with annual turnover of K 200 million or less, a 3 percent tax on turnover is applied. This mechanism is aimed at simplifying the administration for SMEs to encourage more entry into the formal sector. The resulting tax burden may be more or less dependent on the relative turnover and profit levels (World Bank 2004d).

Zambia has adopted numerous tax incentives for nontraditional industries, but these largely exclude services industries, creating a distortion between these industries and their manufacturing counterparts. For example, the reduction in corporate tax to 15 percent for businesses with nontraditional exports (i.e., everything but copper) does not include services exports. This lacuna in the law puts the services sector, including tourism, at a disadvantage as it continues to pay 35 percent corporate tax. Even the traditional mining sector has a lower rate of 25 percent for large mining companies. This oversight of the legislator should be remedied to reflect the increasing role of services trade in the Zambian economy. Similarly, the Zambian Development Agency Act exempts 50 percent of profits from taxes for companies operating under its scheme, suspends import duties for a five-year period, and qualifies capital expenditure on improvements for a 100 percent improvement allowance; however, it appears that priority sectors identified in the Second Schedule of the Act do not include services. This Act is likely to increase further the gap between services and the manufacturing sector.

Some other general exemptions do nonetheless benefit the tourism sector. These include incentives in favor of micro and small businesses, which are exempted from taxes for the first three (in urban areas) to five years (in rural areas) of operation.

Finally, the following diverse wear-and tear-allowances benefit the tourism sector:

- Initial allowance on hotel buildings: 10%
- Annual allowance on hotel buildings: 5%
- Equipment and furniture: 50%
- Commercial vehicles: 25%
- Noncommercial vehicles: 20%

Manufacturing and farming also benefit from these allowances. Previous studies qualified the net result of these incentives as "negligible" because of the low profit margin (taxable income) of the industry (World Bank 2004d, p. 25).

Turning to consumption taxes, the VAT stands at 17.5 percent. Numerous exemptions exist, however, that include most tourism service providers, although none of these exemptions covers the sector as a whole.

Table 6.8. VAT Rates in the South African Region

Botswana	10%
Kenya	16%
Namibia	15%
Malawi	20%
South Africa	14%
Tanzania	20%
Zambia	17.5%

Source: World Bank 2004d.

Regarding customs and excise duties, the Zambian tourism industry does not receive preferential treatment. Some key products for the tourism sector are targets of high excise duties, such as beer (70 percent), wines (125 percent), spirits (125 percent), petrol (30 percent), and diesel (30 percent) making tourism operations expensive (World Bank 2004d). It is estimated that Zambia is at least twice as expensive as South Africa, and the costs of operations are one-and-a-half times higher than in other neighboring countries (Pope 2005). Although this is in part because of the cost of transport and basic services in Zambia, it is also because of the higher level of taxes on basic consumption goods served to tourists and the taxes on fuel.

In addition, a compulsory service charge of 10 percent is applied to all services rendered in hotels, lodges, and food and beverage establishments. The amount collected is then redistributed to the staff of these establishments. Finally, visitors have to pay visa fees that vary from $25 to $100 (for U.S. citizens),[6] and an airport departure tax of $20 for international flights, which is comparable to other countries' practice. To promote Zambian tour operators, however, the government decided to waive the visa fees if the international traveler booked the trip through a Zambian tour operator. Good practice would suggest that the airport departure tax be included in the air ticket price (like in South Africa) with a view to reducing transaction costs (Pycroft 2004).

These consumption and other taxes add to the cost of traveling to Zambia for tourists, who are highly sensitive to price. A Deloitte & Touche study conducted on behalf of the British Tourist Authority determined that the price elasticity of the holiday tourist market was –1.5, that is, a price cut of 10 percent would translate into a 15 percent increase in tourist demand (World Bank 2004d, p. 25). In the case of Zambia, however, the high-end tourists are likely to be less sensitive to price, and although there is an urgent need to address the issue of corporate tax or licensing costs that constitute an obstacle to doing business, taxes paid by tourists are less of an immediate worry.

> ## Box 6.5. Level 2: Subsector and Geographic Tax Exemptions and Other Incentives of Relevance to Tourism
>
> Corporate tax = 30%[a]
> VAT = zero rate[b]
>
> a. For tourism businesses in rural areas during the first five years of operation.
>
> b. For (1) the Livingstone area (initially for two years but maintained by tacit agreement); and (2) package tours sold by licensed operators to international tourists and some tourism activities: boat cruising, microlighting, helicopter tours, and walking safaris.

At the second level, some tourism service providers benefit from specific tax reductions and incentives on the basis of geographic or activity criteria. In the first category, the region of Livingstone has benefited since 1991 from a VAT exemption. This may have encouraged the explosion of tourism in the area and the development of many small businesses. However, this tax holiday has contributed to the further concentration of tourism in the Livingstone area as opposed to other destinations in the country. These concessions should be revisited, with a view toward removing them or extending them to more remote provinces. This harmonization could contribute to stimulating growth in remote areas and alleviating poverty across the country. For example, a study commissioned by the Ministry of Finance and the U.K. Department for International Development (DFID) proposed the granting of tax concessions to enterprises willing to invest in the Kafue National Park. The study recommended offering investment tax credits for a three-year period to those investing in the park (Pycroft 2004).

In the second category of activity-based exemptions, package tours and some tourism activities have benefited from a zero VAT rating: these include boat cruising, microlighting, helicopter tours, and walking safaris. The choice of these subsectors remains arbitrary and again the concessions should be removed or extended to all tourism activities for a limited period of time. According to previous studies, variable VAT rates in the tourism sector encourage corruption at border posts and manipulation of the system. For example, overseas business bookings were declared as packages, and fictitious booking offices were set up in international source markets (World Bank 2004d).

At the third level, a number of incentives have been given to attract foreign investors to Zambia. These incentives were negotiated individually and varied from case to case and from period to period, depending on the strategic needs of the country. Some of these incentives were strongly criticized for being unneces-

---

Box 6.6. Level 3: Individually Negotiated Tax Exemptions and Other Incentives of Relevance to Tourism

Corporate tax = 15%
VAT = zero rate

Below is an illustrative list of some incentives negotiated by major foreign investors in the tourism/hospitality industry. Exemptions and incentives depend on the size and strategic importance of the investment, and the general economic situation/needs of Zambia at the time of negotiations:

- Waiver of import duties on all capital goods to be imported during the construction period
- Waiver of deposit duties in respect of temporary import permits for all capital goods
- Fast-track refunds of VAT paid in respect of locally purchased goods
- Treatment of hotels as "Industrial Buildings" to qualify for a tax allowance of 10 percent
- Treatment as a nontraditional exporter to qualify for the reduced corporate tax of 15 percent on foreign earnings
- Partial relief from the payment of the casino levy
- Reduced fee for the submission of the Environmental Impact Assessment Report
- Inclusion of accommodation as part of tourist services qualifying for zero rating of VAT
- Preliminary grant of a hotel operations license together with the necessary gambling/gaming licenses, liquor licenses, tour operator license, and any other licenses needed to fulfill the investor's development plans
- Grant of work permits (up to 30) for expatriate employees

---

sarily generous, for example, in the Sun International case—the argument is that the investment would have taken place regardless of the incentives. It has even been suggested that Zambia reopen negotiations to charge Sun International the normal tax rate, although it is recognized that, in the short run, this would send a negative signal to potential investors and Sun International is just starting to make profits in Livingstone (thus the DFID study suggested that the agreement could be revisited after 2008 only) (Pycroft 2004).

It seems difficult to second guess today what Sun International or other investors would have decided in the absence of incentives. The massive investment by Sun International (two hotels totaling 385 rooms, representing an initial investment of $65 million, and a total of $120 million) significantly boosted economic activity in Livingstone and the neighboring area (Mosi-oa-Tunya National Park and the rapids). The international group managed to bring a critical mass of tourists to Livingstone by imposing a certain quality of service (the Royal Livingstone is one of the leading hotels of the world) and putting the Zambian side of Livingstone back on the tourism map, for example, by including Zambia in packages offered by the in-house tour operator and investing $3 million in marketing Zambia's tourism potential. Increased demand prompted the decision to expand the capacity of the local airport to make it accessible to long-haul flights. Sun International Zambia has approximately 350 permanent employees, supported by 500 or more casual and contract workers. It has contributed to diverse community projects, for example, the completion of renovations for the children's ward in the Batoka Hospital, the rehabilitation of the Zambezi Basic School, and HIV/AIDS training in Mukuni Village, or actively lobbied in favor of the rehabilitation of Livingstone, for example, for improved infrastructure and street lights. In sum, it is widely acknowledged that the contribution of foreign investment was largely positive.[7]

FDI incentives could be maintained but revisited (with a special emphasis on facilitation of the regulatory process rather than tax incentives), and the first and second levels of taxation should be rationalized to restore equality and competitive conditions in the market.

Zambia Needs to Develop Efficient Policies/Institutions to Manage Resources and Deal with the Myopia of the Market

Reforming the organization and administration of the tourism sector

The organization of the public sector in the tourism area is complex and its fragmentation and lack of coordination have been detrimental to the development and implementation of a coherent sector strategy. As pointed out in previous reports, government agencies are still dominated by bureaucratic procedures, are continuously reorganized, and suffer from frequent and unjustified changes of key political and administrative staff (World Bank 2004a). In general, reforms have not been accompanied by the necessary reallocation of powers and resources. For example, during 2003–04, the Government of Zambia disbursed only 12 percent of planned inputs for the National Tourism Master Development Plan and the Tourism Investment Promotion Project—and, more generally, in all fields of intervention in the tourism sector (infrastructure, promotion of investment, marketing, and promotion), actual output was small (Ministry of Finance and National Planning 2004, appendixes 4 and 5). Evidence suggests a willingness to change. The Visit Zambia 2005 campaign has been a first step toward such change, but marketing of the Zambian tourism product remains poor: lack of awareness of the destination stands, in operators' eyes, as the second most important constraint on tourism development (see figure 6.4).

Box 6.7. Public Sector Organizations

Ministry of Tourism
Zambia National Tourism Board
Zambia Wildlife Authority
National Heritage Conservation Commission
National Museums Board
Zambia National Economic and Tourism Development Committee

The bodies representing the private sector have suffered from the same problems: a plethora of small organizations lack coordination and a common strategy, resulting in weak lobbying power. The Tourism Council of Zambia was allegedly not sufficiently representative and only now has begun to play the catalytic role that it was assigned.

This dissatisfaction with the functioning of regulatory and operator bodies in the tourism sector is reflected in the most recent surveys of the private sector (see table 6.9). It appears that businesses consider these bodies to be (1) unprofessional and obstructive or (2) inefficient and unpredictable in 90 percent of the cases. This dissatisfaction runs across the spectrum of bodies involved in tourism management, including local authorities, national ministries or agencies, and private sector associations. The only three exceptions are the Immigration Department, the Revenue Authority, and the National Tourism Board, which are seen as more

---

Box 6.8. Private Sector Organizations

Tourism Council of Zambia (umbrella organization)
Hotel and Catering Association of Zambia
Tour Operators Association of Zambia
Travel Agents Association of Zambia
Livingstone Tourism Association
Conservation Lower Zambezi
Zambia Horizons
Professional Hunters Association
Wildlife Producers Association
Zambia Sports Fishing Association
Airline Owners and Operators Association
Board of Airline Representatives
South Luangwa Safari Association

Table 6.9. Regulatory and Governmental Bodies as Seen by Enterprises in the Tourism Sector

	Kariba Shore-line	South Luangwa	Northern	Lower Zambezi	Living-stone and the Rapids	Lusaka	Lunga, Kafue, Kafue Flats	National average
Community Resource Boards	0	2	2	2	2	0	3	1
District Councils	2	3	1	2	3	3	3	2
Ministry of Energy and Water Development	1	2	0	1	2	3	2	1
Environmental Council of Zambia	1	2	1	1	3	3	2	2
Fisheries Department	1	1	2	1	0	3	0	1
Forestry Department	1	1	1	1	0	3	0	1
Ministry of Health	3	2	1	1	1	3	0	2
Immigration Department	3	3	2	3	2	3	1	3
Zambia Revenue Authority	4	1	1	3	3	4	4	3
Ministry of Tourism, Environment and Natural Resources	1	2	2	3	2	3	3	2
Zambia National Tourism Board	3	3	3	3	3	2	3	3
Zambia Wildlife Authority	1	2	2	1	3	3	3	2
Professional Hunters Association	0	0	0	1	0	4	0	1
Safari Outfitters Association	0	1	0	1	0	0	0	0
Tourism Council of Zambia	1	3	1	2	3	3	2	2
Tour Operators Association	0	3	1	1	2	3	0	1
Local Tourism Associations	1	3	2	2	2	0	0	1

Source: Pope 2006.

Scores: 0=absent; 1=unprofessional and obstructive; 2=inefficient and unpredictable; 3=professional but unpredictable; 4=professional, efficient, predictable, and proactive.

professional but still unpredictable. It appears that proximity or connectivity with Lusaka significantly increases the level of satisfaction with regulatory bodies, once again reflecting the wide disparity of conditions for doing business across the country.

Improving the management of protected areas

Zambia has 19 national parks and 34 game management areas, which represent a major asset for the country. Like any other asset, wildlife has to be managed to optimize its output and make it sustainable—in particular, the depletion of the animal population and the nonpreservation of natural or historic sites would be detrimental not only to the environment, but also to tourism (Lewis 2005). Studies reveal that Zambia has poorly managed its wildlife over the years.[8] As a result, the government undertook to restructure its park management, and created the ZAWA in 1999. Currently, ZAWA, in cooperation with other actors like the World Bank, is in the process of refining its strategic plan.

Zambia is an interesting case study for wildlife management. Across the country, different methods of management have been adopted to preserve natural assets, including strictly public management by ZAWA, public-private partnerships, strictly private management, involvement of nonprofit organizations, and bilateral and multilateral donors. In preparation for this report, a stocktaking of the different forms of management in existence in Zambia was undertaken and is set out in table 6.10.

However, a comparison of the results achieved under different forms of management was not possible because of the lack of available performance data from donors, private providers, nongovernmental organizations (NGOs), or ZAWA.

One of the main exceptions is the Luangwa Integrated Resource Development Project, launched in the 1980s and funded by the Norwegian Agency for Development Cooperation (NORAD), which first linked poverty with wildlife preservation.[9] In the 1970s, the commercial poaching of elephants and rhinos escalated rapidly in the South Luangwa valley. While the authorities in charge of park management at the time were seriously underresourced and ineffective, local people did not resist commercial poachers or inform the authorities about their activities because the revenues from wildlife (for example, from hunting licenses, park entrance fees, safari earnings) went to central government or businessmen living outside the region. By ensuring a share of benefits of nature tourism for the local communities, the program radically changed the attitude of people, who started to invest in "their wildlife." A better management of the resources resulted in the creation of nearly 350 community projects. Not only did tourism create direct jobs and resources, but also local communities started to better understand potential indirect benefits of tourism: markets for provisions and

Table 6.10. Public-Private Arrangements in National Park Management

National park	Partners	Period of partnership	Management focus
Group 1: Formal Memoranda of Understanding Determine Management			
Kasanka	Kasanka Trust	1988–2006	Research Community outreach Animal reintroductions Law enforcement Infrastructure Tourism
North Luangwa	Owens Foundation, then Frankfurt Zoological Society	1992–97 1997–2006	Law enforcement Community outreach Rhino reintroduction Tourism supervision
Liuwa Plains	African Parks	2004–06	Tourism development Law enforcement Species reintroductions Community outreach
Luambe	Cologne Zoo	2004–06	Research Law enforcement Some tourism
Group 2: Financial Support Arrangements			
South Luangwa	LIRDP, then SLAMU/ Royal Norwegian Embassy	1988–93 1993–2006	Financial support to— Law enforcement Infrastructure development Tourism management Community outreach
Lower Zambezi	Conservation Lower Zambezi/Royal Danish Embassy/ Royal Norwegian Embassy	2001–06	Financial and logistical support to— Law enforcement Research support Community outreach
Kafue	World Bank/Royal Norwegian Embassy	2005–06	Financial support to— Technical assistance Law enforcement Infrastructure development Tourism development
Mosi-oa-Tunya	World Bank	2005–06	Financial support to— Technical assistance Law enforcement Infrastructure development Tourism development

Source: World Bank staff.

Note: LIRDP = Luangwa Integrated Resource Development Project; SLAMU = South Luangwa Area Management Unit.

handicrafts emerged at the margin of wildlife tourism. The serious poaching of animals was also tackled with potentially 3,000 animals saved annually (Lewis 2005).

The Kasanka Park is another example of the possible impact of management change. A purely private initiative, officially registered in Zambia in 1987 (and in the United Kingdom in 1989), the Kasanka Trust was first created to help the government raise funds to develop community projects (build roads, bridges, and camps, employ scouts, and so on). As a result of progress made, in 1990, the government authorized the Trust to fully manage the park (ZAWA confirmed in 2003 this delegation of authority for 5+5 years). As described by the Kasanka Trust, their ultimate goals are to secure the future of biodiversity in Kasanka National Park, funded through tourism revenue, and to sustain as well as stimulate the local economy through improved natural resource management. To date, roughly half of the costs of managing the park are raised from tourism revenue with the balance coming from charitable support. Examples of community projects funded by donors include the following: new lodge buildings, an equipped clinic, a bridge to access the park, facilities and teachers at a local school, infrastructure renovation, equipment (radios, uniforms), and logistic help (helicopter use). The Kasanka Trust was chosen by the Zambian Ministry of Tourism to be included in a Compendium on Ecotourism Case Studies published by the World Tourism Organization, which concluded the following results:

In 1986 there was no tourism, little wildlife, little community development. Kasanka is now firmly on the Zambian tourism circuit with turnover around $80,000 p.a. Wildlife populations are approaching capacity. Income is used for park management and community development. 100 local people were employed. High standard facilities were built.[10]

These two examples show that involvement of third parties (private or donors) can significantly improve the management of wildlife. To draw lessons from different experiences in Zambia and find the optimal form of management for sustainable wildlife tourism, this mission launched in cooperation with ZAWA a study on wildlife management. The objective of the study is to compare the results obtained by different types of park management in three domains: wildlife (animal population), infrastructure (roads), and revenue (public and local). This study could help ZAWA and the government refine their strategy for wildlife preservation and poverty alleviation in the country. Given the absence of data, it may be some time before this study is completed.

*Zambia Needs to Remedy the Weakness of Its Infrastructure
and Complementary Services*

Developing infrastructure and basic services

Tourism trade is highly dependent on infrastructure, and in particular transport. Two aspects are intertwined: access and cost. The implications of costs are straightforward: the choice of destination is partially dictated by the cost of the trip (flight and hotel). Among destinations with comparable features (for example, safari tourism), most tourists will opt for the cheapest package. Numerous cost components considerably vary with the quality of infrastructure: competition on international flights, availability of domestic transfers, telecommunications, and insurance (safety).

On access, it appears that the two major markets for Zambian tourism trade exports are Southern Africa (mostly business visitors and visits to friends and relatives) and Europe (mostly holidays); connection with these two markets is crucial. So far, the only direct flight to Europe is the Lusaka–London line operated by British Airways; other long-haul flights are usually operated in cooperation with South African Airways via Johannesburg. This dependence upon the South African hub creates legitimate concerns (in particular about the enforcement of competition rules and the liberalization of air services). However, there does not seem to be enough room for yet another hub in Southern Africa, considering the roles already played by Johannesburg and Nairobi. A project is under way aiming to expand the capacity of Livingstone Airport to make it accessible to long-haul flights. Although this project will create another port of entry for tourists and facilitate the development of the Livingstone area, some concerns were expressed regarding the potential country-wide effects of this development: Would the viability of the only direct flight from Lusaka to Europe be challenged by the diversion of tourists to Livingstone given that capacity usage already drops by 70 percent during the low season when the prices double? Would this new port of entry increase the gap between the Livingstone area and more remote provinces by facilitating regional hoops and one-day trips to Livingstone and the Falls?

These questions raise another key issue regarding access: domestic transport. One aspect of travel is to bring tourists to Zambia, another aspect is to bring them to tourist attractions (other than the Livingstone area). Zambia has a poor road network, in particular to access the national parks, and the rain season makes many roads impracticable. Train connections are inadequate, and domestic air transport is still too costly. Altogether, it appears that the lack of infrastructure and the inefficiency of domestic transports threaten the harmonious development of tourism. If the number of tourist arrivals is to grow in accordance with projections from 600,000 to 2 million in the next decade, Zambia will have to take the necessary steps to improve the access and mobility of the tourists to diffuse trade benefits across more regions.

Finally, the regional dimension of an infrastructure development strategy should not be overlooked. Already half of the tourists combine their trip to Zambia with a visit to neighboring countries. Zambia has important natural endowments for tourism but no sea beaches, and many tourists want their holiday package to include a beach component. In other terms, Zambia needs to develop links with neighboring countries like South Africa, Tanzania, and Mozambique, which can offer the "beach component" of the package. This regional dimension of the tourism development strategy has a major infrastructure component—for example, the development of a more effective air transit between South Africa, Livingstone, and Mfuwe (south to north) or Tanzania, Mfuwe, and Livingstone (north to south) could be useful to extend the length of tourists' stay in Zambia; similarly, by train, corridors to Dar Es Salaam in Tanzania and Ncala in Mozambique are largely unexploited because of weaknesses in infrastructure. Other dimensions of this regional strategy include better cooperation of tour operators and tourism service providers (marketing of a package, including a truly regional beach, safari, and Victoria Falls experience) or the facilitation of tourists' transit. Zambia has already implemented a visa waiver scheme for tourists arriving in the country with hotel accommodation booked through either a registered tour operator or a registered hotel in Zambia. At the regional level, this initiative could be supplemented by, for instance, the creation of a single tourist visa for countries on the tour. The potential impact of such regional cooperation has been demonstrated elsewhere; see, for example, the success of the single tourist visa in the Greater Mekong subregion.

In addition to transport, other upstream basic services and infrastructure are essential to tourism development. The weakness of the financial sector is a major obstacle to the development of hospitality infrastructures and tourism activities; it also creates a distortion in competition between Zambians and foreign investors, who have access to cheaper capital on top of investment incentives. The Tourism Development Credit Fund was a welcome initiative; however, in practice, access to this fund seems to be difficult for many businesses. Other problems in basic services include high international phone call charges and limited access to electricity, water, sanitation, and medical facilities.

The importance of inadequate infrastructure and basic services among the constraints faced by the tourism sector in Zambia clearly appears in recent surveys conducted in the Livingstone area, which remains better endowed than any other tourism destination in the country (see figure 6.4).

Figure 6.4. Constraints to Tourism Development as Identified by the Hospitality Sector in Zambia

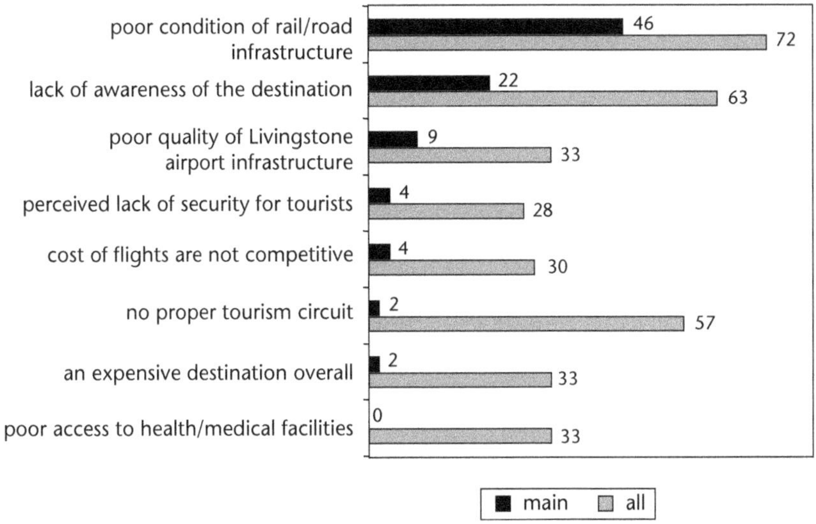

Source: Ministry of Tourism, Environment and Natural Resources 2006.

Note: For example, 46 percent of the businesses surveyed declared that the poor condition of rail/road infrastructure was *the main* obstacle to tourism development, and 72 percent of businesses selected it as *one of the main* obstacles to development. Regarding poor access to health and medical facilities, one-third of the businesses identify it as an obstacle to tourism development in Zambia, but none treated it as the main obstacle to tourism development.

Developing human capital

Human capital is essential to tourism, which is based on direct contact with a clientele of diverse age, culture, and education. Zambian people are a major asset for the country because of their friendliness, peacefulness, and English proficiency. The level of education of Zambians remains low, however, in particular in remote provinces where most of the tourist attractions are located. For example, in the Eastern Province, literacy rates drop to 37.9 percent from a 55.3 percent national average, and school attendance stands at 17.7 percent compared with 25.8 percent at the national level (Pope 2005). Tourism service providers are concerned that qualified personnel from urban areas often refuse to take jobs in remote provinces where basic services and quality of life are not as good as in cities.

Beyond the general gaps in education, which Zambia should remedy to harness the opportunities and benefits of trade in services, the tourism industry requires specific training and qualifications to meet the international standards of service. To date, the industry has not had sufficient supply of properly trained personnel and fears qualified labor shortages if tourism were to develop quickly. For example, Lusaka has only one hotel and tourism training institute, run by the Ministry of Tourism (through a trust arrangement with a modest contribution from the government), whose curriculum has not changed in a decade and does not meet international standards. The donor community has developed numerous projects aimed at improving tourism training in Zambia—so far, however, none of these projects have reached the implementation phase. This lacuna in the training system has two other negative effects: (1) the inadequacy of training results in non-qualified personnel being hired at lower wages level; and (2) a number of private "training" institutions have emerged, which sometimes do not have qualified teaching staff or the proper training equipment. In the absence of any accreditation of tourism training institutions, students are unlikely to meet the international standards of service.

Another aspect of human capital is health. Thus far no well-established relationship exists between a country's HIV/AIDS prevalence rates and its tourism attractiveness. Nonetheless, pandemics like AIDS and malaria could affect a country's image. These pandemics could dissuade foreign companies from investing in a country where staff will have to be treated at high cost or will be missing for a number of working days. Zambia, like many other countries in the region, has been particularly hit by pandemics (see table 6.11). With more than 700 species of birds and a number of migratory species, Zambia is exposed to a spread of avian flu when birds return from infected areas. A tourism strategy should therefore include a health component to disseminate good practices along the development path of tourism activities.

Table 6.11. HIV and Malaria Prevalence (%)

Country	HIV prevalence (percent of adult population, ages 15 to 49)	Malaria prevalence (notified cases, percent of all population)
Botswana	37.3	48.7
Malawi	14.2	25.9
Namibia	21.3	1.5
South Africa	21.5	0.1
Tanzania	8.8	1.2
Zambia	16.5	34.2
Zimbabwe	24.6	5.4

Source: Estimates for HIV from UNAIDS Web site (2003) and for malaria from WHO Web site (2000).

Notes

1. These figures were provided by the Zambia Hotel and Catering Association.

2. UNDP/GEF-funded project on reclassification and sustainable management of Zambia's protected area systems (UNDP/GEF 2004).

3. The concept of "tourism multiplier" is explained in part 1, section 2. The UNDP/GEF study used a multiplier of 4, which is very large.

4. Over the same period of nine years (but in this case from 1990 to 1999), Zimbabwe could achieve the same progression, from 600,000 visitors to more than 2 million—this projection is therefore credible, under the condition that Zambia grasps this opportunity and adopts adequate policies. The quick econometric exercise undertaken below shows a more timid growth perspective for Zambian tourism to reach 900,000 visitors per year.

5. "The Zambian resort continued to enjoy increased demand, with room occupancy at 62 percent—nine percentage points better than last year. Rooms revenue in USD grew by 34 percent as the resort benefited from increased regional and international demand coupled with the contribution of 'Dreams', Sun International's in-house tour operator. . . . This unique African experience is rapidly growing its stature from being a top regional destination to becoming an international destination of choice. Indicative of its success is the fact that when launched, Nationwide flew to Livingstone from Johannesburg only three times per week: now, this airline, together with SAA and British Airways, provides up to 18 flights per week. This complex has added significantly to the Zambian tourism economy and has assisted greatly in the regeneration of the town of Livingstone" (Sun International 2005).

6. A visa waiver program exists for some Commonwealth and Scandinavian countries benefit from free visas.

7. See for instance, OECD (2003), pp. 341, 344, recognizing that the opening of the Sun International hotels in Livingstone "boosted the tourism sector."

8. See for example UNDP/GEF-funded project on reclassification and sustainable management of Zambia's protected area systems (UNDP/GEF 2004).

9. Developments below summarize findings of Dalal-Clayton and Child (2003).

10. Information collected on the Kasanka Trust Web site at www.kasanka.com (accessed April 2006).

References

Civil Society for Poverty Reduction. 2001. *Poverty Reduction Strategy Paper for Zambia.* Lusaka.

Dalal-Clayton, B., and B. Child. 2003, March. *Lessons from Luangwa—The Story of the Luangwa Integrated Resource Development Project.* International Institute for Environment and Development, Wildlife and Development Series No. 13.

Grant Thornton Kessel Feinstein. 2003. *Study for Development and Promotion of Tourism in Zambia.*

Guillon, B. 2005. "Tourism, Growth and National Parks—An Economic Analysis of Nature-Based Tourism Demand in Zambia."

Jacobs, S., and I. Astrakhan. 2006. *Effective and Sustainable Regulatory Reform: The Regulatory Guillotine in Three Transition and Developing Economies.* Jacobs and Associates, Washington, DC.

Lewis, D. 2005. *Can Rural Communities be Partners in Tourism? A Hopeful Model for Zambia.* Wildlife Conservation Society, Lusaka.

Ministry of Finance and National Planning. 2004, December. "Second Poverty Reduction Strategy Paper Implementation Progress Report, July 2003–June 2004."

Ministry of Tourism, Environment and Natural Resources. 2006, March. "Livingstone Tourism Survey." Submitted by DCDM Consulting.

OECD (Organisation for Economic Co-operation and Development). 2003. *African Economic Outlook.* OECD, Paris.

Pope, A. 2005. *Luangwa Safari Association Tourism Study.* Whydah Consulting Ltd., Lusaka.
———. 2006. *A Study of Nature-Based Tourism Supply Side in Zambia–2005.* Whydah Consulting Ltd., Lusaka.
Pycroft, J. 2004. *The Taxation of the Tourism Sector in Zambia.* In conjunction with the Zambian Ministry of Finance and DFID (RIZES Project).
Rosen, S., P. Hamazakaza, and L. Long 2006. "The Impact of HIV/AIDS on the Tourism Sector in Zambia." Tourism Policy Brief, Boston University.
Southern Africa Development Community. 2005. *Regional Biodiversity Strategy.*
Sun International. 2005. *Annual Report.*
UNDP/GEF (United Nations Development Program/Global Environmental Fund). 2004. *A Financial and Economic Analysis of the Costs and Benefits of Managing the Protected Area Estate.* Development Services and Initiatives.
UNESCO (United Nations Educational, Scientific and Cultural Organization). 2006. *World Heritage List.*
World Bank. 2004a. "Framework for Tourism in Zambia." World Bank, Washington, DC.
———. 2004b. *World Development Report 2005.* Washington, DC: World Bank.
———. 2004c. "Zambia Country Economic Memorandum." World Bank, Washington, DC.
———. 2004d. "Zambia Sectoral Study on the Effective Tax Burden." FIAS, World Bank, Washington, DC.
———. 2005. "Development Through Tourism, The World Bank's Role, 1966–2005." World Bank, Washington, DC.
———. 2006. "Overview of Tourist Expenditures in Zambia." World Bank, Washington, DC.
World Commission on Protected Areas. 1998. *Economic Values of Protected Areas, Guidelines for Protected Area Managers.* Best Practice Protected Area Guidelines Series No. 2.
———. 2002 *Sustainable Tourism in Protected Areas, Guidelines for Planning and Management.* Best Practice Protected Area Guidelines Series No. 8.
World Conservation Union. 2004. *Red List of Threatened Species.*
World Tourism Organization. 2006. *Tourism Satellites Accounts.*
World Travel and Tourism Council. 2005a. *Country League Tables.*
———. 2005b. *Zambia Travel and Tourism.*
Zambia National Tourist Board. 2002. *Tourism Statistics.*
———. 2005, *2004 International Visitor Survey Report* (March).
Zimbabwe Tourism Authority. 2006. *Tourism Statistics.* Research and Development Division.

Annex 1. The Zambia Tourism Potential

World-Leading Natural Endowments

- The Kafue National Park, the second largest in Africa
- The South Luangwa National Park, which has a high animal density and diversity
- The Victoria Falls, one of the seven natural wonders of the world
- Lake Kariba, the largest man-made lake in the world
- Lake Tanganyika, the gateway to East Africa and the source of the Nile
- The Zambezi River, the carrier of life in south-central Africa

Comprehensive List of Tourist Attractions

- North Luangwa National Park
- South Luangwa National Park
- Liuwa Plain National Park
- Sioma Ngweshi National Park
- Sioma Falls
- Kafue National Park
- West Lunga National Park
- Mosi-oa-Tunya National Park
- Tiger Fishing in Senanga
- Lochinvar National Park
- Blue Lagoon National Park
- Lower Zambezi National Park
- Kasanka National Park
- Lukusuzi National Park
- Luambe National Park
- Lavushi Manda National Park
- Isangano National Park
- Nyika Plateau National Park
- Sumbu National Park
- Mweru Wantipa National Park Open pit and underground mine tours on the Copperbelt (the Nchanga Open Pit mine offers a unique tour opportunity for a tourist to conduct a once-in-a-lifetime experience)
- Lusenga National Park
- White-water rafting along the Zambezi River
- Bird watching, sailing, and fishing
- Mulungushi/Lunsemfwa Dams
- Itezhi-Tezhi Dam
- Victoria Falls
- Ntumba Chushi Falls
- Lumangwe Falls
- Chishimba Falls
- Kundabwika Falls
- Kundalila Falls
- Nyambwezu Falls and Rock Shelter
- Lake Kariba
- Lake Mweru
- Lake Tanganyika
- Lake Bangweulu
- Lake Kashiba
- Shilengwa Lake
- Shiwa Ng'andu Hot Springs
- Kapishya Hot Springs
- Batoka Gorge
- Kafue Gorge
- Katolola Rock paintings

- Mumbwa Caves
- Kaputa GMA
- Tondwa GMA
- Munyamadzi GMA
- Mukungule GMA
- Lumimba GMA
- Musalangu GMA
- Lupande GMA
- Sandwe GMA
- Chisomo GMA
- West Petauke GMA
- Kafinda GMA
- Bangweulu GMA
- Chambeshi GMA
- Luwingu GMA
- Chikuni GMA
- Mansa GMA
- Luano GMA
- Rufunsa GMA
- Chiawa GMA
- Kafue Flats GMA
- Nkala GMA
- Namwala GMA
- Mumbwa GMA
- Machiya Fungulwe GMA
- Lunga Luswishi GMA
- Musele Matebo GMA
- Chibwika-Ntambu GMA
- Lukwakwa GMA
- Chizela GMA
- Kasonso-Busanga GMA
- Bilili Springs GMA
- Sichifulo GMA
- Mulobezi GMA
- West Zambezi GMA
- Kuomboka Ceremony – Western Province
- Umutomboko Ceremony - Luapula Province
- Cibwela Mushi Ceremony - Northern Province
- Nc'wala Ceremony - Eastern Province

Source: Civil Society for Poverty Reduction 2001.

Note: GMA = game management area.

Annex 2. Tourism Activities in the Livingstone Area

Tourism activity providers	Activities
Abseil Africa	Rope Activities
African Extreme	Rafting/Kayaking
Angle Zambia	Fishing
Batoka Sky	Flying
Victoria Carriage Company	Horse Carriage
Livingstone Quad Company	Quad Bikes
African Queen	Boat Trips
Birding with Bob	Birding
Bundu	Rafting/Kayaking
Bushtracks Africa	Transfers/Drives
Zamcentive	Bush Dinners
Bwaato Adventures	Rafting/Kayaking
Cholwe Adventures	Rafting/Kayaking
Gwembe Crocodile Farm	Crocodile Farm
Jet Extreme	Jet Boating
Kayak School	Kayaking
Livingstone Walking Safaris	Walking Safaris
Local Cowboys Tours	Guided Bike Tours
Makora Quest	Rafting/Kayaking
Plafours	Transfers/Drives
Raft Extreme	Rafting/Kayaking
Ross's Eco-lift	Gorge Lift
Zambezi Elephant Trails	Elephant-Back Rides
United Air Charters	Helicopters
Victoria Falls River Safaris	Boating
Wild Side Tours	Guided Tours
Wilderness Tours	Guided Walks

Source: Pope 2006.

Annex 3. Tourism Direct and Indirect Trade Balance, 2005

Demand-side accounts (K billion)	
Personal Travel and Tourism	1,148.1
This category includes all personal spending by an economy's residents, T&T services (lodging, transportation, entertainment, meals, financial services, and so on) and goods (durable and nondurable) used for T&T activities. Spending may occur before, during, and after a trip. Spending covers all T&T, outbound and domestic.	
Business Travel	258.6
This category of expenditures by government and industry includes spending on goods and services (transportation, accommodation, meals, entertainment, and so on) for employee business travel purposes.	
Government Expenditures (Individual)	21.4
This category includes expenditures (transfers or subsidies) made by government agencies to provide T&T services such as cultural (art museums), recreational (national park), or clearance (immigration/customs) to visitors.	
Visitor Exports	816.2
Expenditures by international visitors on goods and services with the resident economy.	
Travel and Tourism Consumption	2,244.2
Total T&T expenditures made by and on behalf of visitors (goods and services) in the resident economy.	
Government Expenditures (Collective)	48.8
This category includes operating expenditures made by government agencies on services associated with T&T, but not directly linked to any individual visitor, instead these expenditures are generally made on behalf of the "community at large," such as tourism promotion, aviation administration, security services, resort area sanitation services, and so on.	
Capital Investment	506.2
This category includes capital expenditures by direct T&T industry service providers and government agencies to provide facilities, equipment, and infrastructure to visitors.	
Exports (Nonvisitors)	86.1
Consumer goods (such as clothing, electronics or petrol) exported for ultimate sale to visitors or capital goods (such as aircraft or cruise ships) exported for the use of T&T industry providers.	
Travel and Tourism Demand	2,885.3
The nominal aggregate of tourism activity in the resident economy.	

Supply-side accounts (K billion and thousands of jobs)	
Travel and Tourism Industry GDP (Direct)	585.1
Direct GDP (also known as value added) and employment associated with T&T consumption. This is explicitly defined supply-side industry contribution of T&T that can be compared one-for-one with the GDP and employment contribution of other industries in the economy. Establishments in this category include traditional T&T providers such as airlines, hotels, car rental companies, and so on.	(23,700 jobs)
Travel and Tourism Industry GDP (Indirect)	349.7
Indirect GDP associated with T&T consumption. This is the upstream resident economy contribution that comes about from suppliers to the traditional T&T industry. Establishments in this category include fuel and catering companies, laundry services, accounting firms, and so on.	
Travel and Tourism Industry Imports	1,309.5
The value of goods imported by direct and indirect T&T industry establishments.	
Travel and Tourism Industry Supply	2,244.2
Total T&T industry supply.	
Travel and Tourism Economy GDP (Direct and Indirect)	1,361.1
Direct and indirect GDP (also known as value added) and employment associated with T&T demand. This is the broadest measure of T&T's contribution to the resident economy. Establishments in this category include those described above as well as manufacturing, construction, government, and so on, which are associated with capital investment, government services, and nonvisitor exports.	(55,100 jobs)
Travel and Tourism Economy Imports	1,524.2
The value of goods imported by direct and indirect T&T economy establishments.	
Travel and Tourism Economy Supply	2,885.3
Total T&T economy supply.	

Source: World Tourism and Travel Council 2005a.

Annex 4. Zambian Tourism: Poor Performance of Zambian Tourism

	Data source confidence and forecast margin of error	2005 T&T demand ($ million)	2005 T&T demand (% real growth)	2005 T&T industry GDP (% of total GDP)	2005 T&T economy GDP (% total GDP)	2005 T&T industry Jobs (000s)	2005 T&T industry jobs (% total employ-ment)
Sub-Saharan Africa	n/a	73,618	7.9	3.3	8.8	3,877	2
South Africa	High	30,332	7.1	3.9	9.0	522	4
Botswana	Low	1,421	12.8	4.8	10.3	20	7
Namibia	Low	1,004	8,2	5.6	11.2	34	6
Zimbabwe	Low	342	-3.2	1.4	3.3	13	1
Tanzania	Low	1,858	11.5	4.3	9.7	293	3
Malawi	Low	232	9.4	3.7	7.3	67	3
Zambia	Moderate	620	1.3	1.9	4.5	24	2
Zambia regional rank (out of 7)	n/a	5	6	6	6	5	6

Source: World Tourism and Travel Council 2005b.

2005 T&T economy jobs (000s)	2005 T&T economy jobs (% total employment)	2005 T&T capital investment (% total investment)	2005 T&T capital investment (% real growth)	2005 T&T visitor exports (% total exports)	2005 T&T visitor exports (% real growth)	2005 personal T&T (% total consumption)	2005 T&T govt. expd. (% total govt.)
10,647	6.8	11.9	5.8	7.9	11.0	5.8	1.5
1,100	8.3	14.1	5.2	11.0	11.8	6.3	0.5
39	12.7	6.8	5.2	13.4	17.1	10.3	2.3
65	11.3	8.1	3.7	18.9	11.9	5.2	3.7
30	2.9	8.4	-2.6	3.6	-16.4	3.3	2.3
673	7.7	13.0	9.3	33.0	12.4	5.8	5.5
133	5.7	5.5	4.1	9.6	13.9	3.8	1.3
55	3.7	11.4	5.3	9.0	1.5	4.6	2.1
5	6	3	2	6	6	5	4

7

MIGRATION FROM ZAMBIA: ENSURING TEMPORARINESS THROUGH COOPERATION

Mohammad Amin and Aaditya Mattoo

Overview

Overall emigration from Zambia is not high by regional standards, but the pattern of migration in Zambia is skewed toward the skilled. Although international migration offers potentially large benefits to sending and receiving countries, industrial receiving countries have shown little interest in liberalizing the inward flow of the unskilled while being relatively open to the entry of the skilled. The total stock of Zambians living in OECD countries is estimated at 27 per 10,000 of Zambia's population, an emigration rate far below that of many other African countries, such as Kenya (56) and Zimbabwe (47). Currently, about 10 percent of all tertiary educated Zambians live outside Zambia as compared with more than 18 percent for Eastern Africa. The emigration rate among the tertiary educated is about 35 times that for the secondary educated in Zambia, while for most other African countries, the ratio is below 10. The main reason for this is the low level of unskilled migration from Zambia.

A development-friendly migration policy for Zambia would strive to ensure temporariness. On the one hand, industrial countries may be willing to accept a higher level of unskilled immigration if they could be certain that it was temporary. On the other hand, concerns about brain drain in a source country like Zambia would be greatly alleviated if emigration was temporary. The problem is that host countries cannot unilaterally ensure temporariness of unskilled migration because repatriation cannot be accomplished without the cooperation of the source country. And source countries cannot unilaterally ensure temporariness of the skilled because repatriation cannot be accomplished without the cooperation of the host country. Hence, a strong case could be made for Zambia to cooperate with destination countries in the design and implementation of a migration policy so that unskilled migration becomes feasible and skilled migration becomes more desirable.

Zambia may be able to promote more migration of the unskilled if it takes measures, in cooperation with the receiving countries, to ensure that such migration is temporary. Bilateral agreements on these lines have been successfully implemented between the Caribbean and Canada, Ecuador and Spain, and Poland and Germany. Zambia would agree to help with the selection and screening of migrants, provide necessary predeparture training, and cooperate to ensure timely return. Aversion to unskilled immigration in the receiving countries may be reduced through agreements that ensure temporariness.

Although the rate of skilled migration is not high in Zambia, the impact is significant given the country's limited capacity to generate human capital. The adverse effects of brain drain are typically larger when the country has limited human capital and limited capacity to train professionals. These concerns are valid for Zambia especially in the health care sector. For example, there are only 12 physicians per 100,000 population in the country, which is lower than the least developed country average of 18 per 100,000. New health graduates in Zambia number only 7 per 100,000 population which is the eighth lowest in Africa and the world. In terms of the stock of tertiary educated in all disciplines, Zambia's performance is average by regional standards. It ranks 17th among 29 African countries and 5th among 10 Southern African Development Community (SADC) countries.

The current skill shortage in Zambia is primarily due to the inadequate education infrastructure and cannot be solved merely by restricting skilled emigration. Government expenditure on education is currently only 2 percent of GDP, the lowest in Africa and well below the 3.4 percent average level for least developed countries. The problem of low expenditure is compounded by the way it is allocated. Students in health and welfare constitute about 3 percent of all students at the tertiary level in Zambia—only seven countries in the world have a lower percentage. Restricting the outflow of the skilled will address the existing shortages in Zambia only to a limited extent. For example, it is estimated that about 300 Zambian doctors practice abroad while the estimated shortage to meet the basic World Health Organization (WHO) recommended standards stands at 1,654 doctors.

Zambia has taken steps toward retention and voluntary return of those settled abroad but these schemes have had only limited success. The recent National Employment and Labor Market Policy (NELMP) specifically addresses emigration and seeks to attract skilled Zambians home by facilitating their return and reintegration and by providing better working conditions. The country launched a "bonding" system that requires all Zambians who are awarded a publicly funded scholarship to sign an agreement to return after the completion of their studies. Complementary schemes include the International Organization for Migration's (IOM's) Return of Qualified Africans (RQAN) and efforts by Migration for Development in Africa (MIDA). These schemes have had limited success because they require those already settled abroad to return and those who could go abroad to stay in return for certain economic and moral incentives. However, the strong economic motives that propel much of the skilled emigration from Zambia tend to dominate the material and moral incentives to return. These problems apply to exchange programs of the kind negotiated between the United Kingdom and South Africa. One alternative is to make receiving countries pay Zambia for the Zambian professionals they recruit.

Similarly, compensation by host countries like the United Kingdom for Zambian skilled immigrants has proved difficult to negotiate and assistance to build training capacity may be a more feasible solution. Private firms in the receiving countries are often the main beneficiaries of skilled immigration, especially when public health care systems (like the National Health System [NHS] in the United Kingdom) exercise restraint in recruitment. A compensation scheme is then a de facto transfer from taxpayers in the receiving country to these firms, which may not be politically feasible. Problems also persist with identifying the right level of compensation especially because of the large positive externalities arising from the presence of skilled professionals. A better strategy would be for host countries to provide aid to enhance the training capacity in Zambia, which need not be linked to the numbers emigrating. Aid for training, however, will need to be complemented by a more development-friendly migration regime.

The adverse effects on Zambia of brain drain could be alleviated if skilled migration were temporary rather than permanent. Migration offers an opportunity to earn higher income and learn new skills in the host countries. Savings from higher income are a potential source of investment in Zambia, while the skills acquired abroad are a substitute for costly training at home. Although permanent migrants have less incentive to remit earnings, temporary migrants bring their savings home on return. Similarly, compared with permanent migration, temporary migration offers a larger number of individuals the opportunity to learn while abroad and transfer that knowledge and skill to others in Zambia on their return. This circulation enhances the global stock of human capital, and the benefits can be appropriately shared by the sending and receiving countries. These benefits of temporary over permanent migration are lost under other schemes that are based on permanent migration or no migration.

Temporary migration of the skilled cannot be achieved unilaterally by Zambia and requires cooperation with destination countries in the framework of a bilateral agreement. Today, most temporary migration schemes in the OECD countries are in fact stepping stones to permanent migration. Exceptions include certain managed migration schemes, such as the agreement between Poland and the Netherlands on the temporary movement of nurses and the Seasonal Agricultural Worker's Scheme implemented by the United Kingdom for temporary visits by university students in agriculture. A commitment to repatriate by the host, for example, through granting nonextendable visas, can be based either on self-interest or generosity. In some cases, receiving countries find it difficult to implement temporariness of the skilled even when it is the socially preferred outcome. Firms and natives of the receiving countries often invest in the migrants through, for example, costly training or professional relationships. Once such investments are made, they follow the mindset of sunk costs and the continued presence of the migrant is required to reap the benefits of the investments. The government of the receiving country is then forced to grant such migrants permanent residence, although ideally it prefers a no-investment status and only temporary migration. In these cases, sending countries such as Zambia can help ensure temporariness through a bilateral treaty clearly ruling out permanent residence. In other cases, the receiving countries prefer permanent over temporary migration irrespective of relationship-specific investments. These cases relate to the highly skilled professions that require long and extensive training periods. Ensuring temporariness here is more difficult, and Zambia must rely on the goodwill of the receiving countries to repatriate its skilled labor.

Facilitating the temporary movement of the skilled and unskilled is accomplished more easily in a bilateral than regional or multilateral context. Existing international agreements on labor mobility, such as the WTO's General Agreement on Trade in Services, have failed to do better because they seek primarily to induce host countries to make commitments to allow entry. Such an approach is currently ill-suited to unskilled migration because there is no provision for source countries like Zambia to undertake binding commitments on screening, selection, and repatriation. The approach is also ill-suited for skilled migration because it does not enable host countries to undertake binding commitments to ensure the temporariness of skilled personnel from countries like Zambia. In the absence of a dramatic change in the multilateral framework, a development-friendly approach to manage migration is more easily developed in a bilateral context.

Migration pressure in Zambia

International migration is fueled by economic and sociopolitical factors, which typically are classified as push and pull factors. The push factors include poor socioeconomic living conditions, unemployment, drops in real income, currency devaluation and rising cost of living, professional isolation, tribal/ethnic discrimination against the qualifications held, and competition with expatriates. The pull factors include higher salaries, greater job mobility and professional careers, fewer bureaucratic controls, higher standards of living, acquisition of higher skills, foreign scholarships and education support, active presence of recruitment agents, and network effects. These factors work in tandem with each other in generating migratory flows. In a formal empirical study, Hatton and Williamson (2001) analyze the push-pull factors for the Sub-Saharan African countries and find that the real wage gaps between sending and receiving countries and the demographic booms in the low-wage sending regions are the two most important factors in driving migration. The study notes that the situation in the region is similar to the one in Europe in the late nineteenth century that fueled mass migration.

Emigration from Zambia is mostly driven by the economic motives mentioned above with little role of civil unrest, security concerns, and other factors, as the country has enjoyed peace and stability since its independence. Fears of mass emigration from Zambia (and continental Africa) to the rich developed countries seem unfounded at least for the present. In fact, African countries show lower levels of labor mobility than others. Table 7.1 illustrates the point.

The table shows that emigration pressures are lower in Zambia compared with other African countries and the rest of the world. This holds even if we include migration to other African countries (such as South Africa and Botswana). In fact, available data show that between 1995 and 2000 there was a net inward flow into Zambia (annex table A-1.1).

It is well known that overall migration rates do not convey the full picture of the possible impact of migration and the structure of migration is critical. The first element of the structure is the composition of migrants by their skill or the level of education. Table 7.2 provides a snapshot of this.

Table 7.2 shows that tertiary educated Zambians living abroad equal 10 percent of all tertiary educated Zambians in the country and abroad. This rate is not too high when compared with other African countries although it is higher than many countries outside the African continent. For comparison, the corresponding rate stood at 6.2 percent (Northern Africa), 13.3 percent (Central Africa), 26.7 percent (Western Africa), 18.4 percent (Eastern Africa), and 5.3 percent (Southern Africa). For the South-Central Asia region, it equaled 5.1 percent, and for the Eastern Asia region, it equaled 4.3 percent.

Table 7.1. Migrants per 10,000 of Source Country Population, 2000

	OECD	United States	Canada	United Kingdom	France	Switzer-land	Nether-lands
Angola	87.3	1.7	1.1	2.5	4.6	2.7	2.0
Botswana	15.8	5.9	0.2	6.0	0.7	0.1	0.4
Congo, Dem. Rep. of	18.0	0.9	1.1	1.1	3.3	0.6	0.7
Lesotho	3.3	0.5	0.3	1.3	0.1	0.4	0.2
Malawi	11.0	1.1	0.3	8.9	0.0	0.0	0.1
Mozambique	33.7	0.8	0.5	1.5	0.4	0.4	0.2
Namibia	10.6	0.5	0.9	3.9	0.4	0.7	0.4
South Africa	61.1	11.1	6.2	20.5	0.3	0.9	1.2
Swaziland	18.0	9.4	0.7	4.9	0.0	0.4	0.3
Tanzania	18.1	2.7	5.2	8.5	0.1	0.2	0.2
Zambia	**26.5**	**4.3**	**1.4**	**16.1**	**0.1**	**0.2**	**0.3**
Zimbabwe	47.1	6.5	2.2	27.1	0.2	0.4	0.4
All SADC	35.2	4.1	2.9	9.7	1.3	0.7	0.7
Africa	55.9	8.0	2.8	7.7	17.8	0.8	2.9
World	94.0	40.0	7.7	5.8	6.2	2.3	2.1

Source: Docquier and Marfouk 2004.

Table 7.2. Emigration Rates by Education in 2000, SADC Countries (Migrants as percent of all educated [natives plus migrants] in each category)

	Primary educated	Secondary educated	Tertiary educated
Angola	2.10	3.40	25.60
Botswana	0.10	0.80	2.10
Congo, Dem. Rep. of	0.10	0.50	7.90
Lesotho	0.00	0.10	2.40
Malawi	0.00	0.80	9.40
Mozambique	0.50	5.80	42.00
Namibia	0.10	0.20	3.40
South Africa	0.40	0.50	5.40
Swaziland	0.20	0.20	5.80
Tanzania	0.10	1.00	15.80
Zambia	**0.10**	**0.30**	**10.00**
Zimbabwe	0.20	0.70	7.60

Source: Docquier and Marfouk 2004.

With most of the attention focused on skilled migration, migration of the unskilled (and the semiskilled) has been largely neglected. As Winters, Walmsley, Wang, and Grynberg (2002) point out, however, welfare gains at the global level are likely to be larger from liberalizing this form of migration relative to high-skilled migration. Migration of the unskilled is one area in which Zambia has fallen behind most of the other countries. Table 7.2 shows that the migration rate of the primary educated (unskilled) is only 0.1 percent. The corresponding figures for other regions are as follows: 2.3 percent (Northern Africa), 0.3 percent (Western Africa, Southern Africa), 0.2 percent (Eastern Africa), 2.8 percent (Western Asia), and 0.5 percent (South-Central Asia). Similarly, migration rate of the secondary educated (semiskilled) is low for Zambia at 0.3 percent relative to other African countries as shown in table 7.2. Low emigration rates for the unskilled and semiskilled, coupled with the moderate level for the skilled, has skewed Zambia's migration structure in favor of the highly educated. The following figures illustrate the point.

To conclude, overall emigration rates to the developed rich countries are lower in Africa relative to rest of the world. For Zambia, these rates are low even by African standards. For Zambia, the percentage of its tertiary educated citizens living abroad is moderate by African standards but much higher than many countries outside Africa.

Figure 7.1. Tertiary to Secondary Migration Rate, 2000

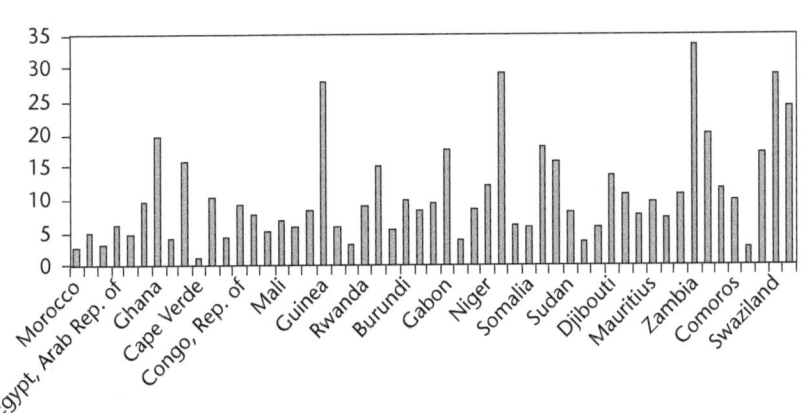

Source: Docquier and Marfouk 2004.

Figure 7.2. Tertiary to Primary Emigration Rate, 2000

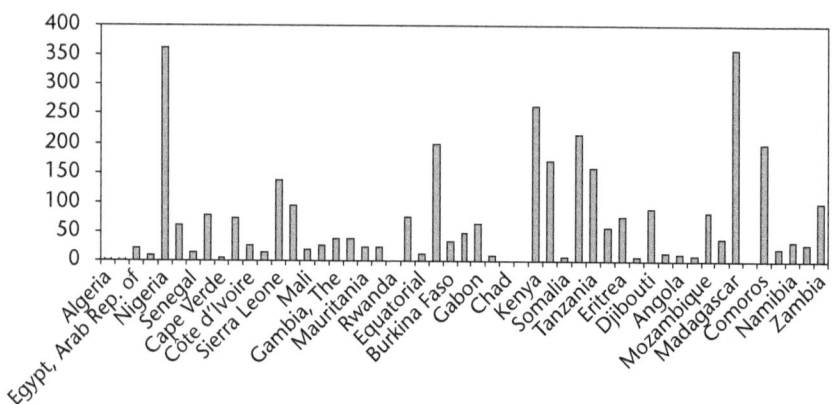

Source: Docquier and Marfouk 2004.

Migration of the unskilled: An opportunity for Zambia

The main cause of Zambia's skewed composition is not that too many of the skilled are migrating but that too few of the unskilled are. Clearly, facilitating the emigration of the unskilled to areas where they have better economic opportunities is desirable. What can Zambia do to achieve this given the highly restrictive immigration policies in richer countries?

One reason for the aversion to unskilled immigration on the part of the receiving countries is their inability to keep this form of migration truly temporary. Guest worker schemes implemented in the past were intended to fill temporary shortages in host country's labor markets. The attractiveness of these schemes to host countries is primarily their temporariness because, unlike permanent migration, temporary migration is more flexible, imposes less burden on the pubic exchequer (like schooling for migrants' children, old-age pension, and so on), and does not threaten the sociocultural-political structure of the host country. The system based on guest worker schemes failed to develop into an efficient and dynamic migration regime precisely because it had no built-in mechanism to ensure the timely return of the migrants, and temporariness remained a distant dream. That the issue of timely return is important to host countries is reflected in the new generation of bilateral agreements. For example, the agreement between Spain and Ecuador signed in 2001 specifically requires that, before seasonal workers are hired, they shall sign a commitment to return to Ecuador when their permit expires (Agreement Between the Kingdom of Spain and the Republic of Ecuador for the Regulation and Control of Migratory Flows, Article 12).

There are, however, examples of successful programs, such as the Canadian Seasonal Agricultural Worker Programme (SAWP). The program started in 1966 and has since evolved in size and geographic reach. For instance, over the last 20 years, the intake increased from just under 6000 in 1980 to 18,700 in 2003. Another successful case is the "German contract worker scheme." The German scheme is implemented through a series of bilateral agreements with Eastern and Central European countries and is perhaps one of the biggest schemes in the world. A key element in the Canadian and German programs is the involvement of sending countries regarding specific obligations and rights over matters related to the selection and screening of migrants, establishment of migrant's rights in the host country, and, above all, assurance of their return. For example, the German scheme delegates the responsibility of recruitment and timely return to the sending country. Anecdotal evidence suggests that the cost of ensuring temporariness is considerably reduced with the effective cooperation of source countries. In fact, the experience so far suggests that it is almost impossible to maintain temporariness without the involvement of the source countries. For example, a report by the Council of Europe (1997) noted that "the return of illegal migrants can be made effective only through the full co-operation of the authorities of the country of origin and, as appropriate, of those of the transit countries."[1]

Sending countries such as Zambia can play an important role in liberalizing the migration of the unskilled. To do so, however, sending countries must shift their focus from getting host countries to open their borders and instead provide a credible case of ensuring temporariness on their own or in cooperation with the host countries. With low-cost temporary migration arrangements in place, demand may grow from labor-scarce richer countries.

To conclude, unskilled migration offers large social benefits to the sending countries that may dwarf those from migration of the skilled. But Zambia lags far behind other countries in this form of migration. Zambia should take initiatives unilaterally and bilaterally with destination countries to keep migration of the unskilled truly temporary. Zambia's own brand of unskilled migration, characterized by timely return, may create its own demand.

Migration of the skilled and brain drain

The issue of brain drain has received extensive attention especially in the African context. From the source country's point of view, brain drain is a problem because it deprives the poor sending countries of valuable skills; increases the burden on the public exchequer, because in many poor countries higher education is publicly funded; and aggravates critical shortages that are beginning to emerge in key sectors such as health care and education.

Box 7.1. A Model Agreement for the Migration of the Unskilled

Host country obligations

- Inform Zambia about the number of guest workers needed.
- Prepare the work contract before the migrant departs, which specifies the duration of stay, wage rate, working hours and working conditions, other benefits, and basic rights to which the migrant may be entitled. Build effective channels of communication with the future employers to facilitate the process.
- Facilitate the processing of contracts (with the future employer's help) and obtaining visas.
- Give preference to those workers who returned on time in the past.
- Seek employers' cooperation in monitoring timely return and compliance with the terms of the contract. Prohibit employers who violated contracts in the past from participating in the program.

Source country obligations

- Set up an agency to which prospective migrants can submit their applications.
- Provide necessary help with the screening, selection, recruitment, and predeparture orientation of the migrants.
- Position a liaison officer in the receiving country to monitor the migrants and the fulfillment of the terms in the contract.
- Ensure the timely return of migrants through monitoring and variety of mechanisms such as withholding of a part of the migrant's income till he returns, "bonding system" with punitive measures, reintegration programs such tax exemptions on return, provision of information on job vacancies, skill training, microcredit schemes for housing, and small business loans.

Potential benefits from the agreement

As the source country, Zambia has a natural advantage in the process of selection, recruitment, and predeparture orientation. Cost savings to employers and host countries through this channel have been an important factor in the success of previous efforts such as the German contract worker scheme.

Ensuring timely return is costly to the host, but this cost can be considerably reduced through the involvement of source by way of monitoring, provision of information, and a streamlined system of repatriating the overstayers.

Host country offers safe, secure, and stable employment opportunities that the source cannot achieve on its own. The host gets truly temporary migration that is safe and orderly and that can be adjusted to the condition of its labor market.

Box 7.2. Past Experience with Managing Temporary Migration of the Unskilled

A number of initiatives have been taken at the unilateral and bilateral levels that incorporate elements of the model agreement listed above. The main strength of these initiatives is the degree of organization and control they offer: they provide effective instruments for monitoring the movement of workers, ensuring their safety and protection, and facilitating return. Some examples are as follows.

The Philippines Overseas Employment Administration (POEA) and the Overseas Workers Welfare Administration (OWWA) provide a number of services that facilitate orderly migration and enhance the gains from migration to all concerned. The agencies conduct intensified skills training and development training programs to improve the competitiveness of Filipino citizens. Foreign employers are able to recruit Filipino workers once their accreditation documents are verified by labor officers stationed abroad and authenticated by embassy officials. Employment contracts are scrutinized to ensure decent pay and working conditions. Return migration is facilitated through a number of reintegration schemes in place. These schemes cover social and economic aspects, and provide counseling to migrants and their families, skills training, educational assistance for children, microcredit assistance, and investment advice.

The Canadian Seasonal Agricultural Workers Program (SAWP) is a highly successful scheme and is often cited as model for similar agreements. The main reason behind this success is the fact that all parties concerned are assigned specific obligations and have a mutual interest in fulfilling these obligations. These parties include Human Resources and Skills Development Canada (the federal employment and labor ministry), Citizenship and Immigration Canada, provincial governments, signatory foreign governments, employers and industry organizations (such as Foreign Agricultural Resource Management Services, FARMS), the liaison officer stationed in Canada by the sending countries, the Internaional Organization for Migration, and others. The local employment office is responsible for approving the offer of employment to foreign workers and transmitting the orders to other participating groups, obtaining the employer's signature on the employment contracts, and sending them to the liaison office. The liaison officer facilitates the recruitment of workers, audits pay, attends to problems on site, and coordinates movement of workers with travel agencies. Cooperation by employers, the liaison officer, and embassy officials greatly helps in the timely return of the migrants.

The seriousness of these concerns cannot be dismissed even for a country with a moderate level of brain drain such as Zambia. Even a moderate rate of brain drain can have a significant impact on the economy if the country is initially scarce in human resources and has limited capacity (educational infrastructure) to produce highly skilled professionals, or if emigration is concentrated in key sectors such as health care and education. In fact, the rate of brain drain tends to be higher in African countries with a lower initial stock of professionals. The picture is similar when we include other countries (see annex 2).

Overview of Skilled Migration and Training Capacity

Zambia has limited capacity to produce professionals and has a low initial stock of professionals even by African standards. We provide some evidence on this after briefly describing the nature of health skills drain from the country.

Hard data on migrants by their profession are not easily available for many receiving countries. Existing work on Zambia is largely based on "guestimates" and anecdotal evidence, which relate mainly to the health professionals. These data estimate the total number of Zambian doctors abroad at 300 or about 46 per-

Figure 7.3. Skilled Migration and Human Capital in Africa, 2000

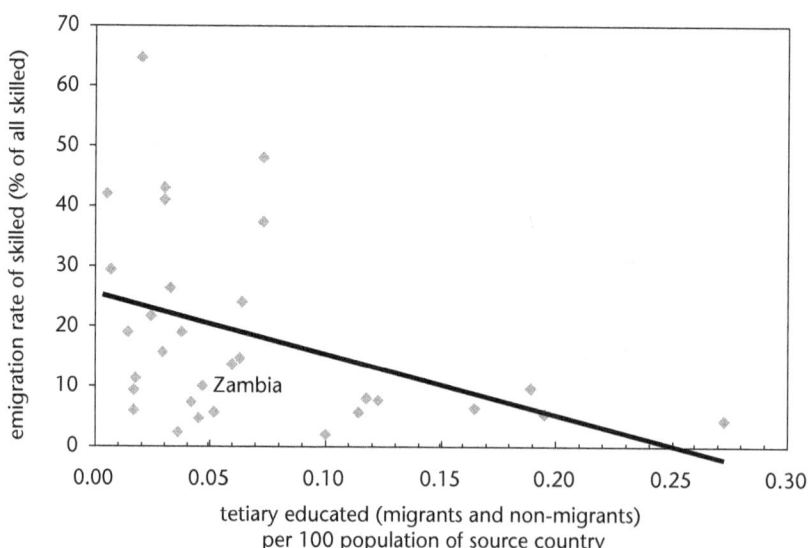

Source: Authors' own calculations using data from Docquier and Marfouk 2004, World Bank, and United Nations 2005.

cent of those currently working in the country's public sector (MoH 2005). According to the Nursing and Midwifery Council of the United Kingdom, a total of 461 Zambian nurses were recruited between 1998 and 2003, which constitutes about 7.6 percent of those currently employed in Zambia's public sector and about 14 percent of Zambia's annual flow of nursing graduates. The following graph shows Zambia's position relative to other countries in the supply of nurses to the United Kingdom.

Zambia is clearly among the main suppliers of nurses to the United Kingdom, and a clear upward trend has emerged since the late 1990s. The total number of nurses in the United Kingdom from Zambia increased from 15 in 1998–99 to 135 by 2002–03, implying that Zambia's share in total foreign nurses in the United Kingdom increased from 0.3 percent to 1.13 percent. Clearly, some corrective steps should be taken to ensure that the trend does not translate into a health crisis in Zambia. Anecdotal evidence on shortages of health professionals is also worrying. For example, a recent study by IOM (2005) noted that international migration of the health workers, mainly to Britain and the United States, has exacerbated staff shortages at major hospitals, such as the Ndola Central Hospital. The hospital requires 567 nurses, but only 133 staff remain to provide the needed nursing services. The Ndola School of Nursing, which should be staffed with 27 tutors, has only three, causing a decline in nursing graduation rates. (Later in this

Figure 7.4. Nurses Recruited in the United Kingdom, 2000

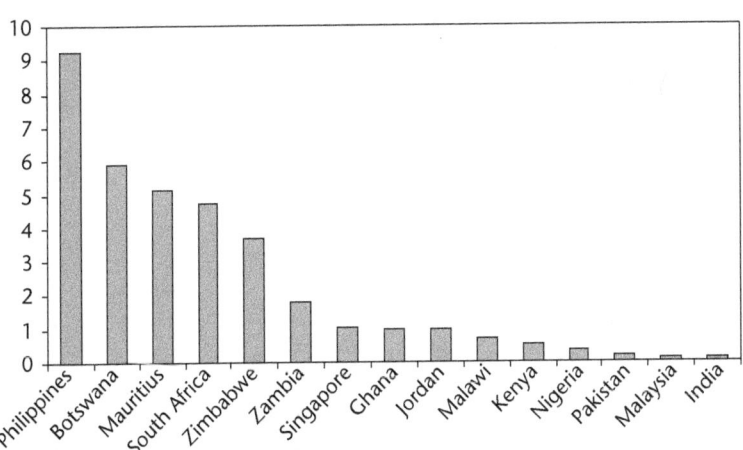

Source: Authors own calculations using population data from World Bank and data on nurses from Buchan and Dovlo 2004.

section, we take a closer look at the graduation rates of health care professionals in Zambia relative to other countries.)

We next provide evidence on Zambia's performance in producing skilled professionals. We believe that this is important not only for Zambia's own professional advancement but also for a better understanding of the likely impact of skilled migration. Table 7.3 shows Zambia's endowment of human capital.

Zambia's performance in generating human capital is mixed. In 1980, Zambia ranked second in the set of 28 African countries for which data are available and first in the set of countries included in table 7.3 in terms of the average years of schooling per capita with the absolute value being 3.9. In terms of tertiary schooling per capita, however, in 1980 it ranked second from bottom within the SADC countries in the table and fourth from bottom in the set of 28 African countries with the absolute value being 0.006. From table 7.3, we can see that both these absolute values have increased significantly in 2000, but Zambia's performance relative to other countries is mixed. Its rank in the set of all African countries for overall schooling slipped to sixth in 2000 and fourth within SADC countries. For tertiary education, the country's rank has improved to seventeenth within Africa (29 countries) and to fifth within SADC. The improvement in tertiary education notwithstanding, Zambia continues to be an average performer in the continent and within SADC.

Table 7.3. Human Capital in 2000, SADC Countries

	Percent of population with no primary education	Average years of schooling per capita	Average years of primary schooling per capita	Average years of secondary schooling per capita	Average years of tertiary schooling per capita
Botswana	24.0	6.279	4.762	1.416	0.100
Congo, Dem. Rep. of	47.7	3.03	2.374	0.619	0.038
Lesotho	28.8	4.232	3.628	0.568	0.036
Malawi	40.7	3.204	3.017	0.170	0.017
Mozambique	63.8	1.105	0.983	0.117	0.005
South Africa	22.1	6.138	4.590	1.353	0.195
Swaziland	21.7	6.010	5.016	0.880	0.114
Tanzania	42.8	2.705	2.515	0.161	0.029
Zambia	**17.3**	**5.457**	**4.296**	**1.113**	**0.047**
Zimbabwe	12.7	5.354	3.456	1.775	0.123

Source: Barro and Lee 2000.

A similar picture emerges when we look at the number of physicians in the country, which is another indicator of skill availability (table 7.4). Currently, Zambia has 0.116 physicians per 1,000 population, which is sixth lowest among the SADC countries in the table. Comparable figures stood at 1.6 (worldwide in 1998) and 0.179 (least developed countries as per U.N. classification in 2004).

In terms of the education infrastructure for health care, Zambia currently has only one medical school, three nursing schools, and three technical colleges graduating doctors, nurses, laboratory technicians, and pharmacists. In 2004, these schools produced 49 doctors, 540 nurses, 20 pharmacists, and 38 laboratory technicians, which equals 647 health care professionals. Data provided by the United Nations on the number of students graduating in health care and welfare per capita show that Zambia ranks eighth from bottom in a sample of 101 countries in the world as well as in the set of 27 African countries (see figure 7.5). These graduation rates are not only low by international standards but also inadequate to sustain acceptable standards of health care. For example, to meet the basic WHO recommendations on staff-to-population ratios (1:5,000 for doctors and 1:700 for nurses), Zambia would require an additional 1,654 doctors and 10,636 nurses, which equals about 34 and 20 times the respective annual graduation rates (MoH 2005).

To conclude, Zambia's performance in generating skilled professionals has improved significantly over the last two decades. The country still remains an average performer by African standards and is not yet equipped to meet its own needs.

Table 7.4. Physicians in Africa, 2004

	Physicians per 1,000 population
Botswana	0.398
Congo, Dem. Rep. of	0.107
Lesotho	0.049
Malawi	0.022
Mozambique	0.027
South Africa	0.770
Swaziland	0.158
Tanzania	0.123
Zambia	**0.116**
Zimbabwe	0.161

Source: World Bank.

Note: Figure for Lesotho is for 2003, and figure for Tanzania is for 2002.

Figure 7.5. Annual Health Care and Welfare Graduation Rate, 1998–2003 (per 1,000 population)

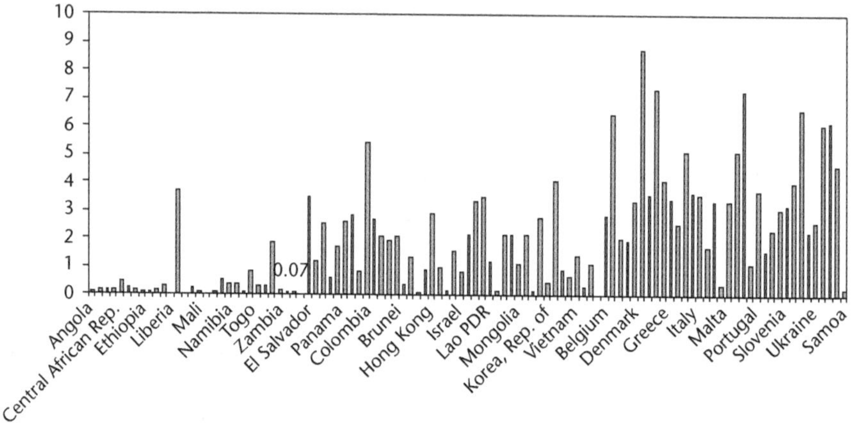

Source: United Nations 2005.

What Is the Solution?

The solution to the skill shortage and brain drain–related problems in Zambia must go to the root of the problem. The main reason for the shortages in Zambia is the country's low capacity to produce skilled professionals, although migration of the skilled tends to aggravate the problem. We suggest two broad principles for the design of an optimal solution to the skill situation in the country.

Increased investment in human capital

The primary solution to the shortage lies in producing more skilled workers. Even in health care, emigration restrictions are unlikely to solve the problem although they may have some impact. For example, the estimated shortage of doctors to meet the WHO recommendations is about 1,654, which is approximately 5.5 times the estimated number of Zambian doctors practicing abroad. As in most developing countries, higher education in Zambia depends critically on financial support from the government. Low incomes and credit constraints deter most students from seeking costly private education. For example, a recent survey conducted by the government to assess the state of primary education in the country revealed that the majority of children who did not attend primary school cited financial difficulty as the main reason (Zambia DHS 2002). Investment in education must not be undermined by the cap imposed on public expenditure. Current public spending on education by the Zambian government is low, even by African standards (see table 7.5).

Table 7.5. Government Expenditure on Education in 2000, SADC Countries

	Percent of GDP
Angola	2.61
Botswana	2.15
Lesotho	10.11
Malawi	4.14
Mozambique	2.36
South Africa	5.58
Swaziland	6.20
Tanzania	2.17
Zambia	**1.99**
Zimbabwe	4.70

Source: World Bank.

Note: Figure for Botswana is for 2001; and figures for Mozambique and Tanzania are for 1999.

Zambia's expenditure on education as a percent of GDP is the lowest among the countries shown. For Sub-Saharan Africa, the corresponding figure stood at 3.4 and for the least developed countries at 2.9. In addition to the low spending on education, resources may not be suitably distributed across various disciplines. Figure 7.6 illustrates the point.

Figure 7.6 shows that Zambia is not doing enough to generate more health care workers. Compared with only 3 percent of the students in health and welfare, the corresponding figure for most of the other countries in the world for which data are available is much higher. For example, the figure stood at 22 percent (Angola), 8 percent (Benin), 11 percent (Ethiopia), 9 percent (Kenya, Swaziland), and 11 percent (Mongolia). For the 73 countries for which data are available, Zambia outperforms only 7 countries: Tanzania, Poland, Uganda, Bangladesh, Samoa, Sierra Leone, and Bangladesh.

Building capacity for greater human capital generation is a long-term and costly process. Given the current cap on public expenditure in Zambia, donor countries can help generate skilled professionals through aid and loans, which could be tied to investment in higher education for health care and other critical professional training.

To conclude, emigration restrictions are not a substitute for building capacity for human capital generation in Zambia. For example, the estimated shortage of doctors to meet the basic WHO recommendation is 5.5 times the number of Zambian doctors practicing abroad. Zambia's public expenditure on education is

Figure 7.6. Students in Zambia by Discipline, 1998/99

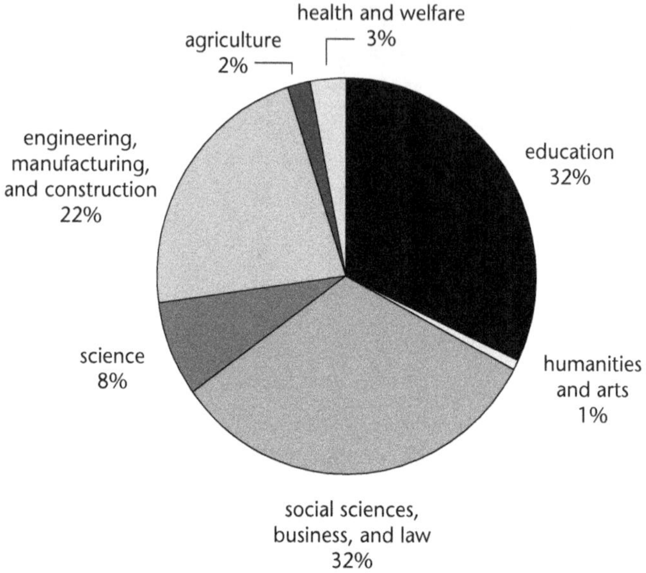

Source: United Nations 2005.

among the lowest in Africa, and even this meager expenditure is not properly distributed across various disciplines.

Migration of the skilled must be managed properly based on the current shortages of professionals in Zambia and the potential benefits offered by such migration. The question that arises is precisely what the proper management of migration of the skilled entails for Zambia.

Emigration restrictions, retention, and voluntary return

A number of countries, including Zambia, have attempted a range of policies to stem excessive outward flows of the skilled and bring back those who have moved abroad. Direct restrictions on emigration have been rare in Zambia and elsewhere. The government of Zambia recently issued an NELMP, which specifically factors in migration. The stated objective of the policy is to attract skilled Zambians back home by facilitating their return (integration) and improving the conditions of employment. Zambia has implemented a "bonding" system that requires all Zambians who are awarded a publicly funded scholarship to sign an agreement before leaving the country promising to return after the completion of their studies. International organizations such as the IOM have implemented programs to encourage return migration. Initially, IOM launched the RQAN program, which was a voluntary scheme that African nationals in Europe and the United States could benefit from if they wanted to return to the continent. Zambia was singled out as one of the target countries. The scheme has now been replaced by MIDA, a partnership of the African Union, the African Development Bank, and several subregional bodies such as the Economic Community of West African States (ECOWAS), SADC, and the East African Community (EAC). MIDA aims to bring the skills of African migrants in Europe and North America to support development projects in Africa.

These schemes are commendable and should be pursued in the future. Their effectiveness, however, presents some concerns. Although no systematic evaluation has been conducted of the efficacy of these polices, anecdotal evidence suggests that their success has been modest. We believe that the limited success could be due to the following two reasons. First, in situations in which punitive measures have been used (for example, bonding schemes), they have been too modest to make any significant impact on permanent outflows of the brains. A recent study by the IOM noted that "the bonding system has never worked effectively in practice. A major problem is the lack of monitoring and the difficulty of enforcing the bonding agreement" (IOM 2005, p. 65). Second, permanent settlement abroad requires substantial sunk cost by the migrant, which once made makes return migration more costly. Most of the schemes discussed above do little to prevent this from happening. The schemes target individuals who are already settled abroad and who seek to achieve a temporary rather than permanent return.

Compensation

One idea that has gained some ground in the recent past is that the receiving countries should compensate the sending countries for the cost they incur in training those who leave. The compensation could be monetary, or of the host country could establish training schools in the sending countries for the would-be migrants.

Thus far such ideas have not found much application, and negotiations between the United Kingdom and Zambia have floundered on the issue of compensation. Host countries are typically averse to compensations in any form. This is not too different from what we observe in other areas, such as trade negotiations, during which cooperation typically takes the form of reciprocal reductions in trade barriers and monetary compensations are rarely observed. There are other problems, too. First, agreement on the right level of compensation can be complicated. For example, source countries incur costs not only in providing technical education but also primary and secondary education. Should the host country compensate for these costs also? Second, in most developing countries, strong externalities result from education. The direct cost of training does not adequately reflect the opportunity cost of skilled emigration to the source. Simply put, if there were no externalities, then there would be no need to manage migration because individual motives would be consistent with social welfare maximization. The problem is that these opportunity costs are hard to evaluate Third, a notable feature of skilled migration is that not only do the highly skilled leave but also the best among. A fair compensation scheme would require transfer amounts linked to the innate abilities of those who migrate, which is perhaps too complicated. Fourth, much of the benefit from skilled immigration is appropriated by the employing firms in the host country. Compensation by the government (of the host country) implies a transfer of resources from the government (taxpayers) to the firms. This has obvious distributional implications that may not be politically feasible. One solution could be to tax the employers for hiring immigrant workers. This is equivalent to a discriminatory tax on immigrant income, which has little history of success.

Establishing training schools that are funded by the host country government is another option. In principle, such measures can reduce some of the adverse effects of brain drain on the source country, but they too have limitations. In fact, the problems mentioned in the previous paragraph with compensation schemes apply as much to training would-be migrants in the source country. For example, we may ask whether the host should establish primary schools because those who migrate embody primary education as well. Additionally, a drawback of relying on compensation and training schemes alone is that they promote permanent migration, at least indirectly, because they do not impose any requirement of temporariness. As we argue below, temporary migration can deliver additional benefits to source countries without significant cost to the host when compared with permanent migration. Thus, compensation-cum-training schemes are best seen as complimentary to a temporary migration regime.

Migration as a supplement

One possibility is that the opportunity to work abroad could be used to induce professionals to serve a minimum number of years in priority areas, including the public sector and underserved rural regions. The scheme can be easily implemented in collaboration with the host countries in cases in which emigration clearance would require evidence of service in certain priority sectors and regions designated by the source country. The scheme is not too different from a tax on emigration because working in the priority sectors entails lower wages or poorer working conditions. Of course, this will not solve the problem of brain drain, but it would ensure that the sending country gets at least something in return for losing its skilled workers, and it helps to channel resources (professionals) to priority areas without places an additional burden on government expenditure.

Emigration restrictions, retention, and voluntary return schemes; compensation through monetary transfers; or establishment of training schools can help reduce the adverse effects of brain drain on the source country. But these are, at best, complimentary measures because they do not exploit the benefits to the source from a truly temporary migration regime.

Exchange programs

Motivated by concerns on the part of source countries about brain drain, some host countries are actively promoting short-term visits by professionals of developing countries to gain valuable expertise and experience. One example of this is the recently concluded bilateral agreement between South Africa and the United Kingdom that gives health care professionals a chance to go on time-limited placements to the other country. The proposed benefits are expected to arise from better information sharing and expertise in such areas as public health, professional regulation, workforce planning, public-private partnerships, and hospital twinning initiatives. The agreement is a two-way arrangement with specific obligations undertaken by both countries. It was motivated, in part, by concerns of brain drain raised by South Africa that resulted from Britain's policy of active recruitment of health professionals in South Africa.

The problem with exchange programs is that they are limited in scope and do not address the strong push-pull factors driving current migration. For example, the bilateral agreement between South Africa and the United Kingdom has no provision to ensure the return of those health care professionals who are not part of the exchange program. Furthermore, it is unlikely that the push-pull factors that fuel migration will, to any significant extent, be diluted by the proposed exchange program. In other words, an effective strategy to combat brain drain must adequately factor in the demand-supply mechanics operating through the global labor market. This brings us to our proposed solution, which seeks to address the major concerns and problems discussed above.

Temporary migration

Many of the concerns raised by skilled migration in source countries could be reduced if the duration of migration were appropriate. In understanding the difference between temporary and permanent migration, it is important to note that a mere rotation of migrants under a temporary scheme does not, in itself, create any extra benefits to either country as compared to permanent migration. If anything, the turnover costs are likely to be higher with the constant rotation of workers. Consider the case of Zambian doctors abroad. As opposed to the current situation in which these doctors are permanently settled abroad, a temporary migration regime would involve all the doctors returning to Zambia and an equal number of new doctors (measured in efficiency units) leaving the country. If the efficiency units of doctors in Zambia and Zambian doctors abroad are unchanged, the switch to temporary migration does not have a positive effect on the welfare of either county.

The key condition for temporary migration to dominate permanent migration is that the benefit of turnover to the source country dominates the cost of turnover to the host country. The former is likely to be high when remittances, as well as learning and learning spillovers, are larger under temporary migration than under permanent migration, although the latter offers scope for cumulative learning and earnings. The cost of turnover to the host is likely to be low in situations in which immigrants acquire host-specific skills quickly and at little cost to the host.

Source country: Impact of temporariness

The first benefit to source from temporariness is a larger inflow of remittances.[2] The propensity to remit is higher when migrants are better connected, for example, through family members living in the source country. Permanent migrants are typically accompanied by their families and have much less incentive to maintain networks in the source country and hence they are likely to remit less. Grieco (2004) provides a useful overview of the relevant literature and concludes that temporary or circular as opposed to permanent and family reunification–based migration is likely to enhance the propensity to remit.

Empirical evidence on the issue comes from two related sources, including the remittance-decay literature and other studies that use a migrant's intention to return home as a proxy for temporariness. Early work on remittance decay produced somewhat mixed results. Brown (1997) looked at the remittance behavior of Tongans and Samoan migrants in Sydney and found no evidence of remittance decay. Funkhouser (1995) found weak evidence of remittance decay. More recent work finds strong evidence of remittance decay. For instance, Brown and Connell (2004) use the same data as in Brown (1997) mentioned above, but they split the migrants into two groups: nurses versus the rest. They find strong evidence of remittance decay for the latter but not for the former. Amuedo-Dorantes, Banska, and Pozo (2005); Fairchild and Simpson (2006); and others find strong evidence of remittance decay.

In the present context, the remittance decay literature suffers from an important shortcoming, because it implicitly treats those who have been in the host country for a short period of time as temporary migrants, even if these migrants have no intention of returning. Our interest is in the difference in behavior between those who know that they are obliged to return and those whose move is more open ended. Two migrants with the same duration of stay may behave differently depending on their intention to stay permanently in the host country. Galor and Stark (1990) developed an early theoretical model showing that the propensity to remit is higher when migrants face a positive probability (intention) of return. Merkle and Zimmermann (1992) used a vast data set from West Germany to test this hypothesis. Controlling for 15 variables, including the number of years spent in the host country, they find that the intended duration of stay had a negative and statistically significant effect on the level of remittances. Brown (1997) and Ahlburg and Brown (1998) reach a similar conclusion in their studies of Tongan and Samoan migrants in Australia. More recently, a supplementary questionnaire on international transfers was added to the Indian Readership Survey by Devesh Kapur and Mark Rozensweig specifically targeted at understanding the link between temporariness (intention to return) and remittances. Rozensweig (2005) summarizes the findings from this survey and notes that, after controlling for a number of factors, the remittance level of intended returnees was about three times the remittance level of those who had no intention to return. Glytsos (1997) contrasts the remitting behavior of Greek migrants to Germany (temporary) and Australia (permanent) and also compares early Greek-German migrants (temporary) and later Greek-German migrants (permanent). He finds strong evidence that temporary migrants have a much higher propensity to remit than permanent ones. Furthermore, because temporary migrants are likely to leave their spouse and dependents in the source country, their propensity to remit is also likely to be higher than permanent migrants. A number of studies confirm this possibility. For example, Amuedo-Dorantes, Banska, and Pozo (2005) look at the remitting behavior of Mexican immigrants in the United States using data from the Mexican Migration Project (MMP) and find that having a spouse or dependents in Mexico has a statistically significant and positive effect on the decision whether to remit.

The second benefit of a temporary migration scheme is that it provides greater scope for learning related benefits. That is, migration serves to enhance the skills and know-how of the migrant, and temporary migration ensures that these enhancements are transferred to the source country.[3] The fact that migrants acquire crucial knowledge and expertise while abroad is confirmed in a number of studies dealing with immigrant assimilation. This literature, however, implicitly assumes that such expertise is "host country specific" and no evidence supports its portability (or lack of it) to the source country. Papers that focus directly on return migrants do shed some light on this point. For example, Barrett and O'Connell (2000) study the performance of return migrants in Ireland and conclude that the returning Irish males earn about 10 to 15 percent more than those who never migrated. They control for a number of observables and (ability-based) selection biases so that the observed earnings differential is primarily due to greater accumulation of human capital abroad. Taylor (1976) and Thomas-Hope (1999) report that Jamaican migrants return home with enhanced skills, experience, and, perhaps most important, leadership qualities. A small but growing body of literature shows that employment choices of return migrants are significantly different from that of the nonmigrants in the source country. In particular, returnees have a higher probability of being self-employed and this phenomenon partly reflects the superior skills and know-how acquired abroad. For example, McCormick and Wahba (2001) study the employment experience of returnees to the Arab Republic of Egypt. Controlling for a host of factors, including education level, they find that the return migrants had a much higher probability of being self-employed, and they attribute this phenomenon to the savings and skills acquired by the migrants while abroad. A recent survey by the IOM of return migrants to Ghana and Côte d'Ivoire reports that many return migrants were keen to start their own business ventures, as opposed to working for others, to implement new the ideas and managerial and technical know-how they acquired abroad.

A number of studies also show that, on their return, migrants bring back valuable "social capital." In one of the earlier studies, Saloutos (1956) argued that return migrants to Greece brought back new ideas on democracy, social behavior, liberal business practices, and so on. Subsequent studies confirmed significant differences between natives and return migrants in Greece with respect to such ideas (Bernard and Comitas 1978). The importance of leadership and social capital should not be underemphasized because it is crucial in the transfer of financial and human capital from the rich to poor countries through return migration (Faist 1997). Existing evidence tends to support this view. For example, the IOM survey in Ghana and Côte d'Ivoire (referred to above) documents a number of returnees claiming to benefit from the social capital and other skills acquired abroad. A 40-year-old Ghanaian who after returning from the United States launched a now-well-established consulting firm stated that,

> [p]eople have come back with different experiences and in fact most of the returnees that I'm aware of have come back to set up their own business, and I think they have been relatively more successful setting up their businesses because ... I think you have an advantage when you're traveled and you've come back, you are willing to take more risk, you are willing to push what you are doing (reported in Ammassari 2003, p. 10).[4]

These benefits of enhanced skills and knowledge need not be restricted only to those who migrate. That is, return migrants can pass on at least some of this knowledge to other Zambian doctors, which is an additional gain to the source country. Of course, such transfers can occur under permanent migration, but it requires elaborate schemes such as RQAN and the migrants' goodwill.

The third reason why temporariness could be attractive for Zambia relates to its egalitarian nature. Permanent migration involves only 300 doctors earning higher wages abroad, and permanently so. In contrast, under temporary migration, such benefits would be distributed over a much larger section of the population. From an individual migrant's point of view, permanent migration is a high-risk and high-return option, because so few get a chance to work abroad. Those who do work abroad, however, earn higher wages for the rest of their life. Temporary migration is a low-risk and low-return option, because more people get a chance to work abroad but over shorter periods. If agents are risk averse, and could choose which type of migration should be allowed in general, then temporary migration may well be the preferred choice in a political equilibrium.

Two related questions that remain to be answered relate to the host country's incentive structure and the feasibility of implementing a temporary migration regime. We discuss these two issues below.

Host country incentive structure: Generosity versus self-interest

Evidence on host's preference between temporary and permanent skilled migration seems to be mixed. On the one hand, concerns exists about permanent immigration, and most international negotiations focus only on temporary migration. On the other hand, many developed countries have created channels through the broader migration policy that allow temporary migrants to become permanent residents. The main concern of the host country about permanent rather than temporary migration is that the former involves additional sociocultural and economic costs like those discussed for the unskilled permanent migrants. Let S_P denote this cost. That is, replacing one would-be permanent migrant by a temporary migrant increases the host country's social welfare by S_P units. The main advantage of permanent migration is that it allows host country to extract some surplus from investing in the migrants' skills. For example, in a two-period game, a firm may invest in firm-specific training to a migrant in period one, which increases his or her efficiency in the next period. Consequently, the firm can extract part of the surplus in the second stage. Suppose the surplus so extracted equals E, while the cost of training to the firm equals c. The values of E, c, and S_P will vary across migrants depending on various characteristics, with the skill content of the migrant (profession) perhaps being most important. Figure 7.7 illustrates the point.

Figure 7.7 shows that S_P decreases with the skill content of the migrant. One reason for this decrease could be that the more skilled and educated are able to integrate more easily with the natives of the host country and impose less of a

Figure 7.7. Temporary versus Permanent Migration from the Viewpoint of the Host Country

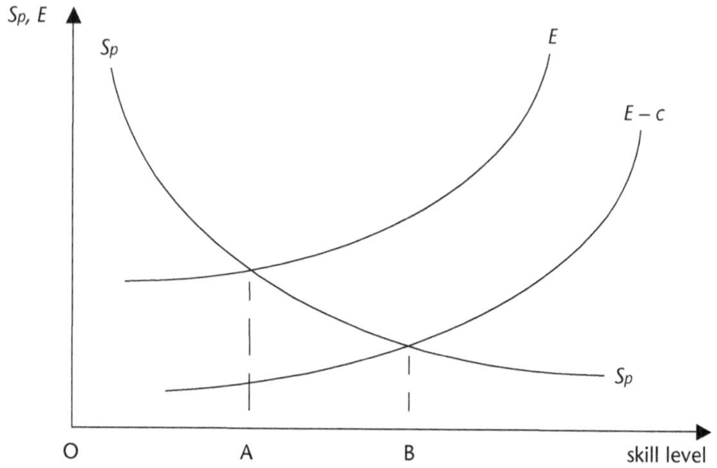

Source: Authors.

long-term fiscal burden. Similarly, training opportunities tend to rise with the skill level of the migrant suggesting that the surplus ex post (E) and ex ante (E − c) are higher the more skilled a migrant is. This gives us the two upward sloping curves. Viewed at the beginning of period one, the host prefers permanent over temporary migrants if and only if $E - c > S_P$, which is the region to the right of B. The opposite holds true for migrants with a skill level less than B and, hence, the host prefers these migrants for a temporary period only. At the beginning of period two, however, the cost of training is already sunk and therefore the benefit from retaining a trained migrant is E rather than E-c, while the cost remains S_P. Applying the same logic again, the host would like to retain all migrants will a skill level to the right of A, where the ex post benefit is higher than the cost of permanent migration, and would repatriate the remaining migrants with a skill level less than A.

This analysis has the following implications for the feasibility of a temporary migration regime. For skill levels less than A, the host country prefers temporary migration only, and this is the equilibrium outcome. Thus, temporariness is guaranteed here. For migrants with a skill level higher than B, we get that the host country would ideally like to keep them permanently, and this is also the equilibrium outcome. Thus, repatriation of these migrants would require an element of generosity on the part of the host country. For migrants with skill levels between A and B, the host country would ideally like temporary migration because the overall benefit from keeping them permanently $(E - c)$ is less than the associated cost (S_p). Such a policy, however, is clearly time inconsistent. Because ex post the benefit (E) is higher than the social cost, the host will be tempted to retain them permanently. Private firms can foresee this temptation and indulge in privately beneficial but socially detrimental (to the host) training of the migrants. For these migrants, a clear case of mutual benefit is evident to both the host and source countries in ensuring their temporariness. One way to achieve this is through a bilateral agreement between the host and source involving an ex ante commitment by the host to repatriate all such migrants.

Successful implementation of migration policies has always been a problem, perhaps because of the sensitive nature of migration. The problem of ensuring timely return, however, is less of an issue with the migration of the skilled. Most of skilled migration occurs through legal channels and skilled migrants are typically employed in the formal sector. Consequently, the cost of monitoring their timely return to the host country is lower and the benefit from overstaying to migrants is also lower because of reduced work opportunities in the formal sector. The host countries' involvement in ensuring temporariness is vital because there is little that source countries can do on their own in this respect. An ex ante commitment by the host, perhaps through a bilateral agreement with the source country, to keep migration truly temporary is crucial. Such a commitment-based migration regime provides a greater degree of certainty and clarity. It avoids the tendency for the host to act opportunistically, ex post, to keep the immigrants permanently, and it also promotes the self-selection of immigrants who are more disposed toward a temporary stay only. The resulting migratory flows would suffice to meet the labor shortages in the host countries, allow source countries and migrants to reap the benefits of migration, and avoid the adverse effects of brain drain. It does go against the individual migrant's incentive to settle abroad permanently, but the migrant community in the aggregate stands to gain because a much larger number of (rotating) workers gets an opportunity to work abroad. A model bilateral agreement aimed to achieve these objectives follows.

To conclude, for certain skill levels, host countries prefer temporary over permanent migration. They cannot, however, implement such a policy on their own. The net outcome is too much permanent migration and too little temporary, overall migration. Source countries like Zambia can help build a credible regime ensuring temporariness in such cases. Source country, host country, and the migrant community in the aggregate are all better off as a consequence of temporariness. For skill levels above a critical threshold level, this temporariness can be achieved only through the generosity of the host countries.

Box 7.3. Model Agreement for the Migration of the Skilled

Host country obligations
- Submit a list of vacancies to the source with details on required qualifications, duration of employment, working conditions, the rights of the migrants, and a copy of the contract between the employer and the prospective migrant.
- Ban employers found in violation of the terms of the contract from taking part in the program in the future.
- Allow migrants in the host country to enroll in training programs to enhance their skills.
- Extend the initial duration of employment when it involves the migrant spending at least three years in the source country from the termination date of the initial duration of the contract.
- Facilitate the temporary movement of Zambian professionals in those areas where on-the-job learning opportunities are high subject to available vacancies and labor market tests that may be in place.
- Bar visa overstayers from taking part in the program in the future.

Source country obligations
- Establish an agency in which prospective migrants could submit their applications. Maintain a database with all relevant information accessible to the employers in the host country.
- Disseminate information on qualifications required to work in the host country and other information to facilitate migratory flows in the future.
- Facilitate the process of screening applicants, recruitment, security clearance, predeparture orientation, and obtaining visa and other travel documents.
- Extend an ex ante commitment to rehire migrants currently working in the public sector on their return.

Gains from cooperation
- Source country has a natural advantage in the screening and recruitment of migrants, which lowers the cost of hiring to employers.
- A stable and secure source of skilled workers to the host. With heightened security concerns after 9/11, Zambia can play an important role in ensuring that the prospective migrants do not pose a security threat to the host.
- Difficult for migrants to overstay knowing that the host is committed not to renew their visa for up to three years. Human capital accumulated by the migrants during their stay is now transferred to the source country.
- Migrants are deprived of the opportunity to stay permanently, but this is more than compensated by a much greater number of rotating migrants who get to spend time abroad. In the aggregate, the migrant community is likely to benefit.

Notes

1. Also see, for example, U.S.-Mexico Binational Study on Migration (1997) and Leiken (2002) for more details on this point.

2. Annex table A-1.2 provides estimates of inward remittances to Zambia and some of the other countries.

3. Temporariness of the skilled is not always a costless process and may even be undesirable (for global welfare) in some cases in which (re)training cost is high, learning periods are long, or the cumulative learning from continued stay in the host country may be large. For many lower-skilled, semi-skilled, and some highly skilled professions, however, transfer of knowledge through temporary migration is likely to be an important benefit.

References

Ahlburg, Dennis, and Richard P.C. Brown. 1998. "Migrants' Intentions to Return Home and Capital Transfers: A Study of Tongans and Samoans in Australia." *Journal of Development Studies* 35 (2): 125–51.

Ammassari, Savina. 2003. "From Nation-building to Entrepreneurship: The Impact of Elite Return migrants in Côte d'Ivoire and Ghana" (mimeograph). International Workshop on Migration and Poverty in West Africa, University of Sussex.

Amuedo-Dorantes, Catalina, Cynthia Banska, and Susan Pozo. 2005. "On the Remitting Patterns of Immigrants: Evidence from Mexican Survey Data." *Economic Review*, First Quarter, Federal Reserve Bank of Atlanta.

Barrett, Alan, and Phillip J. O'Connell. 2000. "Is There a Wage Premium for Returning Irish Migrants?" IZA Discussion Paper No. 135, IZA, Bonn.

Barro, Robert J., and Jong-Wha Lee. 2000. "International Data on Educational Attainment: Updates and Implications." Center for International Development Working Paper No. 42, Center for International Development at Harvard University (CID), Cambridge, MA. http://www.cid.harvard.edu/ciddata/ciddata.html.

Bernard, H.R., and L. Comitas. 1978. "Greek Return Migration." *Current Anthropology* 19(3): 658–59.

Brown, Rochard, P.C. 1997. "Estimating Remittance Functions for Pacific Island Migrants." *World Development* 25 (4): 613–26.

Brown, Richard P., and John Connell. 2004. "The Remittances of Tongan and Samoan Nurses from Australia." *Human Resources for Health* 2 (2): 1–21.

Buchan, James, and Delanyo Dovlo. 2004. "International Recruitment of Health Workers to the UK: A Report for DFID." Final Report, DFID Health Systems Resource Centre.

Council of Europe. 1997. "On the Prevention of Illegal Migration." Conference of Ministers held in the context of Budapest Process in Prague on October 14–15, 1997.

Docquier, Frederic, and Abdeslam Marfouk. 2004. "Measuring the International Mobility of Skilled Workers (1990–2000)." Policy Research Working Paper No. 3381, World Bank, Washington, DC.

Fairchild, Stephen T., and Nicole B. Simpson. 2006. "Variation in the Remittances of Mexican Migrants Across U.S. Regions" (mimeograph). Department of Economics, Colgate University, Hamilton, NY.

Faist, T. 1997. "The Crucial Meso-level." In *International Migration, Immobility and Development*, ed. T. Hammar, G. Bochmann, K. Tamas, and T. Faist. Oxford: Berg.

Funkhouser, Edward. 1995. "Remittances from International Migration: A Comparison of El Salvador and Nicaragua." *The Review of Economics and Statistics* 77 (1): 137–46.

Galor, O., and O. Stark. 1990. "Migrants' Savings, the Probability to Return Migration and Migrants' Performance." *International Economic Review* 31: 463–67.

Glytsos, Nicholas P. 1997. "Remitting Behavior of 'Temporary' and 'Permanent' Migrants: The Case of Greeks in Germany and Australia." *Labour* 11 (3): 409–35.

Grieco, Elizabeth. 2004. "Will Migrant remittances Continue Through Time? A New Answer to an Old Question." *International Journal of Multicultural Societies* 6 (2): 243–52.

Hatton, T.J., and G. Jeffrey Williamson. 2001. "Demographic and Economic Pressure on Emigration Out of Africa." IZA Discussion Paper No. 250. IZA, Bonn.

IOM (International Organization for Migration). 2005. "Migration and Development: New Strategic Outlooks and Practical Ways Forward—The Case of Angola and Zambia." IOM Migration Research Series No. 21. IOM, Geneva.

Leiken, Robert S. 2002. "Enchilada Lite: A Post 9/11 Mexican Migration Agreement" (mimeograph). Center for Immigration Studies, Washington, DC.

McCormick, Barry, and Jackline Wahba. 2001. "Overseas Work Experience, Savings and Entrepreneurship Amongst Return Migrants to LDCs." *Scottish Journal of Political Economy* 48 (2): 164–78.

Merkle, Lucie, and Klaus F. Zimmermann. 1992. "Savings, Remittances and Return Migration." *Economics Letters* 38: 77–81.

MoH (Ministry of Health). 2005, December. "Human Resources for Health Strategic Plan (2006–2010)." Ministry of Health, Republic of Zambia.

OECD (Organisation for Economic Co-operation and Development). 2004. "Migration for Employment: Bilateral Agreements at a Crossroads." OECD, Paris.

Rosenzweig, Mark. 2005. "Consequences of Migration for Developing Countries." Working Paper UN/POP/MIG/2005/08. United Nations Expert Group Meeting on International Migration and Development, Population Division, United Nations, New York.

Saloutos, T. 1956. *They Remember America: The Story of Repatriated Greek American.* Berkeley: University of California Press.

Taylor, E. 1976. "The Social Adjustment of Returned Migrants to Jamaica." In *Ethnicity in the Americas*, ed. F. Henry, 213–30. The Hague: Mouton.

Thomas-Hope E. 1999. "Return Migration to Jamaica and its Development Potential." *International Migration* 37 (1): 183–207.

United Nations. 2002. International Migration Report. United Nations, New York.

———. 2005. Human Development Index Report. United Nations, New York.

U.S. Commission for Immigration Reform. 1998. "Migration Between Mexico and the United States—A Binational Study." http://www.utexas.edu/lbj.

Winters, L. Alan, Terrie L. Walmsley, Zhen Kun Wang, and Roman Grynberg. 2002. "Negotiating the Liberalization of the Temporary Movement of Natural Persons."

Zambia Demographic and Health Surveys. 2002. EdData Survey, Education Data for Decision Making. Central Statistical Office, Lusaka.

Annex 1. Immigration Data

Table A-1.1. Net Immigration Figures

Country/Region	Net immigration in 1990 (per 1,000 population)	Net immigration in 2000 (in thousands)	Net immigration in 2000 (per 1,000 population)
Burundi	−8.5	−80	−12.9
Djibouti	−11.4	4	6.8
Eritrea	−22.5	2	0.6
Ethiopia	3.5	−7	−0.1
Kenya	1.7	−3	−0.1
Madagascar	−0.1	−1	..
Rwanda	−58.4	395	62.8
Seychelles	−1.7	121	1.5
Sudan	−0.8	−77	−2.6
Uganda	1.4	−14	−0.6
Congo, Dem. Rep. of	4.9	−340	−7.1
Malawi	−17.1	−9	−0.8
Mauritius	−3.1	−2	−2.0
Zambia	−0.1	14	1.4
Zimbabwe	−3.3	−3	−0.2
Eastern Africa	−1.5	278	1.2
Southern Africa	0.4	−13	−0.3
North Africa	−1.3	−261	−1.6
Africa	−0.6	−447	−0.6
Less developed regions	−0.6	−2,321	−0.5

Source: United Nations 2002.

Note: Figures for 1990 and 2000 represent averages for 1990–95 and 1995–2000, respectively. Figures for migration in Seychelles are compiled from Migration and Tourism Statistics 2002; the population data are taken from the World Bank's World Development Indicators.

.. = negligible.

Table A-1.2. Average Annual Net Remittance Inflows, 1994–2001

Country	Total ($ millions)	Per capita	Percent of GDP
Zambia	20.7	2.13	0.66
Ethiopia	53.0	0.84	0.82
Madagascar	19.1	1.27	0.51
Rwanda	13.6	1.82	0.70
Seychelles	0.3	3.70	0.05
Sudan	479.1	15.54	4.50
Uganda	317.8	14.08	5.33
Total	882.8	6.36	3.01
Sub-Saharan Africa	2,957.1	4.60	0.92

Source: IMF, UN Wall Chart, GDF 2003; World Development Indicators.

Note: Per capita and percent of gross domestic product (GDP). Figures are obtained by dividing the total remittance figures with population and GDP figures for countries for the year 1999.

The corresponding per capita remittance figures for some other countries stood at 9.3 (India), 67 (Mexico), 80 (the Philippines), 79 (Morocco), 32 (Latin America and the Caribbean [LAC] region), and 10.3 (worldwide). Worldwide figures are based on the figures for world remittances and population data provided by the UN Wall Chart for 2000. As a percent of GDP, the corresponding figures in some other parts of the world are 0.9 percent (LAC region), 2.1 percent (India), 7.9 percent (the Philippines), 1.4 percent (Mexico), 6.3 percent (Morocco), 4.1 percent (Mozambique), and 0.2 percent (worldwide). Thus, official inward remittances in Zambia are, at best, modest.

Annex 2. Migration Data: Skill Migration and
            Human Capital

(Selected countries in Asia, Latin America, Caribbean, and Eastern Europe)

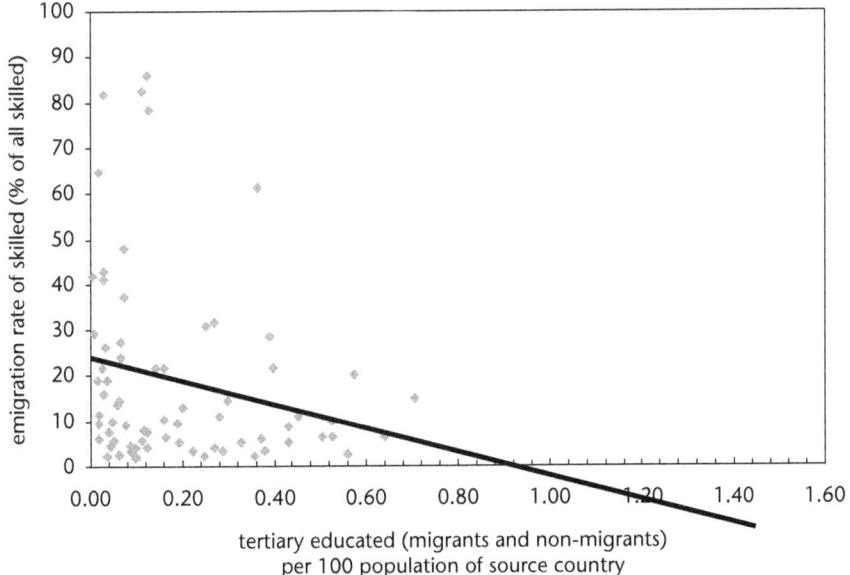

Source: Authors' own calculations using data from Docquier and Marfouk 2004, World Bank, and The United Nations 2005.

www.ingramcontent.com/pod-product-compliance
Lightning Source LLC
Chambersburg PA
CBHW060823170526
45158CB00001B/66